FRANCE IN THE AGE OF ORGANIZATION

BERGHAHN MONOGRAPHS IN FRENCH STUDIES

Editor: Michael Scott Christofferson, Adelphi University

The study of the French past has always functioned as a kind of template for the great historical movements in European history, whether the Renaissance, Absolutism, Enlightenment, Nationalism, Democracy, or Imperialism, while the Great French Revolution still stands as a model for revolution worldwide and evokes debate over the central questions of historiography. And France and French society continue to serve as a laboratory for academic innovation in the study of history and other disciplines. Centralization provides easy access to well-preserved and rich documentary collections in Paris and provinces and departments for all periods; it is no accident that studies of local and social history were pioneered by French historians in the writings of the Annales school. France, the former French Empire, and contemporary Francophonie continue to provide models for modern studies in Imperialism, Postcolonialism, and Multiculturalism.

Volume 1
The Populist Challenge: Political Protest and Ethno-nationalist Mobilization in France
Jens Rydgren

Volume 2
French Intellectuals against the Left: The Antitotalitarian Moment of the 1970s
Michael Scott Christofferson

Volume 3
Sartre against Stalinism
Ian H. Birchall

Volume 4
Sartre, Self-Formation and Masculinities
Jean-Pierre Boulé

Volume 5
The Bourgeois Revolution in France 1789–1815
Henry Heller

Volume 6
God's Eugenicist: Alexis Carrel and the Sociobiology of Decline
Andrés Horacio Reggiani

Volume 7
France and the Construction of Europe, 1944–2007: The Geopolitical Imperative
Michael Sutton

Volume 8
Shades of Indignation: Political Scandals in France, Past and Present
Paul Jankowski

Volume 9
Mitterrand, the End of the Cold War and German Unification
Frédéric Bozo

Volume 10
Collective Terms: Race, Culture, and Community in a State-Planned City in France
Beth S. Epstein

Volume 11
France in the Age of Organization: Factory, Home and Nation from the 1920s to Vichy
Jackie Clarke

Volume 12
Building a European Identity: France, the United States, and the Oil Shock, 1973–74
Aurélie Élisa Gfeller

Volume 13
General de Gaulle's Cold War: Challenging American Hegemony, 1963–1968
Garret Joseph Martin

FRANCE IN THE AGE OF ORGANIZATION

FACTORY, HOME AND NATION FROM THE 1920S TO VICHY

Jackie Clarke

berghahn
NEW YORK · OXFORD
www.berghahnbooks.com

First published in 2011 by

Berghahn Books

www.berghahnbooks.com

© 2011, 2014 Jackie Clarke
First paperback edition published in 2014

Library of Congress Cataloging-in-Publication Data

Clarke, Jackie, 1966-
 France in the age of organization : factory, home and nation from the 1920s
to Vichy / Jackie Clarke.
  p. cm. -- (Berghahn monographs in French studies ; v. 11)
 Includes bibliographical references and index.
 ISBN 978-0-85745-080-7 (hardback) -- ISBN 978-0-85745-081-4 (institutional
ebook) -- ISBN 978-1-78238-091-7 (paperback) -- ISBN 978-1-78238-092-4
(retail ebook)
 1. France--Politics and government--1914-1940. 2. Reconstruction (1914-
1939)--France. 3. France--Social policy--History--20th century. 4. France--
Economic policy--History--20th century. 5. Social
structure--France--History--20th century. 6. Professional employees--France-
-History--20th century. 7. Industries--Social aspects--France--History--20th
century. 8. Technocracy. I. Title.
 DC389.C53 2011
 944.081'5--dc23

                                                                2011018001

British Library Cataloguing in Publication Data

A catalogue record for this book is available from
the British Library.

Printed on acid-free paper

ISBN: 978-1-78238-091-7 paperback
ISBN: 978-1-78238-092-4 retail ebook

CONTENTS

ACKNOWLEDGEMENTS

I would like to thank the British Academy, the Arts and Humanities Research Council and the University of Southampton for providing much needed research time and money to complete this project. I am also grateful to all the staff at the Archives nationales and the Bibliothèque nationale de France who facilitated my work over the years and to Marie Toulouse (daughter of Jean and Annette Coutrot) for granting me an interview. My senior colleagues Clare Mar-Molinero and Patrick Stevenson have had to be rather more patient than I would have wished in waiting for this book to be completed and I thank them for bearing with me. My colleagues at Southampton make it a congenial place to work even when the climate in British universities is as worrying as it is at present. Special appreciation must go to Joan Tumblety and Scott Soo who make Southampton one of the best places in the U.K. to be a modern French historian and who can be relied on for intellectual exchange, moral support or the consumption of red wine as the occasion demands. Rod Kedward, Julian Jackson, Laura Lee Downs and Siân Reynolds have all offered invaluable support and guidance over the years – their wisdom has been much appreciated. I am also indebted to Herrick Chapman, Irwin Wall and an anonymous reviewer for Berghahn Books who made extremely helpful comments on an earlier version of this manuscript. Thanks to all the staff at Berghahn who helped to turn the manuscript into a book. Rod Kedward, Kevin Passmore, Joan Tumblety, Karen Adler and David Meren all made time to offer feedback on chapters, despite having their hands full with projects of their own. A number of the ideas in this book got their first airing over cups of coffee in the BNF with Kevin Passmore, who deserves special thanks not just for these exchanges but for convincing me I had something to say in the moments of uncertainty that are inevitably part of a long research project. I would never have got this far without him or the other friends who have kept my spirits up. Orla Smyth, Karen Adler, Florence Myles, Judith Surkis, my sister Louise Clarke and the 'lovely girls' (they know who they are) have been constant sources of support, intellectual stimulation and laughs. Finally, it was my parents who first kindled my interest in France, so it seems only right that this book is dedicated to them.

Author's Note on Translations

All translations in the text are my own unless otherwise indicated.

LIST OF ABBREVIATIONS

ACJF	Association catholique de la jeunesse française
AN	Archives nationales
BNF	Bibliothèque nationale de France
CCOP	Comité central de l'organisation professionnelle
CEGOS	Commission générale de l'organisation scientifique du travail
CEPH	Centre d'études de problèmes humains
CGPF	Confédération générale de la production française until 1936, then Confédération générale du patronat français
CGT	Confédération générale du travail
CGTU	Confédération générale du travail unitaire
CII	Centre d'information inter-professionnel
CJP	Centre des jeunes patrons
CNE	Conseil national économique
CNOF	Comité national d'organisation française
CNRS	Centre national de la recherche scientifique
COST	Centre national de l'organisation scientifique du travail
CPEE	Centre polytechnicien d'études économiques
CSEIC	Conseil supérieur de l'économie industrielle et commerciale
CST	Conseil supérieur du travail
DGEN	Délégation générale de l'équipement national
EDF	Electricité de France
EHESS	Ecole des hautes études en sciences sociales
ENS	Ecole normale supérieure
IFOP	Institut français de l'opinion publique
ILO	International Labour Office
INED	Institut national d'études démographiques
INETOP	Institut national d'étude du travail et d'orientation professionnelle
INOP	Institut national d'orientation professionnelle
INSEE	Institut national de la statistique et des études économiques
OCRPI	Office central de répartition des produits industriels

MEN	Ministère de l'Economie nationale
MRP	Mouvement républicain populaire
PTT	Postes, télégraphes et téléphones
PUF	Presses universitaires de France
SGF	Statistique générale de France
SIS	Syndicats des ingénieurs salariés
SNCF	Société nationale des chemins de fer français
STCRP	Société des transports en commun de la region parisienne
USIC	Union sociale des ingénieurs catholiques

INTRODUCTION

On the 10th of January 1934 a private view was held at 51 rue Raynouard in the well-heeled sixteenth arrondissement in Paris. On display were mural paintings by the cubist André Lhote, who was also an art critic at the *Nouvelle Revue française*, and by Robert Delaunay, who was later to design the murals for the air and railway pavilions at the 1937 World Fair. Lhote showed a pair of cityscapes, the first featuring the vertical thrust of a towering Notre Dame viewed from the rue de Pontoise, the second treating the horizontal rhythm of the Auteuil viaduct seen from an automobile factory. A certain industrial aesthetic was also in evidence in the very fabric of the premises in which the images hung. Indeed, the private view was unusual not only in the fact that the exhibition space formed part of the exhibit, but in that it doubled as a housewarming party – 51 rue Raynouard was a concrete apartment block designed by the modernist architect Auguste Perret.

Fellow architect, Le Corbusier, who was among the guests, might well have admired the apartment, for it offered the ultimate in rational living space: moveable partitions allowed functional flexibility in the arrangement of the reception rooms and there was even a gym, where the owners could indulge their interest in the scientific exercise methods of experts such as Georges Demeny.[1] This was a household where entertaining was frequent and where housekeeping methods too followed the principles of rational organization. A carefully maintained filing system recorded the dishes served each day, the guests invited and notes on the likes and dislikes of various acquaintances.[2] The lady of the house attended classes with the Ligue d'organisation ménagère (League for Household Organization), which applied industrial efficiency techniques to the home, encouraging housewives to monitor energy consumption and calculate the cost of producing meals, just as industrialists calculated the unit cost of their products. With its ethics and aesthetics of efficiency, this apartment was truly – to use a phrase coined by Le Corbusier – a 'machine for living'. It is perhaps not surprising, then, that it was the home of an engineer, a certain Jean Coutrot.

Coutrot was a former student of the prestigious Ecole polytechnique, France's top science and engineering school. He was also a war veteran, whose right leg had been amputated following an injury sustained in battle in 1915. Having married Annette Gaut in 1917, he became head of the Gaut-Blancan paper company before going on to found one of France's first management consultancy firms, the Bureau des ingénieurs-conseils en rationalisation in 1931. As well as being a notable collector of modern art, he was an energetic publicist and networker, frequenting a host of inter-war organizations, think tanks and reviews including the Comité national de l'organisation française (National Committee for French Organization, CNOF), X-Crise, *L'Etat moderne*, the Plan du 9 juillet group, the Comité central de l'organisation professionnelle (Central Committee for Professional Organization, CCOP) and the Centre national de l'organisation scientifique du Travail (National Centre for the Scientific Organization of Work, known as the COST). What these groups had in common was that they formed part of a movement for 'scientific organization' or 'rationalization' which had focused initially on industry but was ultimately a model for thinking about all kinds of social and economic activity. Much of the rethinking of France's social and economic order that took place in the first half of the twentieth century was informed by the dissemination of models from this movement. And as the example of Coutrot has already hinted, it was not just factories, offices or national economies that were to be planned and rationalized, but homes, minds and bodies.

Historians often think of the period after the Second World War as the key moment in the reorganization of social, economic and political life in twentieth-century France. Indeed, there is no doubt that during *les Trente glorieuses* – the thirty years of economic growth that followed France's liberation from Nazi occupation – the country not only experienced the rapid expansion of mass production and mass consumption, but saw managers, planners and organizational experts of various kinds take on an increasingly central role in directing economic activity, both in businesses themselves and in government institutions. Two social figures have thus been seen to embody France's transformation in the twentieth century – the *cadre* (the term that came to be used for France's managerial class) and the 'technocrat' (a term particularly associated with the role of highly trained engineers and administrators in the French state). In the light of Kristin Ross's work, we might add to this duo, the figure of the 1950s housewife, usually pictured glowing with pride beside a shiny domestic appliance. It is this new postwar middle-class society embodied by managers and housewives that Ross analyses in *Fast Cars, Clean Bodies*.[3] But where did this 'new man' and 'new woman' come from? To what extent did they have an existence before the war? And, more broadly, how were plans for a new social and economic order constructed before 1945?

In the pages that follow, I address these questions by exploring the efforts of a loose coalition of professionals – including engineers, industrialists, trade unionists, psychologists and domestic scientists – to transform France in the period from the 1920s to the eve of Liberation. For the most part, these people saw themselves as technicians, a term which is broader

and carries more prestige in French (*technicien*) than in English. It is a category that encompasses not just those with hands-on responsibility for
machinery or equipment, but the most highly trained graduates of elite
engineering and administration schools. Social professionals, vocational
guidance advisors and domestic science specialists also claimed the label
technicien to emphasize the scientific authority of their interventions.

There are a number of reasons why we might take an interest in the way in
which technicians sought to invent a new order in twentieth-century France,
but one is the fact that their role, particularly as agents of the French state, has
often been seen as a barometer of France's fortunes in this period. More specifically, the 'rise' of a new 'technocratic' and managerial elite has long been identified by historians as one of the primary markers of a major historical
transition in France from prewar crisis to postwar renewal, from stagnation to
renovation. In other words, the story of technicians and their efforts to change
France has played an important part in the construction of a bigger story, about
the very course of French history in the twentieth century.

This narrative of crisis and renewal, which I will outline in more detail
shortly, is in part a product of the way in which two key moments have
structured our thinking about the tumultuous period from the First World
War to the 1960s. Firstly, the defeat of 1940 and the rule of a collaborationist
government based in Vichy, have cast a long shadow over interwar France,
as historians have sought to identify the seeds of what has become known
as Vichy France. Secondly, though it is less commonly acknowledged, the
postwar boom years and the advent of the Fifth Republic (seen as the technocratic regime *par excellence*) have also informed historians' efforts to identify ruptures and continuities in the decades leading up to France's
economic take-off in the 1950s and 1960s. Hence, for thirty years or so following the Second World War, our perceptions of prewar France were
shaped by the work of analysts concerned to explain what they saw as
French economic backwardness and socio-political stalemate. Historians
such as David Landes, Alfred Sauvy and Stanley Hoffmann saw prewar
France as predominantly conservative and excessively individualist. The
country was held back, it was argued, by an abnormally large peasant and
petit-bourgeois population and a risk-averse bourgeoisie that tended (irra-
tionally, it was implied) to put social preservation before economic gain.[4]
Thus, France's aberrational economic development was seen to have contributed to the emergence of a 'stalemate society', a stalemate that would
only be broken after the war, as the old peasant and bourgeois France gave
way to a new 'France des classes moyennes'.[5]

According to this view, while an enlightened few offered a different
vision of France's future before the Second World War – a technicians'
vision of economic dynamism and political effectiveness – these figures
remained on the margins of the Third Republic.[6] While other countries saw
great political experiments in the 1930s, France was deemed incapable of
such dynamism: 'in a world of motion', wrote Hoffmann, 'France and Eng-

land began to appear [...] like big logs of dead wood'.[7] This analysis
allowed the Vichy period (1940–44) to be seen, not simply as an effect of
defeat, but as the product of France's prewar social, political and economic
dysfunction. At the same time, as *les Trente glorieuses* unfolded, such interpretations tended to reinforce the idea of 1945 as a historical watershed.
Only after the war, it was suggested, was France able to 'catch up', overcome its problems and achieve a social, economic and political organization
in sync with history. In this sense, the narrative of a dysfunctional prewar
France was part of a narrative about 'modernization'.

Since the 1980s, this story has been amended somewhat. For one thing,
historians have tried to take on board the criticism that the concept of modernization erected a single model of economic development as normative
for all countries. As a result, they are now more likely to equivocate about
the term, flagging it as problematic without departing entirely from its use
or underlying assumptions, perhaps arguing in terms of different national
'paths to modernity'. Explicit references to French backwardness have
given way, to some extent at least, to the idea of a distinctive French way,
a modernization *à la française* – with the role of technicians and a particular form of state planning being considered as distinguishing features of
the French model of modernity.[8] The periodization of French economic
development has also been revised as historians have reassessed French
economic growth in the nineteenth and early twentieth centuries, arguing
that the picture was less bleak than previous generations of scholars had
suggested.[9] Historians of French political economy such as Richard Kuisel
and Michel Margairaz have begun to focus less on diagnosing the ills of
prewar France and more on identifying the seeds of the country's remarkable 'conversion' to a dynamic state-managed economy in the period
before 1945.[10] Both see interwar technicians' groups such as X-Crise (the
think tank founded by graduates of the Ecole polytechnique) and the
movement for industrial rationalization as laboratories for new forms of
economic organization that would be widely adopted in the changed political context of postwar France. This revision has done little to challenge the
conceptualization of history as modernization – Kuisel's work in particular remained very much within this logic – but, by highlighting the networks of organizations and individuals who were active in promoting
industrial efficiency and economic planning before the Second World War,
these studies have undoubtedly given us a stronger sense of the importance of these groups and of certain historical continuities across the interwar years, the Vichy period and the postwar boom.

Of course technicians and their managerial practices have not only been
considered at state level but in the workplace. Though not really concerned
with questions about economic 'development' or 'modernization', a growing body of research in labour and business history, and in the history of
technology, has also indirectly complicated the picture of a backward France
before 1945. Studies by Aimée Moutet, Yves Cohen, Laura Lee Downs and

Laura Frader, for example, have revealed the extent to which working practices were being 'scientifically organized' between the wars by engineers, industrial psychologists and other managerial intermediaries.[11] Time and motion study techniques were developed and applied, new planning systems adopted, the spatial organization of work analysed, the recruitment and deployment of workers subjected to new forms of aptitude testing – all in the name of efficiency. Whether we call this scientific management, scientific organization, Taylorization or rationalization – all terms that were used at the time to describe this reorganization of work (or aspects of it) – what is not in doubt is that such methods were being applied across a range of sectors in the French economy, from automobile construction to telecommunications, on the factory floor and in the typing pool.

If these histories have extended our knowledge of French workplace practices before 1945 and the work of economic historians has enhanced our understanding of the development of state planning, the role of interwar technical elites has also, since the 1990s, begun to attract the attention of cultural historians. Such studies have focused less on production, planning and the state, and more on ideology, advertising and the development of mass consumption. Marjorie Beale and Robert L. Frost, for example, have added a welcome dimension to the literature by examining the social and aesthetic visions emanating from those who sought to promote scientific mass communication and the mechanization of domestic work.[12] Both link developments in these fields with the movement for industrial rationalization and thus go some way to mapping out an interwar organization project (or set of projects) that extended well beyond the factory and the institutionalization of state planning.

This is an important step. Yet the intervention of cultural historians in a historiography previously shaped largely by economic history and political science, has so far served above all to breathe new life into some rather old ideas. For these historians, what characterized the outlook of French 'modernists' before 1940 was a 'reactionary modernism', a vision of modernity vitiated by what are regarded as nostalgic or reactionary elements – elitism, anxieties about mass society, a desire to reassert gender boundaries. While these interpretations are certainly new in some sense, they have a strangely familiar ring, for they perpetuate the longstanding cliché that the French were peculiarly attached to tradition and that 'the French model' was based on what Landes termed in 1951 a 'modus vivendi' or 'compromise between [...] modern and traditional'.[13] They measure interwar visions of a rationalized order against an imagined purer (often American) version of modernity and find their French subjects wanting.[14] And while earlier accounts reproached mainstream elites for their backward or conservative mentality, often contrasting this with the forward-looking vision of an enlightened (technically orientated) minority, these cultural histories now suggest that in France (unlike elsewhere, it is implied) even those who were in many ways the agents of modernization were also puzzlingly traditionalist. Such, we are told, is the paradox that is French culture.[15]

The question of technicians and their role in political, social and economic life has thus remained at the heart of our stories of crisis and renewal in twentieth-century France for several generations. But these stories have also been shaped by some rather prescriptive assumptions about what constitutes modernity and social, economic or political rationality. Both the earlier generation of political and economic historians, and the new cultural historians have applied a fixed and ahistorical standard for 'modernity' – they imply that there is a normal path of economic and social development, a right way for particular social groups to behave, etc. Moreover, these narratives are characterized by a set of broadly shared assumptions about the direction of history. They reproduce a fundamentally liberal narrative in which history is a movement towards a certain model of capitalism – in this period, Fordism, or some national variant thereof. Indeed, the language of tradition and modernity serves in part to plot national differences along a temporal axis, as though history were a road along which one could only travel forward or back. The analysis is too often conducted as if, to extend Daniel Rodgers' analogy, nations were runners in a race and the job of the historian were to commentate.[16]

The Age of Organization

My ambition in writing this book has been to write a different kind of history of the visions of a new economy and a new society that were developing in France before 1945. Historians like Cohen, Frader and Downs, who have highlighted some of the ways in which techniques of organization constitute and are constituted by relations of power in the workplace, have shown one way of doing this. However, I focus not just on industrial practices but on the ways in which organizers envisaged a new order that exceeded the boundaries of the factory. This is a study of technicians' networks as laboratories for the organization of a new France, but one which defines technicians and their networks more broadly than the previous studies, which focused primarily on the development of economic planning. At the heart of my account lies the scientific organization movement and what might be termed the *nébuleuse organisatrice* which surrounded it. I am borrowing and adapting the latter term from Christian Topalov, who speaks of the turn-of-the-century social reform groups that gathered around institutions like the Musée social as a *nébuleuse réformatrice*. These groups came from a variety of political currents and professions but converged around the idea of social reform and the need for social intervention by professionals to cure the ills of industrial society. They were also agenda setters, helping to shape public debate and policymaking about 'the social'. Topalov uses the cloud metaphor to indicate the fluid frontiers of the networks he sets out to investigate, their varying density and the existence of a certain shared reforming outlook across different groups and sectors.[17] Similarly, while groups like the CNOF might be seen as the backbone of the scientific organization movement in France, other professional milieux and centres of reflection also took up the language and methods of 'organization' or 'rationalization' to formulate their vision of a better social and economic order. Hence we can find organizers in the labour movement, in social Catholic groups, in domestic science education, in applied biology laboratories or vocational guidance centres, among architects and designers, among those who called for reform of the state and among those who frequented the *planiste* groups of the 1930s. Like the turn-of-the-century social reformers examined by Topalov, interwar organizers were agenda-setters, publicists for their cause and sometimes policymakers or government advisors.

It is in this sense that one can speak of the interwar years as part of an 'age of organization'. In adopting this term, I am not endorsing the determinist view, often expressed by organizers themselves, that an age of organization was replacing liberalism and that France must adapt to the new era. Rather, I am registering the centrality of a certain set of ideas and practices in debates about the social and economic order in interwar and Vichy France (and beyond). To conceptualize the period from the 1920s to Vichy in terms of debates about organization has the benefit of moving the discussion away from the hitherto dominant emphasis on backwardness or crisis. This is not to say that there was not a sense of crisis in many quarters, especially at certain points in the 1930s and during the Occupation. On the contrary, there was plenty of crisis talk and it helped bring to the fore a set of interrogations about social, economic and political organization. One can acknowledge the existence of this crisis talk without claiming, as earlier generations of historians did, that there was an *objective* crisis or dysfunction in the French 'system' which serves (implicitly or explicitly) to explain the defeat. Indeed, by defining the period as one of organization projects I am, in effect, paying more attention to proposed solutions than to perceived problems. Some readers may regret that my eye is trained so resolutely on these projects and the networks from which they emerged, rather than on the reception of these ideas among political and business elites more generally, but following projects and people does at least provide a useful way of looking beyond the conventional chronological watersheds of changes of regime, notably those of 1940 and 1944. Though the present study does not go beyond 1944, I will gesture in the conclusion to some of the postwar afterlives of the trends I identify.

I have argued that the projects that emerged from the *nébuleuse organisatrice* should not be measured against a supposedly objective ahistorical standard of what constitutes modernity. This leads me to formulate a different question: what did modernity mean to particular historical actors in this particular historical moment? Or, to use a language closer to that of the period studied here, how were progress and social and economic rationality understood by those who saw themselves as 'rationalizers' or 'organizers'? And how did this colour the techniques they developed in France before 1945? In attempting to answer these questions, I am trying to develop a different kind of cultural history of 'modernization', one in which the notion of modernity, or the conceptions of progress and rationality that came to be associated with it, are *objects* of analysis, rather than analytical categories.[18] If cultural history has a contribution to make to our understanding of what have conventionally been understood as social, economic and political processes, its usefulness surely lies in part in the light it can shed on the historical construction of meaning in these fields.

Experts and Technocrats

At times, I will refer to the people I am writing about as 'experts', but I am conscious that 'expertise' too is historically constructed. The conventional narrative of an enlightened minority of competent and far-sighted individuals, struggling against the prevailing ineffectiveness and economic ignorance of politicians during the interwar period tends to overlook this. It is certainly true that the engineer-planners who emerged in the 1930s tended to see themselves as more competent in economic and organizational matters than the existing political and administrative elites, particularly those trained in the law faculties. But Kevin Passmore has argued that Third Republic parliamentarians, often presented as 'notables' whose power rested more on clientelism than competence also believed that the exercise of power should rest on *compétence*, which for them referred not just to their professional and life experience (often as a lawyer or doctor), but also to a certain ideal of generalism.[19] At the same time, this commitment to generalism, which was shared by many engineers, especially *polytechniciens*, did not preclude the acquisition of specialist knowledge in a particular domain, such as international or financial affairs.[20] Thus, when industrial and engineering elites asserted their own competence and dismissed that of lawyers, they were not inventing the idea of government by competence but *reinventing* it in a way that legitimized their own methods. Their claims rested largely on their supposed *economic* competence, something that tends to be assumed rather than analysed in existing histories. But what made the engineer an economic expert, especially when most economists in France were trained in the law faculties and when the Ministry of Finance could already draw on a highly qualified administrative elite in the form of the Inspecteurs des finances? We can ask the same question about the engineer-organizer or the housewife-manager: all these figures have a history. Hence, when I use the term expert, I am referring to people who positioned themselves as having a certain professional or technical competence and were also recognized by others as having such competence. I am not claiming that they were necessarily better qualified than anyone else to solve the problems they sought to address.

The importance of technical experts in France and particularly their role in the French state have often been conceptualized in terms of the 'rise of technocracy'. Here too one must exercise caution. The term technocrat conjures up a figure whose authority rests on technical/professional competence as opposed to political legitimacy and whose actions are grounded not in a particular social or political ideology but in a concern with effectiveness, rationality and optimization. This usage crystallized in the postwar period. Interwar commentators rarely used the word technocracy and when they did, it had a much narrower meaning: it was the label chosen by Howard Scott and his associates for the doctrine of their little-known American movement, which attracted the attention of some French technicians in the 1930s.[21] In the 1950s and 1960s, the term became common currency, taking on a new, largely negative, resonance, inherited partly from allegations about a secret network of technicians, known as the Synarchy, which was believed to have operated under Vichy. The influence of technicians in planning and development agencies, and the prevailing political consensus in favour of a drive for increased productivity and technological progress in postwar France fuelled continuing anxiety that the country was being taken over by *polytechniciens* and *énarques* (the term used for graduates of ENA, the National School of Public Administration). On the nationalist right, Pierre Poujade railed against the technocratic state, just as he denounced Americanization, seeing both as a threat to the small producers he represented and to their vision of a traditional French way of life. This mythologization of the technocrat rested, as Roland Barthes observed at the time, on an identification of technicians (especially *polytechniciens*) with abstraction, systems and mechanical reason – the technocrat was thus a figure disconnected from the 'real' and rendered inhuman by an excess of intelligence or mathematical training.[22] More moderate and academic voices than Poujade's, such as that of André Siegfried or Jean Meynaud, were also heard in this debate, which was in part a reworking of prewar concerns about the nature of machine civilization, the dehumanising effects of technology and the triumph of quantitative considerations over qualitative ones.[23] Thus, as Gabrielle Hecht has noted, while some technicians had been prepared to try and infuse the term technocracy with a more positive meaning, by the 1960s it had become almost entirely appropriated by their critics.[24]

Given this genealogy, it is striking that the concept of technocracy has been so widely perpetuated by historians, including those who have taken a broadly positive view of the contribution of technicians to French economic organization.[25] Indeed, the idea of technocracy has been particularly prevalent in discussions of technicians at Vichy, where a split is generally identified between technocratic modernizers and social traditionalists, a distinction repeatedly reproduced (albeit with some nuances) since the 1970s in the work of the most authoritative historians of the period – Henry Rousso, Robert Paxton, Julian Jackson.[26] The term technocrat often operates as a kind of shorthand in studies that do not seek to examine the thinking of such figures in detail, but it is a shorthand which effectively imports into these studies many of the assumptions that shaped the polemical debates of earlier decades. Thus, the word still calls to mind a narrow technicism, a purely quantitative or abstract outlook, cut off from social and political realities. In my view, then, it is too marked by its polemical origins to be useful as an analytical category. Hence my adoption of the term 'technician' – in the French sense – throughout this book.

The portrait of the technician that emerges in the chapters that follow departs in some important ways from the stereotype of the technocrat. For one thing, by delineating a broad *nébuleuse organisatrice* and considering technicians of household organization alongside their industrial counterparts, I have mapped out a more heterogeneous group of actors than one might normally consider under the heading of technocracy. Of course, I am not suggesting that all these actors enjoyed the same status, either within the rationalization movement or beyond it, but I do contend that we can learn something by considering them together. From its inception, before the First World War, scientific organization was conceived with reference to a set of principles that were deemed universal and therefore applicable to the organization of all human activity. Between the wars, this aspiration to a 'total rationalization' manifested itself in a huge range of publications and initiatives, notably in a concern with 'human problems' – that is, with the social, biological and psychological dimensions of organization. Indeed, from the beginning, the science of organization was marked by a strong current of social organicism and by a cross-fertilization of ideas from engineering and the biological sciences. Organizers tended to think in terms of systems and the place of human beings within them and by the 1930s this led to developments which paralleled the resurgence of holism within medicine. Medical holists were critical of what they saw as excessive specialization within their profession and were interested in methods such as homeopathy and eugenics which, in their view, offered a more complete understanding of the relationships between mind and body or individual and environment. The publication of Alexis Carrel's best-selling *L'Homme, cet inconnu* in 1935 was symptomatic of this trend and the 'humanist' vocabulary it adopted.[27] The preoccupation with 'human problems' in the organization movement was associated with a similarly holist outlook, but it is important to be clear about the nature of this holism or scientific humanism. The term 'holistic' is often used today in ways that imply a positive value judgement and it has become associated with a certain idea of individual well-being. The holism of the 1930s was more inclined to regard the individual as part of a wider social system, defining rational solutions as those which met the needs of the system (the business, the social organism, the nation's economy etc). When I speak of the 'holism' of organizational thinking, therefore I am not suggesting that such thinking is 'holistic' in today's sense, and to avoid any confusion, I use the adjective 'holist' to designate currents of thinking that make rhetorical claims to holism.

Uncovering these features of organizational thinking not only allows us to reassess its scope but reveals the extent to which organization was conceived as something that must be embodied. The myth of the technocrat, with its emphasis on mathematical abstraction, has tended to obscure this. In what follows, I will show how organizers sought to eliminate social conflict by harnessing class and gender solidarity for productive ends; how they used applied psychology and physiology to develop techniques for enhancing individual and collective efficiency; how they promised to rationalize the middle-class home by re-educating women's minds and bodies; and how they forged a model of economic planning that was closely linked to the study of 'human problems', including population science. Ultimately, I contend, in the minds of these organizers, the new social and economic order required a new man and a new woman, a psychosocial and, in some cases, psycho-biological transformation of the bourgeoisie as well as the worker. If technicians were prepared to work within governments and regimes of various political colours to achieve these goals, their projects were by no means politically and ideologically neutral. In the final chapter I will consider how this vision of a new order found a place among others that competed and sometimes converged with it in Vichy France. This means that the book is organized in part thematically and in part chronologically. While Chapter One considers the origins of the organization movement and Chapter Five its incarnations in Vichy France, the intervening chapters each consider a particular theme or area of activity in the interwar movement and hence have overlapping chronology. To help readers keep track of individual trajectories I have provided brief biographical profiles at the end of the book.

Notes

1. The building also housed Perret's own apartment and studios.
2. Interview with Marie Toulouse, daughter of Annette and Jean Coutrot, 2 August 1996.
3. K. Ross. 1995. *Fast Cars, Clean Bodies: Decolonization and the Reordering of French Culture*, Cambridge, Mass: MIT Press.
4. D. Landes. 1951. 'French Business and the Businessman: A Social and Cultural Analysis' in E. Mead Earle (ed.), *Modern France*, Princeton: Princeton University Press, 334–53; S. Hoffmann. 1961. 'The Effects of World War II on French Society and Politics', *French Historical Studies* 2(1): 28–63; A. Sauvy. 1965–1975. *Histoire économique de la France entre les deux guerres*, 4 vols, Paris: Fayard.
5. Hoffmann, 'The Effects of World War II', 62.
6. Sauvy in particular saw himself as part of this enlightened few and I will consider his position in this historiography in more detail in the conclusion.
7. Hoffmann, 'The Effects of World War II', 33.
8. A useful overview of these shifts in the treatment of 'modernization' within economic history can be found in R. Magraw. 1999. '"Not Backward But Different?" The Debate on French "Economic Retardation"', in M. Alexander (ed.), *French History since Napoleon*, London: Arnold, 336–63. An example of equivocal use of the term can be found in K. Mouré and M. Alexander. 2002. 'Introduction' in Mouré and Alexander, *Crisis and*

Renewal in France 1918–1962, New York and Oxford: Berghahn, 1–13 which revisits Hoffmann's classic framework. On the one hand it is claimed (pp.1–2) that the French 'revolutionary tradition…has made of French experience an exceptional model for political modernization' while 'the French path for economic and social development' was characterized by stability. On the other, the term 'renewal' is offered (p.9) as preferable to 'modernization' because the latter implies an ideal type and a single process of transformation.

9.   See P. Fridenson and A. Straus (eds). 1987. *Le Capitalisme français, 19e-20e siècle. Blocages et dynamismes d'une croissance*, Paris: Fayard.

10.   R. Kuisel. 1981. *Capitalism and the State in Modern France: Renovation and Economic Management in the Twentieth Century*, Cambridge: Cambridge University Press; M. Margairaz. 1991. *L'Etat, les finances et l'économie. Histoire d'une conversion, 1932–1952*, 2 vols, Comité pour l'histoire économique et financière de la France.

11.   A. Moutet. 1997. *Les Logiques de l'entreprise. La rationalisation dans l'industrie française de l'entre-deux-guerres*, Paris: Editions de l'EHESS; Y. Cohen. 2001. *Organiser à l'aube du taylorisme: la pratique d'Ernest Mattern chez Peugeot, 1906–1919*, Besançon: Presses universitaires franc-comtoises; L.L. Downs. 1995. *Manufacturing Inequality: Gender Division in the French and British Metalworking Industries 1914–1939*, Ithaca: Cornell University Press; L. L. Frader. 2008. *Breadwinners and Citizens: Gender in the Making of the French Social Model*, Durham NC: Duke University Press.

12.   R. L. Frost. 1993. 'Machine Liberation: Inventing Housewives and Home Appliances in Interwar France', *French Historical Studies* 18(1): 109–130; M. Beale. 1999. *The Modernist Enterprise: French Elites and the Threat of Modernity 1900–1940*, Stanford: Stanford University Press.

13.   Landes, 'French Business and the Businessman', 350.

14.   In Beale's work the standard for comparison is quite explicitly an American one, in this case a rather idealized notion of 'American mass democracy' (p.6), which allows any form of elitism to be considered as unmodern, a throwback to a deeply ingrained French aristocratic culture.

15.   See also Adam C. Stanley. 2008. *Modernizing Tradition: Gender and Consumerism in Interwar France and Germany*, Baton Rouge: Louisiana State University Press. R. Kuisel. 1993. *Seducing the French: The Dilemma of Americanization*, Berkeley: University of California Press and R.I. Jobs. 2007. *Riding the New Wave: Youth and the Rejuvenation of France after the Second World War*, Stanford: Stanford University Press apply a similar type of analysis to the postwar period.

16.   D. Rodgers. 1998. *Atlantic Crossings: Social Politics in a Progressive Age*, Cambridge, Mass: Harvard University Press, 73.

17.   C. Topalov. 1999. 'Les réformateurs et leurs réseaux: enjeux d'un objet de recherche', in Topalov (ed), *Laboratoires du nouveau siècle: la nébuleuse réformatrice et ses réseaux en France, 1880–1914*, Paris: Editions de l'Ecole des Hautes Etudes en Sciences Sociales, 13.

18.   From two rather different perspectives, Gabrielle Hecht and Kristin Ross have formulated similar questions about the postwar period. See Ross, *Fast Cars, Clean Bodies* and Hecht. 1998. *The Radiance of France: Nuclear Power and National Identity after World War II*, Cambridge, Mass: MIT Press.

19.   K. Passmore. 2004. 'The Construction of Crisis in Interwar France', in Brian Jenkins (ed.), *France in the Era of Fascism*, Oxford: Berg, 167–72. Passmore draws here on the work of Gilles Le Béguec, especially Le Béguec. 1989. 'L'Entrée au Palais-Bourbon: les filières privilégiées d'accès à la fonction parlementaire, 1919–1939', unpublished thesis (doctorat d'Etat), Université de Paris X Nanterre.

20.   We are reminded that lawyers were also experts in this sense in Le Béguec. 2003. *La République des avocats*, Paris: Armand Colin, 147–52.

21.   O. Dard. 2000. 'Les Technocrates: archéologie d'un concept, généalogie d'un groupe social', in Dard, Jean-Claude Daumas et François Marcot (eds), *L'Occupation, l'Etat fran-*

çais et les entreprises, Paris: Association pour le développement de l'histoire économique, 217.

22. R. Barthes. 1970 [1st ed. 1957]. 'Poujade et les intellectuels', in Barthes, *Mythologies,* Paris: Seuil, 182–90.

23. On postwar social scientists and the debate about 'technocracy', see Hecht's lucid discussion in *The Radiance of France,* 28–38.

24. Hecht, *The Radiance of France,* 34.

25. See, for example, G. Brun. 1985. *Techniciens et technocratie en France,* Paris: Albatros; Kuisel, *Capitalism and the State in Modern France* (where Kuisel acknowledges some problems with the term, p.76, but continues to use it). Olivier Dard, having traced the emergence of the term through the Synarchy conspiracy theory, continues to speak of 'la montée des technocrates' and to use the term interchangeably with the more neutral term 'technicien' e.g. O. Dard. 1998. *La Synarchie ou le mythe du complot permanent,* Paris: Perrin, 135–37. He also distinguishes 'les nouvelles relèves technocratiques' from the 'spiritualist' current of *non-conformistes* intellectuals in Dard. 2002. *Le rendez-vous manqué des relèves des années trente,* Paris: Presses Universitaires de France. I have also used the term technocratic myself in the past, albeit in the context of work that sees technicians in a rather different light. In contrast, Hecht studiously avoids the term and speaks instead of 'technologists' and 'techno-political regimes'. See *The Radiance of France,* 15–17, 28.

26. R. Paxton. 1982 [1st ed 1972] . *Vichy France: Old Guard and New Order,* New York: Columbia University Press, 210–20; J. Jackson. 2001. *France: The Dark Years 1940–1944,* Oxford: Oxford University Press, 148–65; H. Rousso. 1987. 'Les paradoxes de Vichy et de l'Occupation. Contraintes, archaïsmes et modernités', in Fridenson and Straus (eds), *Le Capitalisme français,* esp. 72–75 and for a more ambivalent version of Rousso's argument in which 'modernization' is sometimes placed in inverted commas but otherwise retained as an analytical term, Rousso. 1991. 'Vichy et la "modernisation"', in J. P. Azéma, D. Barjot et al., *Reconstructions et modernisation: la France après les ruines 1918...1945,* Paris: Archives nationales, 77–82. Technicians from engineering and industry are not the only kind of 'experts' whose role is highlighted in these studies, but (along with certain *hauts fonctionnaires*) they are the most associated with modernization.

27. On medical holism, see C. Lawrence and G. Weisz. 1998. 'Introduction' and G.Weisz, 'A Moment of Synthesis: Medical Holism in France Between the Wars', in Lawrence and Weisz, *Greater than the Parts. Holism in Biomedicine, 1920–1950,* Oxford and New York: Oxford University Press, 1–22 and 68–93.

Chapter 1

CONSTRUCTING A SCIENCE OF ORGANIZATION

Beginnings

The story of the scientific organization movement begins in the decade or so before the First World War. The theme of organization came to the fore among French elites in this period, manifesting itself not just among business leaders, who played a significant role in articulating this agenda, but on the Right more generally. As Philip Nord has shown, organization in this context implied both the organization of business interests through employers' unions, and a greater role for economic elites in national decision-making. The rhetoric was of a break with (an imagined) pure liberalism: the free play of market forces was seen as anarchic and wasteful, while in contrast an economic order guided by business leaders, deemed to have competence in such matters, would be rational and methodical, promoting the general interest.[1]

This 'organized liberalism', to use Kevin Passmore's term,[2] coincided with and was nourished by a growing body of organizational theory which was being developed notably in engineering networks. From around 1906, the French engineer Henry Le Chatelier had begun disseminating the work of the American engineer-organizer, Frederick W. Taylor, among his fellow professionals.[3] Taylor would become an obligatory reference point and continues to be regarded as one of the 'founding fathers' of the scientific organization movement, but he was by no means the only one.[4] The second acknowledged pioneer of organizational science in France was Henri Fayol – another engineer – whose major work, *Administration industrielle et générale* was published in 1916, at the end of Fayol's long and successful career as an industrial manager.[5] While not all members of the movement would be engineers, the emerging science of organization would be deeply marked by the engineers' preoccupation with systems and efficiency.

Taylorism and Fayolism addressed different kinds of organizational questions. Fayol was primarily concerned with the leadership and coordination of large organizations. He was also concerned with the establishment of management – or administration as he called it – as a professional field in its own right.[6] To this end, he set about defining the essential functions of administration and codifying its principles in terms sufficiently general that the theory could be applied to any area of activity. In what was to become a much-quoted definition, he identified five main managerial functions: planning [*prévision*], organization, leadership, coordination and monitoring.[7] In contrast, while Taylor did conceive of his method as a complete system of organization, his approach centred on the micro-organization of the worker's body and the material production processes in which it was involved. His system had been devised to address the perceived problem of workers 'soldiering' (producing at less than the expected speed) and it sought to take control of the labour process away from workers and foremen.[8] Thus, specially trained engineers were employed to deconstruct the way in which specific tasks were prepared, organized and performed on the shop floor. The flow of work through space was analysed, tasks were broken down into their component movements and the time taken by workers to perform these movements was recorded. The aim was to speed up production by finding the most efficient series of movements for the performance of a given task and establishing these as the required method through a set of detailed written instructions. Hence Taylor's name became synonymous in France with *chronométrage* (time and motion study) and with the use of the stopwatch as a tool of labour discipline, an approach that proved controversial, provoking strike action when it was introduced at Renault in 1912.[9]

The onset of the First World War acted as a stimulus for the dissemination of the methods offered by these engineer-organizers. For one thing, there was a notable cross-fertilization of ideas about organization between the army and industry. This was already apparent in 1910 in General Joffre's reorganization of the French high command, which gave the supreme commander oversight of combat, logistics, training and political liaison, applying a principle of unity of command that was also a key tenet of Fayol's emerging administrative doctrine.[10] Not surprisingly, the military was particularly receptive to Fayolism and made it part of the curriculum at the Ecole de l'intendance and the Ecole supérieure de guerre, where Fayol went on to lecture in 1922–23.[11] It is worth remembering that Joffre was himself an engineer by training, having graduated from the Ecole polytechnique, and some of the early French Taylorists, like Lt-Col Emile Rimailho, were engineers involved in the Taylorization of munitions production during the war. This was facilitated by the wartime partnership between business, labour and the state, embodied by the socialist Minister of Armaments, Albert Thomas, who presided over the drive to increase production through the application of Taylorist methods.[12] If these wartime conditions meant that Taylorization could be carried out with minimal labour resistance, it was also in part because many of the workers in these factories were recently hired women, and ideas about women's natural dexterity or lack of autonomy were used to construct them as having an innate aptitude for Taylorized work. This association would continue to structure the division of labour in French industry for decades to come.[13]

Thomas was not the only minister to promote the organization agenda during the war. Etienne Clémentel, the Radical Minister of Commerce and Industry, and Louis Loucheur, a centre-Right engineer and industrialist who succeeded Thomas at the Armaments Ministry, also made significant contributions. Loucheur had already introduced new technologies to increase production in his capacity as an armaments manufacturer and he used his position as Minister to encourage other industrialists to do likewise.[14] Clémentel's ministry promoted Taylorism, standardization and motion studies during the war and in 1919 published a report which mapped out ambitious plans for the reorganization of the French economy. These proposals implied considerable state intervention and collective action by groups of producers, which did not convince those, such as Loucheur (Minister for Industrial Reconstruction since 1918), who favoured a more liberal approach. Nonetheless, Clémentel's report can be seen as the first of several interwar 'plans' and it reflected a sense among many organizers that concerted action was needed to prevent France falling behind in the international economic race.[15] France emerged from the war significantly weakened economically in relation to the U.S.A. and anxious about the potential reconstruction of German economic and military power.[16] In this context, the belief that the country was lagging behind better organized industrial powers and must somehow catch up provided an important stimulus for the development of the French organization movement.

Institutionalizing the Interwar Movement

If the war allowed scientific organization to gain a foothold both in industry and in government, the interwar years became a crucial period for the institutionalization of scientific organization as a movement in France. The work of Taylor and Fayol was increasingly widely disseminated by this point: by 1925, the French translation of Taylor's major work on scientific management had sold twenty thousand copies and sales of Fayol's theory had reached fifteen thousand – substantial figures for works aimed primarily at a professional, rather than a general audience.[17] Before the First World War, the dissemination channels for these methods were essentially preexisting industrial associations and reviews, such as the Société d'encouragement pour l'industrie nationale and the *Revue de métallurgie*, but the postwar period saw the creation of several groups dedicated specifically to promoting scientific organization in its various forms.[18] Three centres appeared between 1918 and 1924: the Taylorist Comité Michelin, the Fayolist Centre d'études administratives, and the Conférence française de l'organisation, which grew out of conferences held in 1923 and 1924 on the initiative of a group of business journalists and organizational consultants. From 1926, the more durable Comité national d'organisation française (National Committee for French Organization, CNOF) provided a new institutional home for members of all three earlier centres.[19] This was an important moment of consolidation for the movement and the membership of the CNOF rose from 140 to 1200 between 1926 and 1932.[20] The second half of the 1920s also saw a growing interest in scientific organization and mass production methods on the part of employers' organizations, including the Confédération générale de la production française (General Confederation of French Industry, CGPF), which created the Commission générale d'organisation scientifique du travail (General Commission on the Scientific Organization of Work, known as CEGOS) in 1926. Alongside these national organizations, interwar organizers could participate in transnational networks sustained by study trips abroad (often to the U.S.A.) and by international conferences (Prague 1924, Brussels 1925, Paris 1929), as well as by institutions such as the International Labour Office (ILO, headed by Albert Thomas from 1920 to 1932) and the International Management Institute in Geneva (which existed from 1927 to 1934).[21] The two most important interwar institutions created in France for the promotion of scientific organization – the CNOF and the CEGOS – would continue their activities for decades to come and still exist (albeit in a slightly different form) today.[22]

These groups were dominated by engineers and industrialists, but the emerging science of organization also drew increasingly on another significant field of expertise in the interwar period. In France, as in a number of other countries, physiologists had turned their attention to the analysis of the working body and were developing techniques with industrial applications. Ergonomics and fatigue study were important areas of research before the First World War and wartime work on soldiers led Jean-Maurice Lahy and Jules Amar to develop new techniques for aptitude testing (Lahy) and the rehabilitation of the maimed (Amar).[23] Lahy's tests were the forerunners of the psychometric testing which is still used by many employers today, but the term used in France in the 1920s was *la psychotechnique*. This was to be one of the most important fields of applied psycho-physiology in the 1920s, enabling employers to test such qualities as attention, reaction time or dexterity and to deploy staff accordingly.

Industrial psycho-physiology – or work science as it has been more simply termed – was also becoming increasingly institutionalized as a field in the 1920s. Lahy's involvement in aptitude testing in the transport industry from 1921 led to the creation of his psychotechnic laboratory at the Paris public transport company, the Société des transports en commun de la region parisienne, in 1924. This in-house lab was the first of its kind, but by the end of the decade Renault and Citroën had also created their own psychotechnic services and in 1931 Lahy set up another lab at the Chemins de fer du nord.[24] Psychotechnics became the dominant approach in the development of vocational guidance in the 1920s, a trend that was illustrated not just in the psychotechnicians' own publications in this field but in the way this approach was taken up by educationalists and social reformers.[25] In 1922 the government established a system of state-funded vocational guidance offices, which created a demand for advisors trained in the new methods. In 1928, the physiologists Henri Laugier and Henri Piéron and the vocational guidance specialist Julien Fontègne founded the Institut national d'orientation professionnelle (INOP, National Institute for Vocational Guidance) which provided the necessary training and was soon home to a journal that published research by leading psychotechnicians.[26] Like the centres created by engineers and industrialists, INOP has proved a durable institution and continues to exist under the slightly revised title INETOP (Institut national d'étude du travail et d'orientation professionnelle).[27] Similarly, following the creation of the short-lived *Revue de la science du travail* (1929–1930), *Le Travail humain* was founded in 1933 and remains a leading journal in the field of work science today.

Beyond Americanization

The dissemination of these new techniques of industrial organization in the twentieth century has often been explored as a process by which American methods were exported to other countries. This is particularly clear in Richard Kuisel's *Seducing the French* which deals with the Cold War period (when direct American intervention was at its height) and argues that American methods were often resisted in an effort to defend French cultural identity.[28] Even in relation to the interwar period, French thinking about organization has often been seen as being at odds with 'the American way' and interpreted as an attempt to develop or defend a distinctive national (or European) model of organization. Thus, for example, Fayol's interest in leadership and his insistence on the importance of a centralized chain of command has been seen as an expression of a French attachment to hierarchy and centralization in contrast with Taylor's more hands-on, workshop-based system.[29] Quoting Paul Devinat (of the ILO and the International Management Institute) for example, Marjorie Beale observes that Fayol's version of scientific management was 'more attractively expounded from the point of view of the Latin mind'.[30] Likewise, it has been suggested that while American scientific management was an expression of managerial interest itself, work science embodied a disinterested European tradition of humanist scientific research.[31]

In my view we must exercise some caution here. It is true that the United States was a key reference point in debates about industrial organization. It is also true that differences in method, political orientation and institutional or professional context existed among organizers and coloured debates within the movement. The Catholic Taylorist engineer Eugène Nusbaumer, for example, discussed the differences between Taylorism and Fayolism in terms close to those later adopted in the historiography, while the left-wing work scientist Lahy (who was a member of the Communist Party from 1920 to 1923 and would later be a member of the Comité de vigilance des intellectuels anti-fascistes) criticized Taylorism as both dehumanizing and unscientific: he reproached the American engineer for seeing 'man' only in terms of his productive capacity and asserted the scientific superiority of his own discipline as a means of studying the working body.[32] These debates were sometimes framed in terms of an opposition between French and American cultures (or 'civilizations' to use the terminology favoured between the wars). This was certainly the case in the popular literature, where interventions such as Georges Duhamel's sensationalist *Scènes de la vie future* (1930) portrayed the production line as the epitome of an 'American way' that destroyed individuality and threatened the very fabric of French civilization.[33] Even more moderate commentators like André Siegfried (writing before the Wall Street Crash) tended to share a similarly reified conception of old and new-world civilizations.[34] In this context those who promoted scientific organization sought to counter the perception that their methods implied an 'Americanization' of French culture, claiming instead to offer a form of organization *à la française* which could look to a long line of French antecedents – Vauban was even invoked as a pioneer of the time and motion study.[35] But it is possible to acknowledge that these debates about organization took place partly in culturalist terms without adopting the same culturalist outlook as a framework of analysis. Organizers were not just (or even primarily) defending Frenchness; they were defending their own methods and professional competence. Moreover, neither Taylorism, nor any other current of scientific organization, should be seen as a ready-made national product: rather, we might think of the organization movement as a space in which a science of organization was being constructed.

This process was a syncretic one which incorporated techniques developed in a range of geographical, disciplinary and professional settings. In fact, as a number of scholars have acknowledged, Taylorism, Fayolism and work science were in many ways complementary.[36] Taylorization was part of a process that took the division of labour to a new level, fragmenting tasks into simple repeated operations that could be performed with minimal training. Significantly, this fragmentation created a need for new techniques of coordination and planning, directing attention to precisely the sorts of concerns that animated Fayol's work. Likewise, while there were tensions between work scientists and Taylorists, there was also dialogue. Rabinbach has shown how in 1913–14, Le Chatelier was not only promoting Taylorism in France but cultivating the psycho-physiologist Jules Amar in an effort to bring Taylorism and work science together.[37] Amar was less hostile to Taylorism than Lahy initially was, but by the 1920s even Lahy's position became more conciliatory.[38] This evolution was in keeping with the trajectory of the scientific organization movement as a whole, since the latter sought to consolidate itself in the interwar period precisely by synthesizing approaches from different sources. The merger of Taylorist and Fayolist groups into the CNOF in the mid-1920s provided an institutional framework in which this more syncretic science of organization could be constructed.[39] Similarly, by the time the *Revue de la science du travail* was founded in 1929, it was being promoted explicitly as a collaborative project between professions and disciplines. As an announcement in the *Bulletin du CNOF* put it: 'The collaboration at the head of this journal of a psychologist, a doctor and an engineer is not due to mere chance, but rather a reflection of the necessary conditions for the development of the science of work.'[40] Thus, whatever tensions there were between professions and schools of thought existed in the context of an attempt to construct a new field or discipline at the intersection of existing ones.

The adoption and evolution of the term 'rationalization' provides a further indicator of the movement's synthesizing tendency. The term came to France from Germany and was initially associated primarily with the trend towards industrial concentration (cartelization, the formation of conglomerates and the closure of inefficient factories) as the German economy underwent an intense period of restructuring between 1925 and 1929.[41] For this reason rationalization has been identified in the German context not so much with Taylorism but with Fordism – the model of mass production and consumption to which the American industrialist Henry Ford gave his name. In both France and Germany, the early 1920s had been marked by a preoccupation with the immediate financial and material legacies of the war (particularly the problems of war debt and reparations), but this gave way to a period of increased financial stability and prosperity in the latter part of the decade, providing a more favourable context for the promotion of new industrial methods of all kinds. This was particularly apparent from 1926, when the birth of CEGOS and the CNOF in France coincided with the creation in Germany of the Reichskuratorium für Wirtschaftlichkeit (RKW, National Productivity Board), an institution whose generous state funding quickly became the envy of French organizers.[42] As the concept of rationalization was widely adopted in France in the late 1920s, its meaning evolved and it came to be associated not just with industrial concentration but with the pursuit of efficiency at all levels, encompassing everything from the organization of relations among businesses to the standardization of goods and the analysis of the working body.[43]

Putting Organization on the Agenda

Although French organizers worried about falling behind their international competitors, a survey completed by Paul Devinat for the ILO in 1927 reported that France was among the most advanced countries in Europe in the application of scientific organization methods.[44] Recent historical studies have shown that aspects of scientific organization such as organizational theory, time and motion study, psychotechnic testing or assembly-line technology were being applied in industries as diverse as metal-working, automobile construction, the electrical industry, textiles, transport (notably railways), department stores and food processing.[45] If major companies like Renault, Citroën and Peugeot led the way, smaller and less high-profile firms were also using new methods to rationalize production. For example, the Lyon silk company Gillet and the watch and gauge manufacturer Jaeger applied the Bedaux system, which used time study to determine piece rates. The Comité des forges (which represented employers in the steel industry) drew on fatigue studies by work scientists in an effort to reduce waste by preventing accidents. The state postal and telecommunications company, PTT (Postes, télégraphes et téléphones) used psychotechnic tests to determine women's suitability to work as telephonists.[46] As Delphine Gardey has shown, the 1920s also marked a turning point in the mechanization of office work and the introduction of new record-keeping systems, developments which in turn radically transformed the nature and physical space of clerical work.[47]

If scientific organization was firmly on the business agenda between the wars, it also attracted the attention of political and administrative elites, cutting across the political spectrum. According to Stéphane Rials, no less than thirteen ministers were present or represented at the 1923 Congress on scientific organization.[48] Wartime supporters such as Thomas, Clémentel and Loucheur continued to be present either in French politics or, in Thomas's case, at the ILO, at least in the 1920s. The Radical Edouard Herriot and the conservative André Tardieu, each of whom served as Prime Minister on three occasions during the 1920s and early 1930s, were also among those who frequented the movement.[49] The creation of the Conseil national économique (National Economic Council)[50] in 1925 under Herriot's Cartel des Gauches Government and Tardieu's efforts to promote prosperity through a national retooling plan in 1930 reflected a preoccupation with economic organization shaped in part through contacts with the technicians of the scientific organization movement. Paul Devinat's career provides further illustration of the connections between technicians' and politicians' networks: after working with Thomas at the ILO and directing the International Management Institute, he served in a string of government advisory posts in the 1930s (e.g. *Chargé de mission* to the Under-Secretary of State for the National Economy from 1930 to 1933, *Directeur de cabinet* for the Radical Laurent-Eynac first at the Ministry of Commerce in

1933–34 and then at the Ministry of Public Works in 1935–36). He was also close to Henri Queuille, another Radical politician.

Moreover, there were a series of attempts to apply industrial organization methods to public administration in the 1920s and 1930s, beginning in 1920–23, under the right-wing Bloc National Government, when Fayol was recruited to rationalize the postal service and the public monopoly of tobacco (though he was rather dissatisfied with the results).[51] In 1929, the young engineer Jean Milhaud, who had already conducted studies for the CEGOS and the ILO, was given the task of rationalizing the services of the Secretariat for the Protectorate of Morocco and in 1930 he was commissioned by the Conseil national économique to investigate the application of a new system of bonuses in the PTT, illustrating the interest that the Conseil took in questions of organization.[52] Fayolism even inspired right-wing thinking about the organization of political parties among figures like Henri de Kerillis of the Fédération républicaine, Pierre-Etienne Flandin of the Alliance démocratique and Colonel François de La Rocque of the Croix de feu (subsequently the Parti social français).[53] Meanwhile, those who discussed plans for the 'reform of the state' at the review *L'Etat moderne* (founded by a group of senior civil servants in 1928) or who gravitated towards the various enterprises of the national syndicalist Georges Valois also addressed questions of administrative and economic organization in terms that demonstrate a debt to the scientific organization movement.[54]

This resonance of organizational thinking across various sections of the country's economic, political and administrative elite was due in part to the role of members of the scientific organization movement as publicists. This phenomenon was particularly visible in the late 1920s when figures like Hyacinthe Dubreuil and Lucien Romier contributed to the flourishing literature on the American industrial model. In *Standards*, Dubreuil, a trade unionist and former mechanic who was a member of the CNOF and a close associate of Albert Thomas, offered an account of his experience working in American factories in 1927–28. The book sold thirty thousand copies in France as well as being translated into at least six languages.[55] Romier published *Qui sera le maître? L'Europe ou L'Amérique?* in 1927 and is a significant figure because, although he was a historian rather than a technician by training, he was extremely well connected in political and business circles. He had edited *La Journée industrielle*, the CGPF newspaper, and was Editor of *Le Figaro* (1925–27 and again from 1934).[56] Members of the organization movement, including Dubreuil, Nusbaumer, Milhaud, Le Chatelier and the engineer-industrialist Auguste Detoeuf, were also invited to speak about rationalization at the Comité national d'études sociales et politiques, a Parisian centre which organized debates on topical issues.[57] Perhaps the most prolific networker of all was Jean Coutrot, whose contacts extended not just across the worlds of business, engineering and modern art but to a new generation of intellectual and political figures, including Valois, Charles Spinasse and those who gathered at the *non-conformiste* reviews *Plans* and *Ordre nouveau* in the early 1930s.

Think tanks and study groups such as Redressement français (and later X-Crise) also played a vital role in disseminating a broad vision of organization as a source of social, economic and political renewal. Redressement français, created at the end of 1925 by the industrialist Ernest Mercier, was part think tank and part pressure group. Like many prominent figures in the organization movement, Mercier was a *polytechnicien*. He had made his career in the electricity supply industry and risen to become a senior industrial executive who would go on to accumulate a number of business interests (in petrol as well as electricity) in the late 1920s and 1930s. Redressement was dominated by employers' interests and its programme placed economic rationalization – industrial concentration, standardization of goods, increased productivity – at the heart of a vision of national regeneration, arguing that what Mercier called the 'moral law' of efficiency must also apply to areas such as political and administrative reform.[58] Lucien Romier and Auguste Detoeuf were among Mercier's closest associates at Redressement and Romier was an invaluable publicist for the movement. His *Explication de notre temps: idées très simples pour les Français* (1925) was an attempt to popularize the ideas promoted by Redressement and according to Robert Aron (a young intellectual between the wars) it became a touchstone for a generation of political science students in France.[59]

At the height of its success in 1927, Redressement claimed to have as many as ten thousand members and this may well have been due to its impressive communications strategy.[60] As well as organizing regular talks and meetings, especially in the Paris region, the group had a portfolio of official and subsidized publications through which it sought to mobilize support for its programme. In addition to the *Cahiers du Redressement français* which disseminated the work of the many study groups set up to develop the Redressement programme, there was a monthly bulletin which claimed a circulation of between twenty-five and thirty thousand, and a weekly regional publication, *La Région parisienne*, with a run of thirty to forty thousand copies.[61] To this we can add a number of magazines and reviews that disseminated the movement's ideas among particular sections of the population. These included the women's magazine *Minerva*, a publication aimed at veterans and their families called *Nos plaisirs* and a sports weekly for workers called *Le Muscle*. In these publications, material promoting the Redressement vision of productivity, social peace and national renovation by elites sat alongside sports news or fashion items, depending on the target audience.[62]

From the mid-1920s then, the organization agenda became increasingly visible in public debates. In the early 1930s this debate intensified as the spectacle of the Wall Street Crash and the advent of the Depression heightened anxiety about the human consequences of industrial rationalization. This period was characterized by nightmarish visions of scientifically organized work, not just in Duhamel's best-selling *Scènes de la vie future*, but in the illustrated press and in the columns of reviews such as *Esprit* and *Ordre nouveau*. In these sources, the rationalized worker appears as dehumanized, reduced to or consumed by a machine, the ultimate product of (and metaphor for) the depersonalization of mass industrial society. 'The proletarian no longer even lives in the intimacy of his own work', wrote Alexandre Marc, 'specialization gone mad, mechanization and Taylorism make him an automaton, as distinct from the artisan as a calculating machine is from Newton or Einstein.'[63] The figure of the man-machine was also apparent in filmic representations of assembly lines, a technology still rare in French factories but present on cinema screens in home-grown films like René Clair's *A nous la liberté* (1931), as well as Charlie Chaplin's international hit *Modern Times* (1936). This outcry against rationalization in mainstream cultural production serves to underline the public attention that questions of industrial organization now commanded.

Experts and Autodidacts

The engineers and industrialists who took on the role of publicists as well as practitioners of scientific organization have sometimes been dismissed as rather marginal figures, whose activities make them unrepresentative of wider business interests.[64] Such a view doubtless underestimates the extent to which questions of organization preoccupied the business world, and indeed wider audiences, in this period. But my concern here is not to map the views of the business community as a whole, nor to evaluate whether figures like Coutrot and his colleagues were 'typical'. There are other reasons to take an interest in the organizers' public role and one is its contribution to establishing scientific organization (and what would later be called management or *la gestion*) as a new field or discipline. If we think of the task facing interwar organizers in this light, the historical importance of their work in disseminating their methods becomes even clearer.

Study groups and publishing activities were essential in a context where the science of organization was only semi-institutionalized, particularly in terms of its position in the education system. Members of the organization movement often lamented the inadequacies of the training offered in this respect by France's engineering schools. Fayol, for example, had opened his *Administration industrielle et générale* with a call for education in administrative methods from primary to higher education.[65] Le Chatelier, who was not only a graduate of the Ecole polytechnique but taught there and at the Ecole des mines for many years, had long criticized scientific education in France as excessively theoretical and campaigned for a more research-based approach that would train engineers to apply scientific principles to industrial problems.[66] It was only in the 1920s that scientific organization entered the engineering curriculum. Between 1921 and 1925, the Comité Michelin organized a programme of lectures, practical classes and business placements designed to introduce engineering students to scientific management.[67] However, according to Moutet, the sessions laid on by the committee at the Ecole des mines and the Ecole des ponts et chaussées had little impact, perhaps because they were too far removed from the rest of the curriculum at these institutions.[68] Even the Ecole centrale, whose strong industrial orientation was further developed by Léon Guillet from 1922, offered only an introductory overview of scientific organization and did not seem to see a role for itself in training specialist engineer-organizers.[69] Some aspects of the new science of organization, particularly the practical techniques of task analysis that it encompassed, slotted more easily into the curriculum offered at the Conservatoire national des arts et métiers, which traditionally trained lower ranking technicians rather than senior management or state engineers. Even so, it was only from 1927 that such classes were offered, though the significance of the field was subsequently consolidated by the creation of a chair in scientific organization in 1930.[70] Fayolism had made some inroads in the leading business school, the Ecole des hautes etudes commerciales, as well as in military schools.[71] But most engineers and managers in interwar France would not have benefited from such training.

What filled the perceived gap in their education was the activity of the scientific organization movement itself. Michel Margairaz has noted that the engineers who rose to prominence in the 1930s as economic planners and government advisors were essentially auto-didacts in economic matters, even if their formal education already positioned them as part of a recognized technical elite.[72] Much the same could be said about the whole history of the scientific organization movement up to this point. Most organizers learned about these methods through a combination of industrial experience, management literature and attendance at talks, trips and study days organized by various branches of the movement. In fact, the first efficiency consultants to set up in France, such as Paul Planus and Charles Bedaux, were not even graduates.[73] But even for those engineers trained at the prestigious Ecole polytechnique or the Ecole centrale, it was immersion in the literature and activities of the rationalization movement that turned them into engineer-organizers, who, in turn, could use their participation in these networks to disseminate their methods further.[74] The CNOF, for example, laid on regular lectures and screenings of information films, published a bulletin with articles on efficiency techniques and organized a study trip to the U.S.A. in 1930.[75] Many of its members contributed to the growing literature on business organization that was promoted by publishing houses such as Dunod. One contributor to this literature was Joseph Wilbois, who published a series of guides for business leaders and offered classes at his Ecole d'administration et des affaires (School of Administration and Business), a rather grand name for a series of classes that ran from a base in the Musée social.[76] In 1934 the CNOF founded its own school, the Ecole d'organisation scientifique du travail (School of Scientific Organization), at which members gave lectures aimed mostly at professionals already working in industry. Major companies such as Alsthom, Renault, Gnome et Rhône, Hauts Fourneaux de Pont à Mousson, Peugeot, Nestlé and Kodak Pathé sent their staff to attend these classes in Paris and the numbers enrolled rose rapidly, prompting the CNOF to open a sister school in Lille. Eighty-five students attended in the Paris school's first year of operation, exceeding the target of fifty, and by 1938 the intake had risen to 342 in Paris and 150 in Lille. An alumni network was created in June 1936 and by 1941 more than two thousand students had passed through the doors of the two schools.[77] In this sense, the CNOF might be seen, not simply as an association of experts, but as an important means of *producing* expertise.

First Principles: Bodies, Machines and Systems

Since organizers helped to shape public debate and to train a new generation of managers, it is worth understanding a bit more about how they thought, how they constituted themselves as experts, and what assumptions governed their conceptions of social, economic and political rationality. It may surprise some readers that engineering contributed so heavily to the development of what is today an autonomous discipline of management. It should be remembered, however, that, along with the law faculties, the engineering schools provided French industry with much of its leadership and technical expertise in this period. There were very few people trained in management since there was little in the way of formal management education available before the Second World War. If this was seen as a gap in the curriculum in engineering schools, it was not because it was being provided in management schools instead. There was some management training in the *écoles de commerce* and even in one or two pioneering universities but the major expansion of management education in France and the establishment of the field as an academic discipline in its own right came only in the 1960s and 1970s.[78]

We should remember also that the role of the engineer has long been a heterogeneous one, by no means limited to dealing with material artefacts.[79] Indeed, among the high-profile engineers already mentioned above, one spent much of his career as a production engineer (Taylor), one rose to become a mining company executive (Fayol), one was a researcher and teacher (Le Chatelier) and one headed a family business as well as founding an organizational consultancy firm (Coutrot). Two of these figures (Le Chatelier and Coutrot) were *polytechniciens*, and one could make an argument that *polytechniciens* were not really engineers at all, since the training they received was an advanced grounding in general science and mathematics, rather than an applied scientific training of the kind we might expect an engineer to have.[80] Nonetheless, since *polytechniciens* were regarded in France as occupying the pinnacle of the engineering profession, since they played a crucial role in engineering networks and since their vision of the breadth of an engineer's role played a not insignificant part in the story I have to tell in this book, it makes little sense to depart from the conventional usage of identifying them as engineers. Moreover, though the Ecole polytechnique had originally been created to educate state engineers for public service, by the interwar period a significant number of its alumni could be found working in industry, which had more traditionally been thought of as the domain of the *centraliens*.[81]

Whether as senior executives or as middle-tier professionals with responsibility for overseeing particular operations, engineers had increasingly become de facto managers. Part of what the founders of scientific organization sought to establish then was a scientific basis for this role of the engineer as an organizer of processes and people. For Taylor and his French disciples, like Le Chatelier and Nusbaumer, Taylorism was not just a particular technique but, above all, a set of scientific principles. Thus, while critics associated the system primarily with *chronométrage*, its advocates identified it with scientific method itself, even suggesting on occasion that Taylor was simply extending the work of Descartes.[82] Such claims were often to be repeated in the years ahead: indeed the CNOF published a special issue of its bulletin in 1937 to celebrate the tricentenary of *Discours sur la méthode*, claiming that scientific organization was the application of Cartesian principles to social and economic facts.[83] For Le Chatelier the starting point for any science was a belief in determinism: 'chance does not exist', he claimed.[84] Rather, the world was governed by laws and these laws could be ascertained by observation and experimentation. Taylor and Le Chatelier saw their task as bringing the light of science into industry, where, in their view, working practices remained too often the product of habit and misconceptions: industrialists and managers were short-sighted and lacked detailed knowledge of production processes, thereby deferring to workers or foremen who were by nature 'extremely conservative' and moved by 'more or less confused reasoning' about class struggle.[85] Workers were deemed unable to determine for themselves the best way of performing a task.[86] It was those trained in scientific methods who were presumed to hold the key to industrial progress.[87] In this way, Taylorism was able to tap into a well-established discourse about science as arbiter of the general good, an ethos long promoted by the engineering schools, especially the public-service orientated Ecole polytechnique.

The organizers' scientism appealed to a distinction between the rational elite and the unindividuated masses which was common in conservative opinion in the early twentieth century and was most explicitly codified in the discourse of collective psychology. Le Chatelier claimed that 'it is a proven fact that manual workers have few personal ideas; they do not have much time to think and they imitate above all what they see around them.'[88] If this was held to be true of French workers, Le Chatelier also assumed a racial hierarchy, observing that Jules Amar's decision to conduct his physiological research for *Le Moteur humain* in North Africa was motivated by the need for particularly docile subjects, 'presenting undoubtedly, as Taylor puts it, the moral and physical temperament of cattle'.[89] Human behaviour, especially group behaviour, was nonetheless believed to obey certain laws, making it manageable scientifically: 'the actions of men and especially of groups react in a determined fashion to the influences which provoke them', Le Chatelier wrote in another volume. He went on: 'in a mass of gas, molecules wander in all directions ... and yet under the influence of a difference in pressure they move as a unit [*prennent un mouvement d'ensemble*] in an entirely predictable manner.'[90] One implication of this analogy was that workers required leadership. Thus, as Fayol put it in a note written in the early 1910s, the art of leadership or *direction* was to 'try to act on ones collaborators from above. Penetrate their thinking, find the arguments that make up their minds .... It is psychology. Influence, suggestion.'[91] Indeed, there is some evidence that Fayol was familiar with the work of Gustave Le Bon, author of *La Psychologie des foules* (first published 1895), and that this may have had a bearing on his interest in the question of leadership.[92]

There was also a rich vein of organicist thought in the development of management science in the early twentieth century. Fayol, for example, relied heavily on the analogy with the body as a way of conceptualizing the business. 'To organize', he wrote, 'is to constitute the double – material and social – organism of the business'.[93] The term 'organism' may seem banal here. It is an everyday word in French for a collective entity, much as the word 'body' might be used in English in a similar context. But this entry into everyday language of biological analogy has a long history that can be traced notably through the biologism of positivist social theory in the nineteenth century. Fayol and his fellow organizers identified themselves quite explicitly with this tradition, aligning themselves with the methods of Claude Bernard, Auguste Comte and Herbert Spencer.[94] To this extent, Fayol, like Le Chatelier, was part of a broad intellectual culture that asserted the supremacy of scientific knowledge. Indeed, the compatibility of Taylorism and Fayolism was later expressed in precisely these terms by Maurice Ponthière, a specialist in administrative organization, who asserted that both approaches sought to renovate the social and economic sciences 'by giving them a positive and concrete basis. Rejecting the discursive method, they have shown that social organisms ... lend themselves, like any other living bodies to scientific observation, Cartesian analysis, classification and experimental research.'[95]

Fayol's organicist theory was grounded in a particular conception of the unity of nature and society, in which the division of labour was central. 'The division of labour is part of the order of nature', he professed.

[I]t can be observed in the animal world where, the more a being perfects itself, the more it possesses organs differentiated by function; it can be observed in human societies where, the greater the social body, the closer the relationship between organ and function. As a society grows, new organs appear to replace the single organ that had been responsible for all functions in the primitive model.[96]

Thus, organizational complexity was regarded as a feature of both biological and social progress. Such broad social theorizing may seem out of place in a management manual but, according to Fayol's reasoning, this law of nature had direct implications for the principles of sound business organization. It established a functionalist conception of organization, according to which each service or individual must fulfil a clearly defined role. For Taylor, this process of functional sub-division of the business applied to management functions too, so that different managers were given the roles of planning, monitoring and so on. But Fayol argued that 'a body with two heads is, in the social world, as in the animal world, a monster'.[97] It was considered a fact of nature that complex organisms required direction from the centre.

If Fayol's theory defined good management in terms of administrative unity and hierarchy, it also implied a certain model of social relations in the workplace. Individual interests were to be subordinated to the business, which was assumed to represent the collective interest of all employees. Personal ambitions, passions or laziness were thus regarded as damaging or destabilizing, since all effort was to be channelled towards the goals of the business.[98] To combat these dangers a combination of clear administrative systems and personal leadership was required. Indeed, Fayol drew a parallel here between the business and the family, implying (particularly in the context of his statements elsewhere about hierarchy) that the relationship between managers and workers was somehow analogous to that of fathers with their children.[99] Employers thus had an interest in and a responsibility for the private lives of their workers, notably for their health, morality, and general social stability.[100] In this respect, Fayolism was part of a well-established current of social paternalism in French industry.

It should be remembered here that organicism has proved a remarkably versatile framework in modern social and political thought and does not in itself imply alignment with one particular ideological current. As Cécile Laborde has pointed out, in the nineteenth century it served both idealists and positivists, both the laissez-faire arguments of Herbert Spencer and the social interventionist vision of the *solidaristes*.[101] Similarly, while the model of the body was used in part to justify hierarchies, the organicism of scientific organizers was less about the reconstitution of 'natural communities' (a central preoccupation for Maurrasians, for example), than about the management of dynamic working organisms. This reflected in part the changing conceptions of the body itself in the late nineteenth and early twentieth centuries and particularly the tendency to conceive of the body as analogous to a machine or motor. What machines and human beings had in common in this analysis was their capacity for work. Both were sites of energy conversion.[102] Thus, Le Chatelier pointed out, 'like the steam engine, the human organism burns an appropriate fuel' and, as with any other machine, the efficiency of this 'human machine' should be measured.[103]

This analogy provided a rationale for techniques like time and motion study and more broadly helped legitimize the role of the engineer in matters of (human) organization, but it was also the basis for the development of industrial psycho-physiology. As Anson Rabinbach has shown, this field had emerged from physiologists' appropriation of a concept of energy that had been born in nineteenth-century physics. Through the work of Helmholtz in particular, physicists came to conceive of the forces of nature as manifestations of a single universal energy which could be converted from one form to another (but not increased or destroyed) – a worldview that is expressed in the laws of thermodynamics.[104] In this universe permeated by energy, the concept of work encompassed the expenditure of energy in all its forms – in human beings, in machines and in nature more generally.[105] Soon physiologists began to apply the laws of energy conversion and conservation to the study of the working body. In the 1880s, Etienne-Jules Marey used chronophotography to analyse human and animal movement, while Auguste Chauveau studied the efficiency of muscles.[106] By the time the First World War broke out, Jules Amar (one of Chauveau's former students) had carried out extensive experiments measuring the speed, muscle activity, calorific consumption, respiration and morphology of working bodies. He also studied the movements of workers in specific trades to ascertain which gestures, posture and tools resulted in the least fatigue.[107] With such techniques, work scientists sought to enhance the efficiency of the human motor by determining its optimum working conditions. Moreover, for these scientists and for the social reformers who soon began to take an interest in their work, this field of research promised a solution to some of the most profound problems of industrial society: it would increase productivity while sparing the worker, allowing science to reconcile the interests of labour and capital.[108] To this extent, the physiologists shared the engineers' conviction that science would provide the answers to social and economic questions.

Interwar Organization and the Organism-Machine

As the organization agenda evolved in the interwar years it continued to be marked by this transfer of ideas between engineering and the biological sciences. Indeed, arguably, it became increasingly preoccupied with the problem of how to integrate the human (physical, physiological or psychological) elements and the mechanical elements in industrial work. Psychotechnics was certainly concerned with this question of 'fit', and fit with a post could be readily equated in this productivist vision with integration into society more broadly.[109] Organicism too remained a feature, especially in the 1930s. Fayol died in 1925 and it has been suggested that Fayolists lost ground, at least in terms of internal politics, in the merger of groups that produced the CNOF.[110] But the Fayolist approach to business organization still had promoters in high places, including Joseph Wilbois, the Catholic Leplaysian who ran the Ecole d'administration et des affaires, and Maurice

Ponthière, who was one of the founder members of the CNOF and went on to head its School of Scientific Organization in 1934. Ponthière was a Catholic nationalist journalist who had become the managing editor of the magazine *Mon bureau* in 1925.[111] Along with Wilbois, he was one of a group of organization specialists to emerge in the early 1920s from outside the engineering profession, his career trajectory exemplifying the model of the self-made organizational expert.

In the manuals he published and in the core lessons he dispensed at the School of Scientific Organization, Ponthière affirmed a very explicitly organicist theory of organization. 'All living things are organisms', he explained: 'a plant, a dog, each is an organism. Human society is also composed of living things: a State, a town, a factory, a business. These are organisms.'[112] Each of these organisms, he argued, was composed of organs: 'a dog has paws, a stomach, a brain; a factory has machines, workers, accountants, directors. Organization is the organs taken together, their arrangement in relation to each other, the rules that govern their functioning'.[113] Functional organization was seen as a fact of nature: 'Everything that lives is organized. An earthworm is organized for its life as an earthworm. A man is organized for human life.'[114] As in Fayol's work, this was the basis of a theory of organization that emphasized both unity and functional hierarchy.

This holist functionalism of the interwar science of organization was a visual as well as a verbal one. The organigramme, the invention of which has been attributed to Fayol, was used as a means of rendering immediately apparent the lines of communication and command within an organization.[115] It could also serve a diagnostic function: if a clear diagram could not be produced, it was argued, this indicated an organizational confusion which ought to be eliminated. In his lessons at the School of Scientific Organization, Ponthière put the 'organ' back in the term organigramme: his diagrams incorporated pictures of hearts and eyeballs to represent crucial functions of the business (finance and documentation services respectively), providing a reminder that the ostensibly neutral language of the organigramme (which purports to describe rather than prescribe) in fact emerged from a particular historical understanding of the link between the organization of social and economic entities, such as businesses, and the organization of the human body.

Since Ponthière was a specialist in administrative organization, it is not surprising that his theory owed a considerable debt to Fayol's work, but organizers who had worked in other fields or whose conception of scientific organization reflected the more syncretic approach that was emerging between the wars also drew parallels between businesses and organisms. Eugène Nusbaumer, who had pioneered the Taylorization of the French armaments industry during the First World War and was critical of Fayolism, advocated an organicist theory of organization in the late 1920s.[116] He observed that both biological and social organisms evolved from simplicity to complexity, from confusion to precision, from independence to interdependence, cooperation and hierarchy. From this he deduced that the engineer could determine the advantages and disadvantages of different forms of industrial organization through reasoning by biological analogy.[117] Similarly, Paul Planus, whose consultancy firm helped to disseminate time and motion study practices in France, spoke of the complexity of modern businesses in terms borrowed from evolutionary theory – an outlook expressed both in Planus's writings on scientific organization and in his firm's adoption of the slogan 'S'adapter ou disparaître' ('Adapt or die').[118] It was noted earlier that since the First World War, organization had been seen by its advocates as the key to national strength as well as business success and as the threat of another war began to loom in the 1930s, Planus's slogan must have seemed increasingly resonant. Coutrot too was happy to use organic analogies as he demonstrated in *Le Système nerveux des entreprises* (The Nervous System of Businesses) in 1935. What was proposed in this work was an administrative tracking system that would monitor and coordinate a job as it worked its way through the various stages of production, from order to despatch. This approach, which became known as *le planning*, offered a (cheaper) paper alternative to the mechanical coordination system of the production line, but its operation was described in biological terms: 'the circuit is essentially the same as in an organism: the peripheral sensation is transmitted via the nervous system, goes to the brain [*centre cérébral*], [and] is sent back to the muscular system for execution.'[119]

The appeal of this analogy, as Coutrot acknowledged, was that it offered the engineer a compelling way of visualizing abstract processes and conceptualizing the business as a system – i.e. something that must be conceived as a whole, in terms of the interdependent nature of its component parts.[120] What is equally striking, however, is the interchangeability of organic and mechanical metaphors in these interwar writings on business organization. Nusbaumer concluded his argument that engineers and organizers should reason by biological analogy with a quote from the German industrialist Walter Rathenau in which he spoke of society as a 'living machine'.[121] Ponthière blurred the lines between the organic, the mechanical and the social when he compared simple and complex businesses. In a primitive business with one person at its head, he explained, a single human brain was the organ that directed the work. But just as manual work was increasingly done by the power of water, steam or electricity, rather than human muscles, so in more complex and evolved businesses, the human brain was replaced by an office or administration, 'an artificial brain ... a bureaucratic motor'.[122] Here, the double metaphor that allowed the business to be at once an organism and a machine could legitimize the increasingly bureaucratic nature of capitalism, and of course the professional role of organizers. For Coutrot, the whole human history of work could be understood in terms of the blurred lines between bodies and machines:

It is with his hands, his nails, his teeth that man began to work. Then he equipped himself with tools: the knife, the stick, the spade. Then he created machines, metal organisms.

Finally he let businesses be born, and around these businesses, non-material mechanisms, which he did not really see or understand: industrial organizations and economic mechanisms.[123]

These words, spoken in a radio broadcast in 1937 on 'How in the Twentieth Century We Can and Must Produce', articulated a vision of society in which machines, businesses and the economy as a whole were conceived as extensions of a human body defined by its capacity for work.

The work-centred view of the body and of society, outlined in this instance by Coutrot but implicit in all the endeavours of the scientific organization movement, illuminates one final and crucial aspect of the culture of organization between the wars – the universalizing tendency which encouraged organizers to believe that any activity could and should be scientifically organized. This was apparent in the aspirations of early figures like Taylor, who argued that

> the same principles can be applied with equal force to all social activities: to the management of our homes; the management of our farms; the management of the business of our tradesmen, large or small, of our churches, our philanthropic institutions, our universities, and our governmental departments.[124]

A similar outlook will be apparent in the projects of French interwar organizers that I discuss in later chapters.

Many of the examples of interwar holist thinking that I have cited here come from the 1930s. This is not a coincidence, for if a certain holism or systems thinking which blurred the line between the body and the machine was present in the French organization movement from its inception, the fresh wave of accusations about the dehumanizing effects of rationalization which emerged in the early 1930s brought the holist and 'humanist' claims of the movement to the fore. In 1930 and 1931, organizers met at the CNOF for sessions on 'Industrial Organization and the Human Value of the Worker' or 'Has Rationalization Gone Bankrupt?'[125] Several representatives of the movement spoke at a meeting of the Comité national d'études in 1931, which asked, 'Does rationalization necessarily entail economic crises and lower the spiritual level of humanity?'[126] This is not to say that the organizers who participated in such discussions merely succumbed to the anxieties of the moment and abandoned their faith in science. What was at stake in these debates was the legitimacy of scientific organization and its promoters were keen to defend it, however imperfect its current manifestations might be. Demonstrating their attention to the 'human factor' was one way of doing this and the benefits of industrial psycho-physiology were often showcased when the rationalization movement communicated with a wider public in the 1930s – this was the case in a series of radio broadcasts in 1930–31, for example.[127]

What had emerged in France by the time this mood of crisis took hold was a set of networks that promoted a broad syncretic approach to scientific organization rather than a particular method such as Taylorism. The movement's interest in the 'human factor' in the 1930s was not a novelty. But both in France and internationally there were signs that the nature of this interest in the 'human' was shifting. By 1938, a report on recent international trends issued by the Comité international de l'organisation scientifique noted that organizers had begun to pay more attention to the role of the will and affect in production. The term 'human factor' had become virtually synonymous in the 1920s with industrial psycho-physiology, especially psychotechnics, but in the 1930s it became preferable to speak of 'human problems' or 'the problems of man at work'. What this shift in vocabulary signalled, according to the International Committee, was a concern with 'how to adapt business methods to the demands, desires and aspirations of the men with whom they are in relation'.[128] This 'hearts and minds' discourse implied a rather broader psychological agenda than that of aptitude testing, as it focused attention on the motivation and personalities of workers. The person-centred rhetoric was clearly a response to the humanist critique of rationalization but this trend also reflected a heightened concern in the 1930s with class conflict and how to eliminate it. This 'human problem' and the solutions proposed by members of the organization movement are the subject of the next chapter.

Notes

1.   P. Nord. 1991. 'Social Defence and Conservative Regeneration: The National Revival, 1900–1914' in R. Tombs (ed.), *Nationhood and Nationalism in France: From Boulangism to the Great War, 1889–1918*, London: Harper Collins, 210–28.
2.   K. Passmore. Forthcoming. *The Right in the French Third Republic*.
3.   G. Humphreys. 1986. *Taylorism in France 1904–1920: The Impact of Scientific Management on Factory Relations and Society*, New York and London: Garland, 57–58. Translations of Taylor's work began appearing from 1907 and included two works on scientific management prefaced by Le Chatelier just before the First World War: F.W. Taylor. 1913. *La Direction des ateliers*, Paris: H. Dunod & E. Pinat; and idem. 1912. *Principes d'organisation scientifique des usines*, Paris: H. Dunod & E. Pinat. On Le Chatelier, see M. Letté. 2004. *Henry Le Chatelier (1850–1936) ou la science appliquée à l'industrie*, Rennes: Presses universitaires de Rennes.
4.   Yves Cohen shows how another early engineer-organizer, Ernest Mattern, came to questions of organization through his industrial experience and his reading of French writers on organization such as Jules Simonet. See Y. Cohen. 2001. *Organiser à l'aube du taylorisme: la pratique d'Ernest Mattern chez Peugeot, 1906–1919*, Besançon: Presses universitaires franc-comtoises, 165–66. Cohen also points to earlier precursors of scientific organization, citing Michelle Perrot. 1976. 'Travailler et produire: Claude-Lucien Bergery et les débuts du management en France' in F. Bédarida (ed.), *Mélanges d'histoire sociale offerts à Jean Maîtron*, Paris: Editions ouvrières.
5.   First published in the *Bulletin de la société de l'industrie minérale*, Fayol's *Administration industrielle et générale* went on to be published in book form and went through multiple editions, the latest of which was in 1999, reflecting the book's status as a classic.

References here are to the edition published by Bordas in 1979, which is a facsimile of the Dunod 1918 edition. On the relationship between Fayol's industrial management experience and his theory of administration, see D. Reid. 1986. 'Genèse du fayolisme', *Sociologie du travail* 1, 75–93.

6. Fayol's use of the term 'administration' was quite particular and it has been suggested that it derived from Saint-Simon. See J.-L. Peaucelle. 2003. 'Saint-Simon, aux origines de la pensée de Henri Fayol', *Entreprises et histoire* 34, 68–83. The other articles in this special issue also focus on Fayol.

7. 'Administrer, c'est prévoir, organiser, commander, coordonner et contrôler.' Fayol, *Administration industrielle et générale*, 5.

8. F.W. Taylor. 1907. *Etudes sur l'organisation du travail dans les usines*, Paris: H. Dunod & E. Pinat, 5.

9. On the early development of Taylorism in France see, P. Fridenson. 1987. 'Un tournant taylorien de la société française (1904–1918)', *Annales ESC* 42(5), 1031–60; A. Moutet. 1975. 'Les Origines du système Taylor en France: le point de vue patronal (1907–1914)', *Mouvement social* 93, 10–45; Humphreys, *Taylorism in France*; Cohen, *Organiser à l'aube du taylorisme*, esp. 163–92.

10. J. Joffre. 1932. *Mémoires du Maréchal Joffre, 1910–1917*, Paris: Plon, 12–14. For Joffre (35–36) this was a way of building doctrinal unity in favour of an offensive strategy. Joffre was later promoted to the rank of Field Marshal. Although *Administration industrielle et générale* was not published until 1916, Fayol had begun to express his managerial thinking in public lectures from 1900.

11. On this cross-fertilization, see F. Blancpain. 1973. 'Les Carnets inédits de Fayol: présentation', *Bulletin de l'Institut international d'administration publique* 28, 602; S. Rials. 1977. *Administration et organisation: de l'organisation de la bataille à la bataille de l'organisation dans l'administration française*, Paris: Editions Beauchesne, 70; Peaucelle, 'Saint-Simon', 80–81 and K. Passmore. Forthcoming. 'La Droite, l'organisation et la psychologie collective dans l'entre-deux-guerres'.

12. R. Kuisel. 1981. *Capitalism and the State in Modern France: Renovation and Economic Management in the Twentieth Century*, Cambridge: Cambridge University Press, 34–37. See also M. Fine. 1977. 'Albert Thomas: A Reformer's Vision of Modernization, 1914–1932', *Journal of Contemporary History* 12(3), 545–64.

13. On this renegotiation of gender boundaries in the workplace see L.L. Downs. 1995. *Manufacturing Inequality: Gender Division in the French and British Metalworking Industries 1914–1939*, Ithaca: Cornell University Press. As a new productivity drive got underway in France after World War Two, low-grade production line jobs continued to be gendered as feminine particularly in the rapidly expanding household electrical goods sector, while in automobile construction a racial division of labour was also apparent in the high proportion of immigrant men doing production-line work.

14. Kuisel, *Capitalism and the State*, 48–49.

15. Kuisel, *Capitalism and the State*, 39–48, 50–52.

16. On economic relations between Europe and America in the aftermath of the First World War, see F. Costigliola. 1984. *Awkward Dominion: American Political, Economic and Cultural Relations with Europe 1919–1933*, Ithaca: Cornell University Press.

17. Rials, *Administration et organisation*, 133. The war had also brought translations of works by other American organizers: Henry L. Gantt's work was published in the *Revue de métallurgie* in 1915 and Frank Gilbreth's in the *Revue générale des sciences* in 1916. See Rials, *Administration et organisation*, 54–55.

18. The translations of Taylor's work cited earlier were published in association with the *Revue de métallurgie*. Le Chatelier was the founding editor of the review from 1903 and was elected President of the Société d'encouragement in 1904.

19. For further detail on the earlier movements and creation of the CNOF, see A. Moutet. 1997. *Les Logiques de l'entreprise: la rationalisation dans l'industrie française de l'entre-deux-guerres*, Paris: Editions de l'EHESS, 36–40. On Michelin's role in promoting Taylorism see

S.L. Harp. 2001. *Marketing Michelin: Advertising and Cultural Identity in Twentieth-Century France*, Baltimore: The Johns Hopkins University Press, Chapter 6.

20. Moutet, *Les Logiques*, 42–43.
21. Many of the leading figures in the interwar movement, including Auguste Detoeuf, Jean Coutrot and Hyacinthe Dubreuil, visited the U.S.A. The International Institute in Geneva was founded in association with the ILO and the Comité international d'organisation scientifique which organized many of the international conferences on scientific organization. It was funded by American industrialist Edward Filene's Twentieth-Century Fund but this funding was eventually withdrawn during the Depression.
22. The CEGOS is today an international training and consultancy group. The CNOF continued to promote scientific organization throughout the postwar period before being subsumed into the Institut français de gestion in 1997.
23. See G. Ribeill. 1980. 'Les Débuts de l'ergonomie en France à la veille de la Première Guerre mondiale', *Mouvement social* 113, 3–36 and A. Rabinbach. 1992. *The Human Motor: Energy, Fatigue and the Origins of Modernity*, Berkeley: University of California Press.
24. On the institutionalization of psychotechnics and related specialisms, see William H. Schneider. 1991. 'The Scientific Study of Labor in Interwar France', *French Historical Studies* 17(2), 410–46. Peugeot created a psychotechnic service in 1938 under Raymond Bonnardel who had trained with Lahy.
25. See, for example, J. Amar. 1920. *L'Orientation professionnelle*, Paris: Dunod; J. Fontègne. 1921. *L'Orientation professionnelle et la détermination de l'aptitude*, Neuchâtel: Delachaux et Niestlé, prefaced by the pedagogue Ferdinand Buisson; J. Fontègne. 1923. *Manualisme et éducation*, Paris: Librairie de l'enseignement technique, Léon Eyrolles Editeur, prefaced by the Director of Technical Education, Edmond Labbé. Mary Louise Roberts discusses the gender implications of *orientation professionnelle* and women's educational reform in M.L. Roberts. 1994. *Civilization Without Sexes: Reconstructing Gender in Postwar France*, Chicago: University of Chicago Press, 183–96.
26. *Bulletin de l'Institut national d'orientation professionnelle* (published from 1929).
27. Since 1941, INETOP has been an institute of the Conservatoire national des arts et metiers.
28. See especially R. Kuisel. 1993. *Seducing the French: The Dilemma of Americanization*, Berkeley: University of California Press.
29. M. Beale. 1999. *The Modernist Enterprise: French Elites and the Threat of Modernity 1900–1940*, Stanford: Stanford University Press, 8, 100–101 and J. Merkle. 1980. *Management and Ideology: The Legacy of the International Scientific Management Movement*, Berkeley: University of California Press, 158–60.
30. Beale, *The Modernist Enterprise*, 100.
31. See Rabinbach, *The Human Motor*, 242–3; Schneider, 'The Scientific Study of Labor', 444.
32. E. Nusbaumer. 1924. *L'Organisation scientifique des usines*, Paris: Nouvelle Librairie nationale. This volume was based on Nusbaumer's lectures as part of the series organized by the Comité Michelin and was prefaced by Le Chatelier. J.-M. Lahy. 1916. *Le Système Taylor et la physiologie du travail professionel*, Paris: Masson, viii–x.
33. See, for example, Duhamel's famous description of the Chicago stockyards in G. Duhamel. 1934. *Scènes de la vie future*, Paris: Arthème, Fayard et Cie, 65–66.
34. A. Siegfried. 1931. *Les Etats-Unis d'aujourd'hui*, Paris: A. Colin, 347. First published in 1927.
35. Charles de Fréminville. 1934. 'Discours à l'Assemblée générale de la Société des ingénieurs civils', *Bulletin du CNOF* February 1934, 53–5.
36. Blancpain, 'Les Carnets inédits', 597 and Rials, *Administration et organisation*, 105 assert the complementarity of Taylorism and Fayolism. This was also acknowledged by many writers at the time such as: J. Wilbois and P. Vanuxem. 1919. *Essai sur la conduite des affaires et la direction des hommes*, Paris: Payot, 125–39; J. Chevalier. 1928. *La Technique de l'organisation des entreprises*, Paris: Librairie française de documentation commerciale et industriel, Editions Langlois et Cie, 30 and Charles de Fréminville in his preface to Chevalier, *La Technique*, iii.

37. Rabinbach, *The Human Motor*, 246–47.
38. The trend towards rapprochement is noted by P. Devinat. 1927. *L'Organisation scientifique du travail en Europe. Bureau international du travail, Etudes et Documents Série B (Conditions économique)*, Geneva: Bureau international du travail, 32–3 and is discussed in Rabinbach, *The Human Motor*, 273–74.
39. Moutet notes the tensions between different currents as they jostled for position within the new organization but acknowledges that a range of approaches continued to be covered, 40–44.
40. *Bulletin du CNOF* June 1929, 14. Lahy was the psychologist in question.
41. Nolan, *Visions of Modernity*, 131–32.
42. On the RKW, see Nolan, *Visions of Modernity*, 134–37.
43. E.g., one member of the movement defined rationalization in 1931 as including not just industrial and commercial concentration but Taylorism, business organization and normalization. J.-P. Lugrin. 1931. 'La Rationalisation a-t-elle fait faillite?' *Bulletin du CNOF* June 1931, 167.
44. *L'Organisation scientifique du travail en Europe*, Geneva: Bureau international du travail, 80.
45. See Moutet, *Les Logiques* and L.L. Frader. 2008. *Breadwinners and Citizens: Gender and the Making of the French Social Model*, Durham and London: Duke University Press for a detailed portrait.
46. Frader, *Breadwinners and Citizens*, 72 (Jaeger), 199 (Gillet), 115 (Comité des Forges) and 124–27 (testing of telephone operators).
47. D. Gardey. 2001. *La Dactylographe et l'expéditionnaire: histoire des employés de bureau 1890–1930*, Paris: Belin, 127–38.
48. Rials, *Administration et organisation*, 140.
49. Herriot served as Président du conseil in 1924, 1926 and 1932, Tardieu in 1929, 1930 and 1932. On Tardieu and organization, see F. Monnet. 1993. *Refaire la République. André Tardieu, une dérive réactionnaire*, Paris: Fayard, esp. 27–33, 87–94. Loucheur, Thomas and Clémentel died in 1931, 1932 and 1936 respectively.
50. The Conseil national économique was an advisory body which included representatives of labour, capital and consumers and was symptomatic of a desire to involve economic interest groups in policy making
51. See Rials, *Administration et organisation*, 70, 174–80.
52. See O. Dard. 2002. *Le Rendez-vous manqué des relèves des années trente*, Paris: Presses Universitaires de France, 89–90. On Jean Milhaud's work for the ILO see J. Milhaud. 1956. *Chemins faisant. Tranches de vie*, Paris: Editions Hommes et Techniques, 47–62.
53. Passmore, 'La Droite, l'organisation et la psychologie collective'.
54. See Dard, *Le Rendez-vous manqué*, 29–34, 47–49.
55. H. Dubreuil. 1929. *Standards*, Paris: Grasset. J. Maîtron. 1986. *Dictionnaire biographique du mouvement ouvrier. Vol 26*, 64; Fine, 'Hyacinthe Dubreuil', 56 says the book was translated into seven languages, while Maîtron counts six.
56. Romier returned to *Le Figaro* in 1934.
57. The Comité was founded by Albert Kahn, a financier who sponsored a range of social and cultural intitiatives, and its activities are discussed in G.B. Berthier. 1995. 'Le Comité national d'études sociales et politiques, 1916–1931' in J. Beausoleil and P. Ory (eds), *Albert Kahn, 1860–1940: réalités d'une utopie*, Boulogne: Musée Albert Kahn. Dubreuil worked as a rapporteur to the committee.
58. R. Kuisel. 1967. *Ernest Mercier, French Technocrat*, Berkeley: University of California Press, 54, 57–60. The electricity industry was particularly strongly represented at Redressement and interest in rationalization in these quarters reflected the fact that this was an industry concerned with the development of infrastructure. In these days before EDF (Electricité de France), electrical supply was the responsibility of a patchwork of small suppliers and it is not hard to see why industrial concentration seemed to make sense as a way of developing a coherent network and offering more even provision.
59. Robert Aron cited in Kuisel, *Ernest Mercier*, 64–65.

60.   Kuisel, *Capitalism and the State*, 89.
61.   Kuisel, *Ernest Mercier*, 65.
62.   Kuisel, *Ernest Mercier*, 66, 77.
63.   A. Marc. 1933. 'Le Prolétariat', *Esprit* 4, 560. Similarly, a photomontage by Marcel Ichac on the cover of *Vu*, 1 March 1933 featured a man being swallowed up by enormous cogs and wheels, with the caption 'The End of Civilization'. This echoed Duhamel's representation of abattoir workers reduced to killing machines by repetitive labour in *Scènes de la vie future*, 65–66.
64.   Richard Vinen makes this observation about Jean Coutrot, for example. See R. Vinen. 1991. *The Politics of French Business 1936–1945*, Cambridge: Cambridge University Press, 63–67.
65.   Fayol, *Administration industrielle*, 14–17.
66.   Le Chatelier also occupied a chair at the Collège de France from 1897 and a chair at the Sorbonne from 1907. On his criticisms of scientific teaching, especially at the Ecole polytechnique, see Letté, *Henry Le Chatelier*, 168–70 and F. Le Chatelier. 1968. *Henry Le Chatelier, un grand savant d'hier, un précurseur*, Paris: Revue de Métallurgie, 163–76.
67.   Le Chatelier, *Henry Le Chatelier*, 177–87, 253; Moutet, *Les Logiques*, 36–37.
68.   Moutet, *Les Logiques*, 36–37.
69.   Moutet, *Les Logiques*, 28–31.
70.   Moutet, *Les Logiques*, 30–31.
71.   Rials, *Administration et organisation*, 70. Fayol had been invited to give a series of lectures at the Ecole des hautes etudes commerciales in 1918–19 and one of his best-known disciples, the engineer Joseph Carlioz, also taught there. The lectures given by the Carlioz in 1919 were published as J. Carlioz. 1921. *Le Gouvernement des entreprises commerciales et industrielles*, Paris: Dunod.
72.   M. Margairaz. 1995. 'Les Autodidactes et les experts: réseaux et parcours intellectuels dans les années 1930' in B. Belhoste et al. (eds), *La France des X. Deux siècles d'histoire* Paris: Economica, 169–74.
73.   Moutet, *Les Logiques*, 38. Odile Henry has recently shown that among *ingénieurs-conseils* there was a high proportion of auto-didacts and 'engineers' who had not actually completed their studies because of the war. This reflects the fact that this was an emerging profession, especially compared to the prestigious *corps* of state engineers. See O. Henry. 2006. 'L'Impossible Professionnalisation du métier d'ingénieur-conseil (1880–1954)', *Mouvement social* 214, 37–54.
74.   On the importance of consultancy firms in the spread of scientific organization in interwar France, see Moutet, *Les Logiques*, 32–33.
75.   See *Bulletin du CNOF* (from 1927) for a flavour of the group's activities.
76.   See, for example, Wilbois and Vanuxem, *Essai sur la conduite des affaires*; J. Wilbois. 1926. *Le Chef d'entreprise: sa fonction et sa personne*, Paris: Alcan; J. Wilbois and A. Letixerant. 1928. *Comment faire vivre une entreprise*, Paris: Alcan; J. Wilbois. 1934. *La Psychologie au service du chef d'entreprise*, Paris: Alcan.
77.   *Bulletin du CNOF* October 1938, 1, 35. A number of professional training schools and government departments also sent students or employees for training at the school in the 1930s. The 1941 figures are from 'Assemblée générale du 6 novembre 1941', *Bulletin du CNOF* November 1941, 3, 5.
78.   M.-E. Chessel. 2001. *Le Technocrate, le patron et le professeur: une histoire de l'enseignement supérieur de gestion*, Paris: Belin, 12–13.
79.   This point is also made by Gabrielle Hecht in G. Hecht. 1998. *The Radiance of France: Nuclear Power and National Identity After World War Two*, Cambridge, Mass: MIT Press, 25.
80.   On the Ecole polytechnique and the education dispensed there see B. Belhoste, A. Dahan Dalmedico and A. Picon. 1994. *La Formation polytechnicienne 1794–1994*, Paris: Dunod; and T. Shinn. 1980. *L'Ecole polytechnique*, Paris: Presses de la Fondation nationale des sciences politiques. It might also be noted that Coutrot was part of a cohort whose education at the Ecole polytechnique was interrupted by World War One, but who were nonetheless treated as engineers and as members of the school's alumni networks.

81. In his study of French *patrons* between 1912 and 1973, Maurice Lévy-Leboyer found that 48.3 per cent were educated at the Ecole polytechnique, 16.5 per cent at the Ecole centrale and 18.2 per cent at other engineering schools. For the year 1929, Lévy-Leboyer's sample revealed 55.4 per cent were engineers. The other main route into management was through the law faculties. See M. Lévy-Leboyer. 1979. 'Le Patronat français 1912–1973' in M. Lévy-Leboyer (ed.), *Le Patronat de la seconde industrialisation*, Paris: Les Editions ouvrières.

82. See H. Le Chatelier. 1928. *Le Taylorisme*, Paris: Dunod, 7; Nusbaumer, *L'Organisation scientifique*, 317.

83. *Bulletin du CNOF* November 1937.

84. Le Chatelier, *Le Taylorisme*, VII.

85. Le Chatelier, *Le Taylorisme*, XII–XIV; Taylor, *Etudes sur l'organisation du travail*, 25, 319. Le Chatelier's enthusiasm for Taylorism was just one expression of his ongoing quest to strengthen links between science and industry. See Letté, *Henry Le Chatelier*.

86. Le Chatelier, preface to F.W. Taylor, *Principes d'organisation scientifique*, 2, cited in Letté, *Henry Le Chatelier*, 213.

87. Taylor asserted the superiority of the engineer's knowledge in *The Principles of Scientific Management*, 103, collected with other works in F.W. Taylor. 1947. *Scientific Management*, London: Harper and Row.

88. Le Chatelier, Preface to J. Amar. 1914. *Le Moteur humain*, Paris: H. Dunod & E. Pinat, xvi.

89. Le Chatelier, Preface to Amar, *Le Moteur humain*, x. On 'race' and work science see Frader, 'From Muscles to Nerves'.

90. H. Le Chatelier, Preface to E. Nusbaumer. 1924. *l'organisation scientifique des usines*, Paris: Nouvelle librairie nationale, x.

91. Note from the Fayol papers cited in Y. Cohen. 2003. 'Fayol, un instituteur de l'ordre industriel', *Entreprises et Histoire* 34, 47.

92. Cohen observes ('Fayol, un instituteur', 46) that the focus on the role of the '*chef*' is not apparent in the early notes in Fayol's papers from around 1892 but is apparent by the 1900s. He notes that the archives contain a note headed 'Psychologie. Psychologie des foules – Gustave Le Bon', suggesting that Fayol was at least familiar with Le Bon's work (though the content of the note does not refer directly to it). Cohen therefore hypothesizes that the emergence of the theme of leadership may have been shaped in part by Le Bon's theory.

93. Fayol, *Administration industrielle*, 5.

94. See Rials, *Administration et organisation*, 96.

95. M. Ponthière. 1942. 'Principes généraux d'OST et leur évolution. Leçon 12' in *Leçons de l'Ecole d'organisation scientifique du travail*, 15. The lessons from this school were deposited at the Bibliothèque nationale in 1942 but it appears that much of the material originated before the war and was updated only very minimally during the Occupation. I read this source in this light.

96. Fayol, *Administration industrielle*, 20.

97. Fayol, *Administration industrielle*, 27.

98. Fayol, *Administration industrielle*, 27–28.

99. Fayol, *Administration industrielle*, 27–28, 127.

100. Fayol, *Administration industrielle*, 35.

101. C. Laborde. 2000. *Pluralist Thought and the State in Britain and France, 1900–1925*, Basingstoke: MacMillan, 13. The *solidariste* tradition is discussed further in Chapter Two.

102. Le Chatelier, Preface to Amar, *Le Moteur humain*, V.

103. Le Chatelier, Preface to Amar, *Le Moteur humain*, VI–VII.

104. Rabinbach, *The Human Motor*, 3.

105. Rabinbach, *The Human Motor*, 59–60.

106. Rabinbach, *The Human Motor*, 84–119, 127–28.

107. Rabinbach, *The Human Motor*, 185–88.

108. Rabinbach, *The Human Motor*, Chapter 8 esp. 234–37.

109.   Matthew Price makes this point in relation to some of the pioneers of psychotechnics who were involved in rehabilitation science during World War One and I would like to thank him for his generosity in providing me with a copy of his dissertation. See M. Price. 1998. 'Bodies and Souls: The Rehabilitation of Maimed Soldiers in France and Germany During the First World War', Ph.D. Dissertation, Stanford University.

110.   Moutet, *Les Logiques*, 42; Taylor had died in 1915 but Le Chatelier would live until 1936.

111.   On interwar Leplaysianism and Wilbois's place in it, see B. Kalaora and A. Savoye. 1985. 'La Mutation du movement le playsien', *Revue française de sociologie* 26(2), 257–76.

112.   M. Ponthière. 1931. *Le Nouvel Esprit des affaires*, Paris: Nouvelle librairie commerciale, 17.

113.   Ponthière, *Le Nouvel Esprit*, 17.

114.   Ponthière, *Le Nouvel Esprit*, 18.

115.   See Cohen, *Organiser à l'aube du taylorisme*, 321–29.

116.   Nusbaumer's role in the development of Taylorism in France is discussed, along with that of his fellow engineer Charles de Fréminville, in A. Moutet. 1984. 'La Première Guerre Mondiale et le Taylorisme' in M. de Montmollin and O. Pastré (eds), *Le Taylorisme*, Paris: La Découverte.

117.   E. Nusbaumer. 1929. 'De l'idée d'organisation dans son application à l'industrie', *Bulletin du CNOF* November, 3–4, 7.

118.   P. Planus. 1937. 'S'adapter ou disparaître', *Méthodes* March, 40.

119.   J. Coutrot. 1935. *Le Système nerveux des entreprises*, Paris: Delmas, 26. The comparison with the production line is made by Coutrot on p.28 and informs Aimée Moutet's discussion of the implementation of *le planning* in French industry. See Moutet, *Les Logiques*, 284–302.

120.   Coutrot, *Le Système nerveux*, 1, 20.

121.   Nusbaumer, 'De l'idée d'organisation', 12.

122.   M. Ponthière. 1935. *Le Bureau moteur*, Paris: Delmas, 85–86.

123.   J. Coutrot. 1937. *Comment, au XXe siècle, on peut et doit produire*, Paris: COST, 1. Broadcast on 2 July 1937.

124.   Taylor, *Principles of Scientific Management*, 8.

125.   J. Coutrot. 1930. 'L'Organisation industrielle et la valeur humaine de l'ouvrier', *Bulletin du CNOF* May; J.-P. Lugrin. 1931. 'La Rationalisation a-t-elle fait faillite?' *Bulletin du CNOF* June, 166–79.

126.   'Le Problème de la grande industrie. La Rationalisation implique-t-elle nécessairement des crises économiques et un abaissement du niveau spirituel de l'humanité?' *Comptes rendus du Comité national d'études sociales et politiques* 15 June 1931.

127.   The texts of the broadcasts, organized by the Institut d'organisation commerciale et industrielle, were published in the CNOF bulletin. See 'Comment la physiologie du travail peut aider à la rationalisation. Causerie faite au Poste national de la Tour Eiffel, le 10 décembre 1930', *Bulletin du CNOF* January 1931; 'Le Rendement du travail et l'hygiène mentale. Conférence par radio-diffusion du 14 janvier 1931', *Bulletin du CNOF* March 1931; 'La Psychotechnique et l'organisation scientifique du travail. Conférence par radio-diffusion, 21 janvier 1931', *Bulletin du CNOF* May 1931; 'La Mesure de l'intelligence. Causerie du 4 février', *Bulletin du CNOF* June 1931; 'La Sélection de machinistes de tramways et d'autobus. Causerie du 18 février 1931', *Bulletin du CNOF* July 1931.

128.   Secrétariat général du Comité international de l'organisation scientifique. 1938. 'Les Tendances actuelles de l'organisation scientifique', *Bulletin du CNOF* October, 26. Charles Maier noted this international trend towards social and psychological approaches to management in C. Maier. 1987. *In Search of Stability: Explorations in Historical Political Economy*, Cambridge: Cambridge University Press, 53–63.

Chapter 2

PSYCHOLOGY, MASCULINITY AND THE SOCIAL POLITICS OF ORGANIZATION

The network of groups that made up the organization movement existed to promote technical practices such as time and motion studies, standardization or aptitude testing, but they also concerned themselves with rather broader questions of social and economic organization. Indeed, much of what would be promoted after World War Two under the heading of 'modernization' was already being discussed by interwar organizers. One element of this embryonic vision of 'modernization' was the idea of a 'third way' between liberal capitalism (or at least one version of it) and communism. A feature of the interwar movement was the relative political diversity of those who believed that organization offered the key to a third way: socially conservative and (comparatively) progressive employers and engineers came together with reformist socialists and social Catholics, who saw in organization the possibility of a reformed capitalism in which social conflict could be replaced by peaceful class collaboration. In this sense, 'the social question' was crucial to the organization movement's ability to garner support across certain political boundaries. The only major political current that was not represented in the movement as I have defined it was communism. Although the Parti communiste and the communist-led Confédération générale du travail unitaire (CGTU) embraced scientific organization in principle in a socialist form, they denounced the capitalist version and were not part of the networks examined here, operating largely within their own organizations.

One of the most obvious ways in which the possibility of class collaboration was debated in interwar France was through a renewal of corporatist thinking, a trend that was particularly evident in Catholic circles by the 1930s. But the question of how to organize for social peace cannot be reduced to the question of corporatism. In fact, as this chapter will make clear, the elimination of conflict was an issue which appeared among organizers in a number of different guises. Conflict was considered pri-

marily as a psychological phenomenon and hence as one that could (potentially at least) be managed or organized out of existence. This linkage of
organization and social peace was something that could be found in the
paternalist view of business espoused by Henri Fayol and in the visions of
rationalization that emerged in the late 1920s. But the heightened interest
in 'human problems' in the 1930s brought a new level of interest in psycho-
social and psycho-biological techniques of organization, while the social
upheaval of 1936 brought the questions of human relations and class conflict into even sharper focus. In order to highlight the scope and evolution
of the organizers' engagement with these issues, therefore, this chapter
takes up the story in the period 1926–28, when Redressement français was
the most visible group in the organization movement, before tracing some
of the proposals that emerged over the ensuing decade.

Rationalization and 'Solidarity'

The connection made between scientific organization and social peace may
not be an obvious one, especially since the imposition of certain organizational practices, such as Taylorism or *chronométrage*, provoked considerable
conflict. But the techniques and ideology of scientific organization took
shape in France in an environment where 'the social' was already marked
out as a field of scientific or technical intervention. The networks of social
professionals who gathered around the Musée social at the turn of the century, for example, included architects, doctors and engineers, united by a
sense that their professional competence could be deployed to solve social
questions, or indeed, '*the* social question' – the problem of how to achieve
social peace in an industrial society in which conflict appeared to be
endemic.[1] These 'techniques of the social' occupied a significant place in
business culture as major employers such as the Schneider family or André
Michelin (an early supporter of Taylorism) sought to integrate and stabilize
their workforce by providing housing, medical services and family
allowances.[2] Social workers or *surintendantes d'usine* were appointed in
many factories to oversee the welfare of women workers from the First
World War onwards and rapidly became involved in applying techniques
such as psychotechnic testing – indeed since factory social policies themselves followed a similar productivist logic to that of scientific organization,
the line between the two was often blurred.[3]

Not surprisingly then, when Redressement français began to flesh out its
vision of national renewal based on technical competence in the late 1920s,
it turned to those who had already established themselves as social experts.
The Redressement programme was developed by a series of commissions
staffed by recognized experts on a variety of social, economic and political
questions. Kuisel has calculated that some 223 experts participated in these
study groups, the results of which were edited into thirty-five *cahiers*.[4] The

section on 'social life' was chaired by Georges Risler, head of the Musée social, and included commissions on housing and urbanism, social hygiene, family and the birth rate, the use of leisure and popular education, immigration and social insurance.[5] Among those who served on the social commissions were Jacques Lebel of the Central Committee for Family Allowances, Fernand Boverat of the National Alliance Against Depopulation, Léonie Chaptal, a prominent figure in nursing education, Cécile Brunschwicg, one of the forces behind the introduction of the *surintendantes* in French industry (among other roles), and Raoul Dautry, then an engineer-manager in the railway industry who had developed a particular interest in workers' housing.[6]

Redressement was a socially conservative movement (from which Mercier went on to join the Croix de feu in 1933). Its social section did not challenge existing hierarchies but rather set out to create a France of socially functional, productive and fecund bodies. In this respect the longstanding hygienist concern with 'social scourges', such as alcoholism and tuberculosis, merged with the organizers' concern for efficiency. A report from the social section written by Dautry argued that: 'No political or economic resurgence is possible if social life is not organized first, for a country is strong only if its children are united, numerous and healthy.'[7] When Dautry spoke of the organization of social life, he was arguing for greater coordination among the different actors already involved in social projects – the state, labour, employers and individuals or philanthropic bodies. In the field of housing, for example, it was suggested that piecemeal efforts were no longer sufficient and that a national housing policy was required. Along with this systematization of the policy framework, he argued, 'rationalization has just as much a role to play in housing as in industry', ensuring the construction of 'large estates of healthy homes, equipped with a complete organizational infrastructure for collective life (hygiene, education, transport, food, leisure)'.[8] Similarly, arguments for a pro-natalist bolstering of the family allowance system and for further development of family associations were framed in terms of the need for 'the French family' to become 'a strongly organized and constituted force'.[9] In this way, the idea of organization as a means of enhancing efficiency coincided at Redressement with the notion of an order based on the organization of natural social bodies. This reflected perhaps the extent to which Dautry's vision was shaped both by his training as an engineer and by Catholic social thinking – a subject to which I will return in a moment.

A less obvious feature of Redressement's engagement with the social reform movement was that Detoeuf and Mercier appropriated the vocabulary of *solidarisme* to articulate the case for a coordinated economy. *Solidarisme* was an influential current of Republican social thought whose importance lay in its effort to articulate a 'third way' between individualism and collectivism, thereby providing a philosophical rationale for social intervention. Noting that Léon Bourgeois and other *solidaristes* had already gone some way to developing a spirit of social solidarity in France, Detoeuf argued in 1927 that rationalization was ushering in a new era of *economic* solidarity.[10] Similarly, Mercier urged businessmen to conceive of all the businesses in their industry not as competitors but as 'un tout solidaire'.[11] What solidarity meant in this context was industrial concentration and cartelization; coordination was favoured over individualism and the free play of competition. For Mercier this extended to the international level, where he tried to foster a rapprochement between French and German industry after the Locarno treaties of 1925 and supported international agreements among producers, inspired by his experience in the organization of provisions for allied forces at Loucheur's armaments ministry during the war. From 1931 he succeeded Loucheur as President of the French branch of Richard Coudenhove Kalergi's Pan-Europe Movement.[12]

Indeed, in this analysis, almost anything that could be construed as a brake on productivity or efficiency could be constructed as a breach of solidarity. Detoeuf argued, for example, that workers who limited production, bosses who paid their technicians badly or companies that criticized the quality of their competitors' products were guilty of a lack of solidarity because they failed to promote the general interest in rational production.[13] This argument clearly imbued rationalization with moral significance, but it is notable also that Detoeuf and Mercier identified the principle obstacles to efficiency as mental or attitudinal ones. French industrialists were accused of excessive 'individualism' and of lacking a taste for risk, for example, while workers and consumers were reproached for attaching too much importance to originality, when standardization should be the order of the day.[14] The inverted commas around 'individualism' here are Mercier's, as he was using the term as shorthand for the alleged failure of businessmen to conceive of their interests in terms of the organization of the economy as a whole. This was seen as a retrograde habit, an outlook ill-adapted to the age of organization – hence its association with aversion to risk. The true entrepreneurs and risk-takers, for Mercier, were those with a willingness to embrace a new order based on collective self-discipline. It was not unusual for organizers to reproach French economic actors in such terms and this was one of the ways in which they cast organization as a 'human problem', a problem of mentalities. What is also apparent in Mercier's formulation is that this implied a certain ideal of what it was to be a 'modern man' in the business world.

While these discussions about 'economic solidarity' were not constructed specifically around the problem of *class* conflict, the term 'solidarity' certainly seemed to suggest that conflict or internal frictions of any kind were a threat to the smooth running of the economic system. Other sources too reveal an outlook in which 'rationalization' was closely identified with the reduction of conflict and competition, not least as organizers responded to their increasingly vociferous critics in the early 1930s. For example, when J.-P. Lugrin of the International Management Institute in

Geneva was invited to discuss the perceived crisis facing the scientific organization movement at a meeting of the Comité national d'organisation française (CNOF) in 1931, he spoke of a new collaborative mentality that would emerge from the introduction of science as an arbiter of social and economic problems, a mentality that would in turn facilitate the implementation of scientific solutions.[15] At a subsequent meeting Lyndall Urwick (a British engineer who was Lugrin's colleague in Geneva) went further, highlighting the extent to which social conflict itself was viewed as an irrationality that must be engineered out of existence. For him, rationalization was, above all, about the elimination of waste and the definition of waste included any form of conflict or lack of coordination:

> There is jealousy among different people who work in the same business, there is the lack of collaboration or a common policy among manufacturers, wholesalers, retailers; there is the lack of collaboration between technicians and workers, between technicians and managers, between managers and the boss; and finally there is, from a broader perspective, the lack of collaboration among peoples.[16]

What characterized this generation of organizers then was not just the tendency to think in terms of the interdependence of different elements within a system, but the belief that the mentality of economic actors and relations among them were crucial factors in determining the efficiency of these systems.

To aspire to an order of peaceful collaboration among economic actors (locally, nationally and internationally) was one thing. To agree on how such an order might be constructed was another. At Redressement the rhetoric of 'solidarity' was not accompanied by any real attempt to engage with workers or organized labour. In 1927, one member of the group, the founder of the Catholic employers' federation, Joseph Zamanski, proposed a form of tripartite corporatist organization, in which employers, technical/managerial staff and workers would all be represented. Such schemes ostensibly made the *cadres* social arbiters between capital and labour but in effect offered the prospect of a built-in managerial majority. Zamanski envisaged that these representative bodies would initially have responsibility for fixing salaries and resolving conflicts but that their powers could be extended over time as workers were educated by the experience and a new collaborative mentality established itself.[17] Rationalization and corporatism went hand in hand in this analysis because both were conceived in terms of an evolution away from liberal individualism towards an organized economy.[18] But others at Redressement were more reticent. Mercier did suggest that the confrontation of labour and capital would eventually be diluted in large corporations by the opportunities for shareholding and the replacement of the owner-employer by the salaried manager.[19] In the meantime, however, he argued that the working class remained too attached to the ideology of class struggle and that corporatist structures were therefore unworkable.[20]

Social Catholicism, Management and Masculinity

If corporatist forms of class collaboration had limited support among organizers in the late 1920s, the question of how work might be organized and managed in ways that tended to reduce conflict remained on the agenda nonetheless. One particularly rich current of this discussion centred on the social role of the engineer, a theme developed at Redressement by Dautry. Dautry emphasized the role of *young* engineers, whom he considered better equipped to promote collaboration in the workplace. Like many of his colleagues in the organization movement, he regretted that engineers did not, in his view, receive sufficient training in managing people, but believed that some did possess the leadership qualities to 'create a happy order', through a combination of technical competence, character and experience.[21] If young professionals were seen as particularly well qualified in this respect, it was in large part because of their presumed experience as officers in the war. 'Having shed their uniforms, they have remained leaders of men, in the factory, in commerce, in banking', wrote Dautry. 'From the discipline and camaraderie of combat, they have retained the habit of a positively and actively ordered environment and a desire for generous action .... Having seen so much, they are less confined within their specialism.'[22] Action, breadth of vision and an ability to ensure order in a spirit of camaraderie and mutual respect were thus seen as the key features of this new generation of engineer-managers.

Although, there were large numbers of women workers in French industry and even a few female engineers, the social question was conceived here essentially in terms of relationships among men.[23] This tendency to exclude women from the imagined category of 'workers' was part of what allowed them to be constituted as an exceptional group requiring specific forms of intervention and supervision in the workplace (supervision that was to be provided by female social workers rather than male engineers).[24] It also meant that the models of management developed by social engineers were simultaneously models of masculinity. What Dautry articulated was an ideal of middle-class masculinity in which the young engineer-officer was supposed to embody a style of management that rested on everyday contact with workers and with the organization of production, a style that was presented as less distant, less rigid and more open than that of the older generation. In this respect, he continued the work of Marshal Hubert Lyautey, whose famous essay of 1891 on the social role of the officer set out a vision of the army in the Third Republican age of universal male military service and mass democracy. Lyautey emphasized the role of officers in the socialization of the masses and the need for them to take an interest in their men.[25] Extending this to the workplace, Dautry reiterated a call for the renovation or re-education of the French technical elite that had regularly been heard in the organization movement since the early days of Fayol and Le Chatelier. This was not just a question of familiarizing engineers and business leaders with basic methods for enhancing efficiency; it meant giving managers the means to shape the motivation of the worker and the social climate of the workplace.

As the examples of Dautry and Zamanski illustrate, Catholics had established themselves as significant contributors to the debates about organization by the interwar period and their influence was not confined to confessional movements. This pattern emerged early. Indeed, if one were to take away the Catholics from the first generation of Taylorists and Fayolists before 1918, one would wipe out much of the (admittedly small) movement. Henry Le Chatelier was a Catholic, as was Charles de Fréminville, who had been among the first engineers in France to apply Taylorism before World War One and went on to serve as President of both the CNOF and the Société des ingénieurs civils.[26] Other Catholic promoters of scientific organization included Eugène Nusbaumer, whose combination of Taylorism and social organicism was highlighted in the previous chapter, and the military engineer Lt Col Emile Rimailho, who became active in the interwar movement (CEGOS, CNOF), following his work in the organization of armaments workshops before and during the First World War. The key promoters of Fayolism – Joseph Carlioz, Joseph Wilbois and Maurice Ponthière – all of whom were influential in management education, were also Catholics.

Science and religion are sometimes thought of as opposing forces in French history, or at least as separate cultures. Yet such cultures do not exist in isolation from one another and historical actors do not position themselves neatly in such abstract categories. Catholic engineers in particular were likely to be deeply immersed both in the culture of scientific methods that they had absorbed in the engineering schools and in the social doctrine of their Church, itself by no means closed to secular influences. By the interwar period there was a well-developed culture of applied social science and social action within French Catholicism, which had its doctrinal roots in the encyclical *De Rerum Novarum* (Of New Things) of 1891. Catholic social doctrine was critical of economic liberalism and posited a communitarian ideal of society in which class conflict was regarded as one of the most disturbing social consequences of industrialization. What was crucial about *Rerum Novarum* was that it encouraged Catholics to participate in social action to alleviate the problems of industrial society and to foster social reconciliation. Organizations such as the Patronages catholiques, Action catholique and the Association catholique de la jeunesse française (Catholic Association for French Youth, ACJF) were important vehicles for this action and in the interwar years the ACJF gave way to new movements such as the Jeunesse ouvrière chrétienne (Young Christian Workers) which strengthened the presence of social Catholicism in the industrial workplace partly as a response to the rise of communism.[27] The extent to which Catholic action was legitimized by an appeal to social science was apparent at the Semaines sociales, an annual congress on contemporary social issues. For Marius Gonin, who founded the Semaines sociales, the meetings were about 'Science for Action'. Likewise, an early keynote address explained: 'our method consists of observing social facts scientifically, so that we can interpret, correct, and improve [those facts], placing ourselves within a Catholic atmosphere and clarifying the rules of thought and action which derive from Catholicism.'[28] This attachment to the method of social observation points to the legacy of Frédéric Le Play, a nineteenth-century engineer and pioneering social researcher who was a common reference point of both Catholic and secular social researchers and activists.[29] Indeed, Charles de Fréminville told colleagues at the Société des ingénieurs civils that Le Play should be seen as a precursor of Taylor, since both men were fundamentally concerned with the application of scientific methods to social questions.[30]

While Catholics were present in non-confessional groups such as the CNOF, confessional movements such as the Union sociale des ingénieurs catholiques (Social Union of Catholic Engineers, USIC) were also part of the wider networks through which the organization agenda was disseminated. Although social Catholics cautioned against possible abuses of scientific organization, warning that the production and accumulation of material wealth should not be seen as an end in itself, they embraced the organizers' critique of liberal individualism, their holism and their professed commitment to class collaboration. One engineer writing in the *Echo de l'USIC* summed up this view, arguing that rationalization constituted a move away from the anarchy of liberal economics and hence, so long as it was applied in accordance with God's ends rather than those of businessmen, was in perfect harmony with Catholic doctrine.[31] The Jesuit priest Henri du Passage had no hesitation in recommending that all members of USIC read the work of organizers such as Taylor, Le Chatelier and Wilbois, while the President of the Semaines sociales, Eugène Duthoit, welcomed the scientific organizers' attachment to discipline and coordinated action, their emphasis on organization and management of the whole, rather than individualism, freedom and competition.[32] Rather preposterously, De Fréminville even credited Taylor with demonstrating that the duty of the engineer lay not just in seeking the best possible material organization of a task, but in realizing a close collaboration between workers and employers.[33] Since Taylor's method was more about ensuring compliance with managerial dictates and speeding up production than about engaging the worker in anything that could meaningfully be called collaboration, this raises questions about what the rhetoric of collaboration actually meant. Nonetheless, the holist conception of organization that was taking shape in interwar France, in part through the work of Catholic technicians, could be readily incorporated into the social Catholic vision of a 'third way'.

The model of the social engineer set out by Dautry should be understood in this ideological context. As Luc Boltanski has shown, Catholics were the most significant contributors to a flourishing interwar literature on the role of the engineer which served to delineate the *cadre* as a new social category.[34] As salaried managers or technicians, positioned between labour and capital, these engineers conceived of their role as social intermediaries whose scientific training made them the servants of rationality and the laws of nature, rather than the financial interests of capital.[35] This engineer-manager was, as one writer put it in the *Echo de l'USIC*, at once a leader and a mere cog in the great engine of modern production.[36] Already present in the 1920s, this discourse about the social engineer gathered momentum in the 1930s and achieved its most widely circulated form in Georges Lamirand's *Le Rôle social de l'ingénieur*, first published in 1932 with a preface by Lyautey.[37] More active in the social Catholic Equipes sociales than in the organization movement proper, Lamirand was nonetheless familiar with the work of Taylor and Fayol and his book emphasized the role of the engineer as an organizer: the essence of the engineer's function, he insisted, was to maximize efficiency.[38] His portrait of the social engineer was almost indistinguishable from Dautry's: it was a portrait of an officer close to his troops, a heroic man of action, a man who made progress possible thanks to the discipline he was able to impose on himself and the trust he therefore inspired in others.[39] This was a model of a muscular social masculinity, an engineer who would inspire respect by his unassailable moral probity and his technical competence, but also by his physical stature and energy, maintained through regular exercise. Leadership, in this analysis, was an ethos that must be embodied.[40]

The affinity with Fayol's theory of organization is apparent here. What was presented in this management literature was an ethos of leadership that was a *technique* of people management.[41] The engineer's role was to act 'not just on machines, numbers and the forces of nature but on men'.[42] In this respect his task was compared to that of an educator, but also to that of a doctor, in that the engineer contributed, through his action on the workers, to the 'moral hygiene' of the business.[43] Interwar engineers and industrialists tended to see workers as a 'type' and the more conservative among them certainly believed that the stability of the worker depended on appropriate leadership. Having grown up and been educated in a largely separate bourgeois world and come into real contact with working-class people, probably for the first time, when they entered the factory, these young engineers interpreted the social gulf between themselves and their working-class subordinates in essentialized and psychologized terms, as if encountering a foreign culture. Lamirand referred to the gulf 'of nature, of education, of taste, of civilization' that confronted the engineer on taking up a post in industry for the first time.[44] Even the more progressive Gérard Bardet (whose reforming approach to management will be discussed further in a moment) recalled his entry into the family firm as a 'brutal' encounter with working-class society, followed by a period in which he tried to reach a deep understanding of 'the working-class mentality' by observing his workers' behaviour.[45] Embodying the required ethos of leadership was conceived as a way of managing this 'working-class mentality' to minimize conflict.

This is particularly clear in Lamirand's book which was not just a portrait of the social engineer, but a manual providing practical tips designed to teach young engineers what they did not learn at the *grandes écoles*: how to inhabit the role of class intermediary in the exercise of their daily functions and successfully manage relations with their potentially volatile subordinates. The first step, he advised, was to persuade the workers to accept the technical superiority of the engineer, a delicate task since they were deemed to suffer from an inferiority complex, which was blamed for much of the day-to-day conflict that could arise in the workplace. Hence, Lamirand counselled, the engineer must not blind the workers with science, nor should he attempt to communicate with them in their own colloquial language: the former could lead to resentment, the latter to ridicule. Colloquial terms used in the trade for particular machinery or manoeuvres could usefully be employed, it was suggested, as this would establish a sense of shared technical knowledge, but otherwise one must not try to speak like a worker. Indeed, the engineer's language must be scrupulously correct at all times.[46] Similarly, while the social engineer was to cultivate cordial rather than autocratic relations, the question of when to use the familiar *tu* form and when to use *vous* to a worker was a vexed one, for the working-class type was divided by Lamirand into racial and regional types who were liable to react in different ways: the Lorrainer could not bear to be called *tu*, he claimed, while the Flemish 'needed' to be *tutoyé* and the north-African worker (pejoratively referred to as *le bicot*) would scarcely know what to do if addressed as *vous*, since his French (imitated in Lamirand's text) was so rudimentary.[47] Lamirand even provided tips on the appropriate vestimentary signifiers of the engineer's vocation as a man of action: dress should be smart but not too chic or well groomed, for it must signal both the engineer's managerial status and his readiness to 'get his hands dirty' if necessary.[48]

Joseph Wilbois sought to instil a similarly embodied ethos of leadership, though he focused more on the role of the *patron* than that of the *cadre*: the qualities he demanded of the business leader were the familiar ones of physical dynamism, intellectual rapidity, strength of will, decisiveness, love of action and a youthful, risk-taking spirit.[49] A member of Fayol's Centre d'études administrative immediately after the First World War, then Secretary of the CNOF following its creation in 1925, Wilbois was a professional educator, rather than an engineer or businessman. He had taught at the Ecole des Roches, a boarding school modelled on the English public school system, and his idea of education for leadership was shaped by the New Education movement, which flourished in Europe in the early twentieth century, promoting a form of education that emphasized the development of the 'whole person' and the benefit of learning through activity.[50] He also believed that the managerial elite must be educated in the social sciences.[51]

Hence at his Ecole d'administration et des affaires and in manuals like *La Psychologie au service du chef d'entreprise* (published in 1934, but based on a series of classes Wilbois had offered in 1920–21 and 1929–30), his pedagogy relied heavily on practical exercises that drew on psychological techniques.[52] What he offered were lessons in self-management (*administration de soi*) which included not just the application of Fayolist principles (analysis, planning, monitoring etc.) to personal organization, but the use of visualization and autosuggestion techniques to promote positive thinking and 'correct' bad habits or personality traits such as shyness.[53] For Wilbois, the leader's personality must 'penetrate the souls of his subordinates', turning weak elements into strong ones.[54] Thus, while he and the social engineers spent rather a lot of time forging a model of managerial behaviour, this was ultimately a strategy for influencing the behaviour of workers and employees.

Hyacinthe Dubreuil and the Psycho-social Organization of Work

If the above attempts to develop a model of social management often assumed that workers required leadership by those deemed socially and technically superior, a rather different vision of organization for social peace emerged between the wars from a section of the labour movement. Workers' responses to scientific organization varied somewhat. Among the rank and file, many followed the analysis offered in a famous essay by Emile Pouget, condemning 'the organization of overwork'.[55] Male skilled workers in particular denounced time and motion studies as dehumanizing and deskilling. As Laura Frader has shown, this sometimes enabled them to gain a right to consultation about new working practices (in disputes at Citroën in 1924 and 1927, for example) but women's status as unskilled workers prevented them from making similar arguments and obtaining the same concessions.[56] While the CGTU resisted scientific organization within capitalism, the Confédération générale du travail (CGT) leadership was more favourable, as they calculated that efficiency gains obtained through rationalization offered the possibility of securing reductions in working hours without lowering pay.[57] The CGT position hardened in periods of depression, notably in 1931 when the union adopted a policy of 'permanent and determined resistance' against the demands of employers and the state, though it reverted back to its earlier line to defend the forty-hour week in 1936.[58] Albert Thomas and Hyacinthe Dubreuil, on the other hand, maintained their favourable position even when the Depression hit, Dubreuil distancing himself from the CGT in 1931 and joining Thomas at the International Labour Office. The former factory worker had become the most visible spokesperson for the pro-rationalization current of the labour movement following the success of *Standards* in 1929, a position that was reinforced when Thomas died in 1932.

Like Thomas, Dubreuil integrated scientific organization into a reformist social philosophy which embraced class collaboration. What was distinctive about his analysis was the emphasis it placed on the psycho-social dimensions of work. In the mid-1920s he criticized many of his CGT colleagues as misguided in privileging demands for shorter hours and higher wages, when, in his view, the value of the wage was now less important than the psychological conditions in which waged labour placed the worker.[59] When he travelled to the U.S.A. in 1927–28, he returned to France impressed not just by the material organization of work and the standard of living of the American worker, but also by the collaborative climate that seemed to prevail in American business. Interactions among workers and managers in the U.S.A. struck him as less constrained by hierarchical relationships and more cordial than in France – something that was also apparent, he claimed, in the spatial organization of the workplace, where managers and workers might use the same drinking fountain, for example.[60] 'In America', he argued, 'since the worker does not feel the weight of contempt bearing down on him, neither does he feel envy or bitterness in return.'[61] This psychologized view of class relations had something in common with that of social Catholic organizers though Dubreuil did not see leadership as the solution. Nor did he see the forms of organization he observed in American factories as sufficient in themselves, though he did assert that scientific organization was 'the indispensable tool of true socialism'.[62]

Dubreuil belonged to a tradition of communitarian socialism whose reference points were Proudhon and Fourier, rather than Marx. He also conceived of work in terms of a gendered humanism which identified labour as the primary site of masculine fulfilment. He praised technology as an expression of man's creative power over nature and believed in its liberational potential.[63] Responding to bourgeois critics like Duhamel, who evoked images of working men reduced to machines in the rationalized factory, he argued that what degraded modern work was not an excess of technological development but the loss of community in work.[64] Like so many organizers, he conceived of businesses as analogous to bodies: 'in the human body, it is the state of perfect solidarity which ensures good health and it is this sign of physical harmony that we must take as a model in our search for a better organization of work'.[65] But in Dubreuil's vision, unlike that of Fayol or Le Chatelier, workers were not just the unthinking hands of the business but its eyes and ears, sentient organs in close liaison with the brain.[66] He admired the sense of fraternal community embodied in the *compagnonnage* tradition and the cooperative movement and aspired to an industrial order that would combine the technical progress of scientific organization with the spirit of solidarity embodied in these movements.[67] Crucially, this implied a much greater commitment to worker autonomy than could be found in orthodox Taylorism or Fayolism. Dubreuil argued that the next stage of industrial organization would be one in which the emphasis on external constraints or stimuli to work would give way to a system which harnessed the 'internal motivations' of the worker, tapping into a new source of 'productivity and joy'.[68]

In practice, what Dubreuil envisaged was a system of business organiza-tion in which workers were organized in small autonomous groups and were contracted to complete a job at a particular price, the proceeds being shared among the group according to criteria determined in advance by its mem-bers. He first set out a version of this system in his 1924 book *La République industrielle*, which received little attention outside his existing audience within the labour movement.[69] In 1935, however, he revisited the subject in *A Chacun sa chance* and enjoyed greater success. By sub-dividing businesses into autonomous groups, he argued, one could put workers in a psychological position analogous to that of the artisan or entrepreneur, since all members of the group would share in the price paid for the task, benefiting from any effi-ciency savings. This would not only provide an incentive to work efficiently and create bonds of camaraderie among workers, but would change the workers' relationship to the business in such a way as to generate a new kind of corporate loyalty.[70] Anticipating perhaps the objections of managers, Dubreuil did not assume that workers would develop this new outlook immediately, but argued that his organization project was also a pedagogical one: the reorganized workshop, he proclaimed, was to be 'the school of social life'. This was partly a question of scale. In a small group, he suggested, the worker learned the discipline of living and working with others, adapting to the needs of the group. With the discipline of cooperation would come a sense of a stake in a common project. Authority would no longer be embodied in the arbitrary rule of an individual but rather would obey laws of organization to which the worker would willingly consent.[71] In this way, moving from an imposed discipline to a form of self-discipline, a discipline based on consent, the worker would at last 'become a man'.[72] Indeed, Dubreuil even envisaged that a renewal of elites would flow from this renewal at the base.[73]

If this commitment to worker education, autonomy and social mobility distinguished the former CGT official's vision from that of bourgeois organizers, including many social Catholics, it did not prevent a certain convergence between the latter and the pro-rationalization section of the labour movement. Certainly, both believed that the rational organization of production required a collaborative climate in the factory, envisaging this in terms of an organic work community as well as an ideal of masculinity in work. This perhaps explains why Dubreuil and Thomas were among the few speakers from outside the fraternity of Catholic engineers or the priesthood to be invited to address USIC meetings.[74] Thomas's talk on 'The Spirit of Collaboration in the International Labour Organization' appears to have been particularly eagerly awaited as there was standing room only in a venue crowded with more than four hundred people.[75] Dubreuil's work was also referenced in articles and reviews in the *Echo de l'USIC* throughout the 1930s.[76] Moreover, these were not the only technicians to take an interest in his work or in the subject of group organization.

Experiments with Group Organization in the 1930s

Groups – or teams, as management schemes often preferred to call them – were in fact rather in vogue in the 1930s, perhaps because they offered a unit of organization between the individual and the 'mass', appearing as a means of harnessing social or collective behaviour for productive (rather than conflictual) ends. To take an international perspective, Dubreuil's approach could be compared to the findings of the Human Relations School at Harvard, in that both posited a correlation between group relations and productivity. In the American case this was based on the Hawthorne experiments, carried out by Elton Mayo and his colleagues at the Hawthorne plant of the Western Electric Company in Chicago between 1927 and 1932. These experiments investigated the impact of assorted variations in working conditions on a test group of workers who were separated from the other workers in the factory. The initial results were found to be perplexing, for although improvements in productivity were detected there was no simple correlation between these variations and the changes in physical conditions. Instead, Mayo concluded, the productivity gain could be explained by the sense of group solidarity and the opportunities for expression which the research itself had provided for the test group (whose members were interviewed regularly). Like Dubreuil, Mayo located the problem of productivity in the psycho-social position of the worker in industrial society. He argued that industrialization had brought social disintegration, leaving the worker unable to find meaning in work. More rooted in the elitism of collective psychology and Paretan sociology than Dubreuil, however, he saw irrational fears and lack of understanding on the part of workers as the source of social conflict and the restriction of output. What the Hawthorne experiments were believed to show was that such conflict could be avoided and productivity increased by managing human relations, by fostering a sense of group solidarity in the workplace and, importantly, by mounting a communications strategy which ensured that worker solidarity would not be turned against the interests of the firm.[77]

If there was some awareness of the Human Relations School in France, it was Dubreuil's proposals and other similar forms of group organization that received most attention there. One factor that lent authority to the former mechanic's work, apart from his own credentials as a technician, was his reference to the practices adopted by the Czech shoe manufacturer Bat'a, whose sub-division of his massive business into autonomous workshops had attracted the attention of a number of French observers. Paul Devinat had written a report on the Bat'a model for the ILO, for example, and Dubreuil himself followed the publication of *A Chacun sa chance* with an account of the Bat'a system.[78] Bat'a had sub-divided his factory at Zlin in what was then Czechoslovakia into several hundred separate workshops and each workshop housed a team responsible for manufacturing a particular model of shoe. To this extent the work of the team was highly standardized. Each team had a budget to buy in materials from the Bat'a leather shop and tannery and if the workers were able to make savings, for example, by improving their cutting technique to get more pairs of shoes from the same amount of materials, the team shared in the additional profit. These teams did not have the level of autonomy envisaged by Dubreuil, as their pay was largely determined by rates fixed by management, and the team itself did not decide how profits were split.[79] Nonetheless, the commercial success of Bat'a even in the difficult economic context of the 1930s, and its owner's reputation as Europe's answer to Henry Ford, suggested that sub-division was not an unrealistic proposition.

Several French engineers and industrialists, including Emile Rimailho and Gérard Bardet, carried out their own experiments with group organization. While these schemes had something in common with Dubreuil's – Rimailho cited Dubreuil favourably and later published a book with him[80] – the engineers did not devolve the same amount of responsibility to workers. Rimailho applied the team-working method at the Compagnie générale de construction et d'entretien de matériel de chemins de fer and gave classes on his method at the Ecole nationale supérieure de l'aéronautique from 1930 to 1934, before publishing a book on it in 1936.[81] In terms of the amount of autonomy given to workers, his approach seems to sit somewhere between Taylor's version of scientific management and Dubreuil's 'industrial republic'. In Rimailho's workshops, representatives of both labour and management participated in the preparatory process of determining the best method for completion of a given task. Productivity and salary norms for the completion of the order were then set by management on the basis of these calculations. An amount of time was allocated for the work and bonuses could be gained if the team completed the task satisfactorily in less than the allocated time.[82] Rimailho summed up his method as 'efficiency [*rendement*] through collaboration'.[83] The basic premise was similar to Dubreuil's to the extent that organizing workers into small groups was supposed to develop team spirit, a sense of responsibility and an investment in quality workmanship.[84] Likewise, Rimailho insisted on the primary importance of social and affective factors in productivity. Work could only be performed efficiently, he argued, if it was performed 'with joy: that is, freely accepted by a "team" of colleagues, confident in the value and equity of their leaders.'[85] The affirmation of the freedom or autonomy of the team was tempered here by an attachment to the authority of the leader that was typical of social Catholics and of the pre-First World War generation of organizers to which Rimailho (born 1864) belonged.

This tension between an appeal to the productive potential of autonomy and the defence of managerial authority was present in other group organization projects proposed by engineers. Nonetheless, Bardet, a young engineer-employer who had graduated from the Ecole polytechnique in the class of 1922, struck the balance in a slightly different place to the older Rimailho, giving workers an institutionalized voice in his business. A member of the CNOF and X-Crise and a close associate of Jean Coutrot, Bardet adopted team organization as part of a series of reforms implemented at his engineering firm between 1927 and 1935. He had begun by altering the pay scale to put greater emphasis on skill than years of service, and by introducing a limited system of paid holidays. He went on to introduce a forty-hour week and a workers' council, well before the Matignon settlement of 1936 forced employers throughout the country to implement a similar model. In conjunction with these changes in pay and conditions, Bardet divided his workforce into small teams of five or six. Each team had a worker appointed as leader and was given responsibility for the completion of a particular task, though there is no mention in Bardet's account of the type of wage reform envisaged by Dubreuil. What Bardet's system did have in common with Dubreuil's was that it sought to capitalize on the strong sense of professional solidarity and pride in quality workmanship that existed among male skilled workers – much of the workforce at Bardet's machine tool company (which manufactured tailor-made products) appears to have been in this category. The aim was to generate productivity not just with the incentive of material gain but by appealing to the notions of collective effort and pride in a task: 'there must reign a mentality of solidarity', wrote Bardet, 'for the overall *œuvre* is a shared *œuvre*'.[86] If we believe Bardet's own account, it appears that he was successful in generating this sense of collective loyalty, as he not only reported improvements in both quality and productivity but also was spared any disruption in June 1936 when much of French industry ground to standstill.[87]

From Psycho-social to Psycho-biological Organization

Group organization schemes posed the problem of the organization of work in psycho-social terms but there were also new developments in the psycho-biology of work in the 1930s. In the 1920s, the key development in work science had been the spread of psychotechnic aptitude testing, but by the early 1930s there was a growing interest in methods for assessing 'personality', 'character' and 'temperament', categories which acknowledged that human behaviour was driven by non-rational as well as rational factors. One of the clearest indicators of this trend was the emergence of the new field of *biotypologie*, which aimed to establish correlations between physical and psychological characteristics and provide a method for classifying individuals into psycho-biological types. Leading biotypologists Henri Laugier, Edouard Toulouse and Dagmar Weinberg spoke of their desire to measure 'all aspects of the personality, physiological, psychological, pathological and psychiatric'.[88] This medicalized conception of personality and the accompanying effort to transcend the boundaries between specializations were indicative of a certain influence of medical holism on work science.[89] In fact, several of the prominent French experts in the psycho-biology of work in the interwar period were trained in medicine, including Laugier and Toulouse. Laugier, one of the founders of the Société de biotypologie and head of the Biometrics Laboratory at the Chemins de fer de l'Etat, summed up the significance of the move from psychotechnics to biotypology when he expressed the ambition to assign workers to jobs not just on the basis of their aptitudes, but according to their 'character' and 'tastes'.[90]

The Société de biotypologie was created in 1932 and all France's leading work scientists became members – Laugier, Toulouse and Weinberg were joined, for example, by J.-M. Lahy and Henri Piéron (co-founder of the Institut national d'orientation professionnelle).[91] Laugier was the chief spokesperson in this group and like Lahy (and Toulouse) he was left of centre in his politics – close to the Radical Party, he had served as *Chef de cabinet* to Yvon Delbos under Paul Painlevé's government in 1925. He saw biotypology as part of a socially progressive agenda, promising a rational organization of work in the interests of workers. He was also particularly interested in potential educational applications of biotypology, suggesting that teachers would be able to adapt their methods to fit the psycho-biological profile of the individual child.[92] At the same time, he subscribed to a functionalist view of society similar to that espoused in other branches of the scientific organization movement, as he made plain in a radio broadcast in 1934: biotypology, he explained, was a response to 'the need for human classification which has manifested itself throughout history and which becomes more demanding every day as a strict adaptation of individuals to highly differentiated and specialized functions appears as the fundamental condition of a rational organization of society and human progress.'[93] Ultimately it was anticipated that psycho-biological typologies could be applied not just in education, vocational guidance and recruitment but also in psychiatry, criminology and public health.

Laugier and his colleagues were academic scientists whose work to establish biotypes was still at an experimental stage and not readily applicable in industry. However, more rudimentary (and less academic) human typologies already existed and these methods were picked up in the management training courses provided at the Ecole d'administration et des affaires and the Ecole d'organisation scientifique du travail. In addition to providing self-improvement exercises for business leaders, Wilbois recommended that the recruitment of employees should be based not just on psychotechnics and intelligence tests of the kind developed by Lahy or Alfred Binet, but also on the use of morphology and graphology. Though he acknowledged that these methods had not been fully tested scientifically, he espoused them in part because they could be applied quickly and easily.[94] Citing examples from the graphologist Jules Crépieux-Jamin and the morphologist Dr Louis Corman, he claimed that one could identify a weak-willed man by the way he crossed his *t*s, and a 'combative type' (one of eight types defined by Corman) by features such as a thick neck, small eyes and short thumbs.[95] These methods were not aimed only at the recruitment of manual and clerical workers but were seen as particularly useful for determining the suitability of 'elite associates'. This notion of elite had both a social and a biological dimension for Wilbois, who emphasized the influence of social environment on behaviour but considered certain morphological types innately unsuitable for leadership roles – the 'combative type', for example, was said to make an excellent soldier but was not considered to be officer material.[96] Such typologies also essentialized racial and sexual difference, linking these differences to suitability for particular social functions, even where the sexual and racial division of labour were not the explicit focus. Frizzy hair was another indicator of the 'combative type', for example, while Corman classified his eight types as masculine or feminine (the latter types being defined by sexual instincts and an artistic tendency to dream).[97]

If Wilbois's interest in such methods were an isolated case and did not parallel in some ways the development of biotypology (albeit from a more socially conservative perspective than Laugier's) it would be easy to dismiss it as mere quackery. However, quackery has historically had (and continues to have) a certain place in business culture, and endorsements of the managerial benefits of morphology came from other organizers too, including Jean Coutrot and Paul Planus.[98] The appeal of these methods was that they promised to make employees psychologically knowable in their entirety, rendering their moods and behaviour predictable, and it appears that this heavily psychologized approach to management was promoted most visibly in 1937–38, in the years after French businesses had been shaken by the major strikes of 1936. The endorsements from Coutrot and Planus came in 1937, when the CNOF organized a workshop on the study of 'man at work' for the World Fair (Exposition internationale des arts et techniques) in Paris. Similarly, it was in 1938 that the CNOF's School of Scientific Organization began to offer a new course on 'The Personnel Service and the Psychology of Man at Work'. Alongside a lesson from Dubreuil which questioned whether one could speak of such a thing as the psychology of the working class, students at this school took several classes on applied psychology including two from Madame Ch. Billard on the measurement of 'Human types and the psycho-physiological stimulants to work'. Billard was aware of the work being carried out by Laugier and cited it in her class but when it came to offering techniques for application in the business world, like Wilbois, she turned to the established typologies of morphology (in this case the work of Ernst Kretschmer).[99] Students at the Institut national d'orientation professionnelle, which trained many of France's vocational guidance officers, were also introduced to the notion of psycho-biological types and items in the Institute's bulletin reported on studies that used both questionnaire methods and psychobiological examinations to classify school children according to 'temperament' and 'character'.[100] By the late 1930s, then, holist currents of psycho-biology that typologized their subjects and addressed non-rational factors in productivity had clearly found a place within the range of techniques being offered to technicians and business people through these educational networks.

Organization and the Social Question in the Aftermath of 1936

There is no doubt that the wave of strikes and factory occupations that followed the election of the Popular Front gave a new urgency to the question of how to deal with social conflict in the workplace. Both the strikes themselves and the Matignon settlement that brought them to an end forced employers to take greater account of workers' voices. The settlement imposed a system of workers' delegates, with whom employers were obliged to consult, notably to establish collective agreements about working conditions. Given the authoritarian climate that prevailed in many French factories before 1936 and the relative weakness of the unions, these were significant changes. For many employers, this was an intolerable attack on their prerogatives as owners and/or managers. At the same time, the introduction of workers' delegates and the more amenable position of the CGT leadership on finding efficiency savings moved the question of worker collaboration in organization up the agenda, at least for those already sympathetic to such a view. On the shop floor managers confronted the issue of class relations on a very practical level as they sought to get factories working productively again after the strikes. Even after the official return to work there were many incidences of small-scale disputes over the organization of work, as well occasional examples of the kind of festive behaviour that characterized the factory occupations: at Renault there was a report in January 1937, for example, of two workers' delegates dressing up and regaling their colleagues with drunken singing and dancing.[101] At Peugeot, engineers like Ernest Mattern were still preoccupied in early 1937 with the problem of getting production back to 'normal' levels.[102] Against this backdrop, it was not just psycho-biological techniques that received renewed attention but also the social role of the engineer, the benefits of group work and the question of corporatist structures, or 'professional organization', as it was more commonly termed at the time.

All these trends were embodied to some extent in Coutrot's response to the events of June 1936. Coutrot and Bardet were the most visible representatives of the reformist *patronat* in 1936, largely because of the publication of Coutrot's *Leçons de juin 1936* and *L'Humanisme économique* (which appeared in a single volume towards the end of the year). Among the Coutrot papers at the Archives nationales are forty-three cuttings about this book from thirty-six different publications, including national and regional newspapers (*Le Figaro, Marianne, La Dépêche du Midi*), the industrial press, and reviews such as *Mercure de France, L'Etat moderne* and the social Catholic *Dossiers de l'Action populaire*.[103] Coutrot's vision of 'economic humanism' is discussed in more detail in Chapter Four, where I consider the development of economic planning in the 1930s. For now it is worth noting that the question of organization for class collaboration was at the heart of Coutrot's agenda. Worker solidarity was, he argued, 'one of the axes of the economy of the future'.[104] With this in mind, he drew further attention to models of group organization, firstly by adopting Dubreuil's proposals and secondly by including Bardet's account of his experiments in class collaboration alongside his own essays. Other endorsements of group organization followed from Ernst Hijmans (a Dutch engineer and associate of Coutrot's) and later from Wilbois.[105]

Many employers were deeply hostile to the Popular Front reforms and some members of the organization movement became disillusioned in the later 1930s, denouncing the irrationality of 'mass politics' (Mercier) or the continued attachment of the French working class to the 'foreign' doctrine of class struggle (Dubreuil).[106] Yet Coutrot and Bardet – whose notion of managerial authority rested as much on the idea of technical competence, which was dear to engineers, as it did on the prerogatives of ownership – saw June 1936 as a moment of opportunity, a moment in which France was shaken from its torpor, making new forms of social and economic organization conceivable. Coutrot interpreted the events in heavily psychologized terms, seeing the working class as an element of social health in a rather ailing society, praising its instinctive attachment to the values of work and solidarity. In his view, this provided a much-needed counterweight to the excesses of liberalism and the prevailing conservatism of much of the French bourgeoisie.[107] This was a rather primitivist view of the working class which remained marked by a tendency to conceive of workers collectively in terms of a shared mentality but it was a more 'workerist' version of collective psychology than that which had informed the thinking of the pre-First-World-War generation of organizers, such as Le Chatelier. Coutrot's interpretation was also more favourable towards workers than that offered by Wilbois, who saw the social movement of 1936 as the expression of a set of complexes on the part of the masses – that is, in terms of pathology rather than health.[108] However, the momentum in the organization movement was now with the younger more reformist current rather than those (like Wilbois, born 1874) who had begun their careers before the Great War. The emergence of the *polytechniciens'* economic think tank X-Crise since 1931 had helped bring Coutrot and Bardet to the fore, while the conservative Redressement français had run out of steam and been dissolved in November 1935. The success of Coutrot's book in the wake of 1936 confirmed his status as one of the men of the moment.

Leçons de juin 1936 was one of several volumes published in 1936–37 which reflected on the role of technicians in social and economic organization in the broadest sense. Other contributions came in the form of a new edition of Georges Lamirand's *Le Rôle social de l'ingénieur* and a collection of essays and lectures by Raoul Dautry gathered under the title *Métier d'homme* (both published in 1937).[109] While there was a certain optimism in this literature, it can also be seen as a response to the challenges that faced engineers and other *cadres* in the post-Matignon landscape. The bipartite structures created by Matignon made no provision for the representation of a group that saw itself as the intermediary between labour and employers. Concern among engineers at this perceived marginalization led USIC to form the Syndicats des ingénieurs salariés (SIS) within days of the Matignon Agreement being signed. The SIS went on to unite with other groups in the Fédération nationale des syndicats d'ingénieurs, while the emergence of a series of other unions, calling themselves *syndicats de cadres* resulted in 1937 in the creation of the Confédération générale des cadres de l'économie française.[110]

There were changes among employers' organizations too as a result of the experience of 1936 and figures from the organization movement were at the heart of these developments. The existing employers' organizations, particularly the Confédération générale de la production française (CGPF, which now changed its name to the Confédération générale du patronat français), were seen as too weak, loosely organized and ill equipped for the new phase in French industrial relations.[111] As a result, René Duchemin was replaced at the head of the CGPF by the more corporatist Claude-Joseph Gignoux, while a newly created Comité central de l'organisation professionnelle (Central Committee for Professional Organization, CCOP) emerged with the specific aim of strengthening links among employers. The motivations for this were mixed. For one thing, the agreements among employers fostered by the CCOP were partly about banding together for technical and economic advantage, since increased labour costs (shorter hours and higher wages) created pressure to find savings elsewhere. Organizing employers' interests was also seen as a way of restoring a more favourable balance of power in industrial relations and being better equipped for social conflict, especially in the face of sharply rising membership of labour unions.[112] Nonetheless, for figures like Coutrot and Detoeuf, both of whom were active members of the CCOP, employers had to find a way of working with organized labour, rather than merely seeking to exact revenge. Hence, the CCOP rapidly made overtures to the CGT via a receptive René Belin in July 1936.[113] It also provided the springboard for the emergence in 1938 of the Centre des jeunes patrons (Centre for Young Business Leaders), whose philosophy of cross-class partnership was influenced by social Catholicism.[114] This group, whose name linked its social ethos with a generational identity, sympathized with the emphasis on developing greater worker autonomy and representation that we have seen in the efforts of Dubreuil and Bardet. It would go on to occupy an important place in the postwar business world in France.[115]

Though he was more reticent about embracing the labour movement than Coutrot and had previously been sceptical about the prospects for corporatist organization, Detoeuf came to see a kind of corporatism, based on negotiation between organized business and organized labour, as a necessity after 1936. He set out this vision in 1938, arguing that the workers and employers in a given 'profession' (branch of activity) should each be represented by a single, obligatory, 'apolitical' union.[116] Detoeuf was instrumental in developing contacts between labour and employers through the *Nouveaux Cahiers* group, which had been meeting informally since 1934 but came to prominence in 1937 when the review which retrospectively gave it its name was launched.[117] Figures from business, such as Detoeuf, Guillaume de Tarde and Jacques Barnaud, came together in this group with some of the more intellectual and non-conformist elements of the labour movement such as Lucien Laurat, Robert Lacoste, Paul Vignaux and Boris Souvarine. Detoeuf also sustained a significant correspondence with Simone Weil, author of *La Condition ouvrière*, and some of the letters were published in the review.[118] In 1938, the group participated in a meeting of labour and employers' representatives from France and Sweden, which followed a study trip to Sweden the previous year by the organizational consultant Paul Planus. Planus subsequently published a book on Swedish industrial relations, prefaced by Detoeuf, providing further evidence of the interest that members of the scientific organization movement took in the organization of class collaboration in the post-Matignon world.[119]

While this interest in developing a model of negotiation between organized labour and organized business may seem some way from those organization projects that constructed social conflict as a psychological problem that required a managerial solution, the two approaches coexisted in the organization movement in France in the late 1930s. Indeed, it will be clear from the projects outlined in this chapter that the movement explored a wide variety of techniques for the social, psychological and biological organization of work. We could label these approaches as post-Taylorist, though they drew on social techniques and currents of thinking that predated and shaped the reception of Taylor's work in France.[120] The assumptions about leadership and collective psychology that informed much interwar organizational thinking were not new in themselves but there was certainly an evolution in the way the psychology of work was conceived and in the techniques proposed to solve 'the social question' in the 1930s. This was illustrated in the way that debates about group organization and the social role of the engineer took off in this period, as well as in the turn to applied psychology and psycho-biology as means of assessing personality or cultivating leadership qualities. What the psycho-social and psycho-biological techniques had in common was that they sought to harness non-rational or affective sources of motivation and productivity – team spirit, creative instincts, loyalty, personal tastes, the individual's whole personality.

The differences among the approaches discussed here lay not just in their methods, but in the social politics within which these methods were inscribed. The scientific organization movement was a loose coalition of social Catholics, Republican scientists, the reformist labour movement, and conservative and reformist elements within the *patronat* and the engineering profession. The construction of organization as a social and psychological problem – the appeal to 'solidarity' and the 'social' or 'human' role of the manager – played an important part in building this coalition. But there was considerable political ground between Wilbois's construction of workers as a homogenous mass in need of leadership, for example, and Dubreuil's vision of productivity generated through working-class solidarity and subjecthood. One development that cut across any divisions between the Left and the Right of the movement was the interest in psychobiological profiling, but the research scientists certainly took this up in a more cautious way than those involved in management education and did not envisage it simply as a tool of management. In terms of the political dynamics of the movement, what is notable is the emergence of a small but high-profile group of reformist employers who were able to capitalize on the situation created by the events of May and June 1936 to promote their vision of organization for social peace. So, while some of the first generation of Taylorists and Fayolists, such as Rimailho and Wilbois, were still active in 1936, these men were now in their sixties and seventies, and younger men like Bardet (born 1903) and Coutrot (born 1895) brought a less conservative outlook to the leadership of the movement.

A final striking feature that unites several of the projects discussed in this chapter is the tendency to imagine a rational social order in terms of cross-class solidarity among men. Technical competence and the potential to achieve subjecthood in work were understood as masculine attributes; a harmonious organization would be created by men who achieved self-discipline (though there was disagreement about whether or not this applied to *working-class* men). Laura Frader has recently argued that discourses about skill, competence and fulfilment in work were closely linked to a male breadwinner model which operated to limit women's access to full social and economic citizenship between the wars.[121] Another aspect of the gendered organization of work is apparent in the construction of 'modern management' in terms of a particular ethos of masculinity. I have suggested that we should view this not just as a question of gendered representations but as a question of management techniques, techniques that were not merely to be studied and applied, but embodied. As the next chapter will illustrate, it was not just men who were called on to participate in this embodied organization project. Nor was the world of paid employment the only sphere in which it was to be carried out.

Notes

1. See Topalov (ed.). 1999. *Laboratoires du nouveau siècle: la nébuleuse réformatrice et ses réseaux en France, 1880–1914,* Paris: Editions de l'Ecole des hautes études en sciences sociales; Y. Cohen and R. Baudouï. 1995. *Les Chantiers de la paix sociale 1900–1940,* Fontenay-St-Cloud: ENS Editions; J. Horne. 2002. *A Social Laboratory for Modern France: The Musée Social and the Rise of the Welfare State,* Durham, NC: Duke University Press.

2. See S.L. Harp. 2001. *Marketing Michelin: Advertising and Cultural Identity,* Johns Hopkins University Press, 143–52; L. Bergeron. 2001. *Le Creusot. Une ville industrielle. Un patrimoine glorieux,* Paris: Belin, 137–62.

3. Report by Mlle Catelet on 'sélection professionnelle' at Association des surintendantes d'usines et de services sociaux. Assemblée générale 21 February 1928. J.-M. Lahy was invited to give classes at the Ecole des surintendantes and addressed the General Meeting of the same Association in 1930. See Dossier on Association des surintendantes d'usines et des services sociaux at Bibliothèque Marguerite Durand. See also L.L. Downs. 1993. 'Les Marraines-élues de la paix sociale? Les Surintendantes d'usine et la rationalisation du travail en France, 1917–1935', *Mouvement social* 164, 53–76; L.L. Frader. 2008. *Breadwinners and Citizens: Gender in the Making of the French Social Model,* Durham, NC: Duke University Press, 120–21.

4. R. Kuisel. 1967. *Ernest Mercier, French Technocrat,* Berkeley: University of California Press, 50.

5. Commissions listed on reverse of cover page in Redressement français. 1927. *Cahiers du Redressement français* 24, no page number.

6. These figures may not be social professionals of the kind that exist today but they held the status of experts nonetheless. Like the first generations of industrial organizers, they were sometimes self-taught experts, whose specialist competence rested on their experience of social action and associational activities as much as on their formal training or professional field – this at a time when new social professions and specialisms were just taking shape.

7. R. Dautry. 1927. 'L'Organisation de la vie sociale', *Cahiers du Redressement français* 24, 4.

8. Dautry, L'Organisation de la vie sociale', 8.

9. Dautry, 'L'Organisation de la vie sociale', 13.

10. A. Detoeuf. 1927. 'La Réorganisation industrielle', *Cahiers du Redressement français* 7, 37. On *solidarisme,* see C. Bouglé. 1907. *Le Solidarisme,* Paris: V. Giard & E Brière; and J. Donzelot. 1984. *L'Invention du social: essai sur le déclin des passions politiques,* Paris: Fayard, 73–120.

11. E. Mercier. 1927. 'Les Conséquences sociales de la rationalisation', *Cahiers du Redressement français* 10, 4.

12. Kuisel, *Ernest Mercier,* 72–3.

13. Detoeuf, 'La Réorganisation industrielle', 35.

14. Mercier, 'Les Conséquences sociales', 2; Detoeuf, 'La Réorganisation industrielle', 10, 12, 36.

15. J.-P. Lugrin. 1931. 'La Rationalisation a-t-elle fait faillite?', *Bulletin du CNOF,* June, 167.

16. L. Urwick. 1931. 'La Rationalisation et la crise économique', *Bulletin du CNOF,* July, 198.

17. J. Zamanski. 1927. 'Les Rapports organisés entre le capital et le travail', *Cahiers du Redressement français* 10, 43–78.

18. J. Zamanski. 1930. 'La Rationalisation peut-elle influencer les rapports du capital et du travail dans la profession? A-t-elle commencé à les influencer?', *Semaines sociales de France. Compte rendu in extenso des cours et conférences,* Lyon: Chronique sociale de France, 280; idem, 'Les Rapports organisés', 44.

19. Kuisel, *Ernest Mercier,* 54.

20. Kuisel, *Ernest Mercier,* 95–96.

21. Dautry, 'L'Organisation de la vie sociale', 30.

22. Dautry, 'L'Organisation de la vie sociale', 31.

23. Several engineering schools, including the Ecole centrale, had begun accepting women in 1917, though it was only in 1972 that the Ecole polytechnique did likewise. C. Marry. 2004. *Les Femmes ingénieurs: une révolution respectueuse,* Paris: Belin, 3.

24. Downs, 'Les Marraines-élues de la paix sociale?'; Frader comments on the tendency to imagine 'workers' as male in Frader, *Breadwinners and Citizens,* 142.

25. H. Lyautey. 1891. 'Du rôle social de l'officier dans le service militaire universel', *Revue des deux mondes* 15 March, 443–59. On Lyautey's influence on Dautry, see R. Baudouï. 1995. 'Un technicien social du service public: Raoul Dautry (du Chemin de fer de l'État au CEA)' in Cohen and Baudouï, *Les Chantiers de la paix sociale,* 195–203.

26. According to Aimée Moutet (*Les Logiques de l'entreprise: la rationalisation dans l'industrie française de l'entre-deux-guerres,* Paris: Editions de l'EHESS, 34), De Fréminville first applied Taylor's system at Panhard and Levassor in 1910. The Société des ingénieurs civils was an organization of non-state engineers (this is the sense of the term 'civil' engineer in French), for whom the Ecole centrale was the most prestigious school.

27. See G. Cholvy. 1999. *Histoire des organisations et mouvements chrétiens de jeunesse en France (XIXe-XXe siècle),* Paris: Editions du Cerf for an overview of these developments.

28. Both Gonin's slogan and this quotation from Henri Lorin are cited in Beale, *The Modernist Enterprise,* 113.

29. On Le Play and his influence over later generations, see B. Kalaora. 1989. *Les Inventeurs oubliés: Le Play et ses continuateurs aux origines des sciences sociales,* Seyssel: Champ Vallon.

30. C. de Fréminville. 1930. *Le Rôle de l'ingénieur dans l'organisation rationnelle du travail. Extrait du No. du Cinquantenaire du Génie Civil,* Paris: Publications de Génie Civil, 9.

31. P. Pezeu. 1929. 'Qu'est-ce que la rationalisation?', *Echo de l'USIC* June, 334.

32. H. du Passage. 1920. 'L'Organisation intérieure des entreprises', *Echo de l'USIC* 18 January, 9–10. Du Passage was Director of the Jesuit review *Les Etudes.* E. Duthoit. 1930. 'La Rationalisation est-elle un progrès? Leçon d'ouverture de la Semaine sociale de Besançon 1929', *Semaines sociales de France. Compte rendu in extenso des cours et conférences,* Lyon: Chronique sociale de France, 52–55.

33. De Fréminville, *Le Rôle de l'ingénieur dans l'organisation rationnelle du travail,* 2.

34. L. Boltanski, *Les Cadres: la formation d'un groupe social,* Paris: Minuit, 63–153. This usage of the term seems to have emerged in the 1920s. It appears repeatedly, for example, in E. Rimailho. 1926. *L'Union entre les collaborateurs de l'industrie par l'organisation du travail. Conférence faite le 27 janvier 1926 à l'USIC et le 2 février à la Ligue républicaine nationale,* Besançon (no publisher).

35. Some of the tensions in the engineer's position in relation to capitalism are evident in A. Isaac. 1932. 'Le Capitalisme vu par l'ingénieur', *Echo de l'USIC* June, 367–70.

36. M. Perrin-Pelletier. 1922. 'L'Ingénieur devant la société moderne. Résumé de la conférence de M. Perrin-Pelletier (P 1908) à la réunion du 21 mai 1922 de la section alsacienne de l'USIC', *Echo de l'USIC,* October, 602.

37. Lamirand was a *centralien* who worked in the steel industry in Lorraine and would later hold the post of Minister of Youth at Vichy.

38. Lamirand's connections with Garric's Equipes sociales are referred to in H. Lyautey, Preface to G. Lamirand. 1932. *Le Rôle social de l'ingénieur: scènes de la vie d'usine,* Paris: Editions de la Revue des Jeunes, VII. In his introduction to the 1937 edition of *Le Rôle social de l'ingénieur* (pp.6–7), Lamirand defended his many references to the need for 'maximum efficiency', arguing that organization was one of the keys to success in the international economy.

39. Lamirand, *Le Rôle social de l'ingénieur,* 51.

40. Lamirand, *Le Rôle social de l'ingénieur,* 226–29.

41. I develop here an idea from Y. Cohen. 2001–2. 'Les Chefs, une question pour l'histoire du vingtième siècle', *Cités* 6, 74–76.

42. Perrin-Pelletier, 'L'Ingénieur devant la société moderne', 602.

43. P. Neve. 1932. 'Le Rôle social de l'ingénieur. Rapport présenté par Paul Neve au Congrès international de l'Enseignement technique de Bruxelles', *Echo de l'USIC* December, 630–31; J. Gay. 1922. 'Le Rôle social de l'ingénieur', *Echo de l'USIC,* October, 607.

44. Lamirand, *Le Rôle social de l'ingénieur*, 17.
45. G. Bardet. 1936. 'Une expérience de la collaboration ouvrière à la direction d'une usine' in J. Coutrot, *Leçons de juin 1936. L'Humanisme économique*, Paris: Editions du CPEE, 34–5.
46. Lamirand, *Le Rôle social de l'ingénieur*, 37, 63.
47. Lamirand, *Le Rôle social de l'ingénieur*, 65.
48. Lamirand, *Le Rôle social de l'ingénieur*, 62–5.
49. See J. Wilbois. 1926. *Le Chef d'entreprise: sa fonction et sa personne*, Paris: Alcan, 92–3.
50. N. Duval. 2002. 'L'Education nouvelle dans les sociétés européennes à la fin du XIXe siècle', *Histoire, économie et société* 21(1), 71–86.
51. J. Wilbois and P. Vanuxem. 1919. *Essai sur la conduite des affaires et la direction des hommes*, Paris: Payot, 178. Wilbois himself had studied science at the Ecole normale supérieure.
52. J. Wilbois. 1934. *La Psychologie au service du chef d'entreprise*, Paris: Alcan. This was part of a seven-volume series (*Le Vade-mecum du chef d'entreprise*) based on courses at the school.
53. Wilbois, *La Psychologie*, esp. 49–50, 80, 115, 121.
54. Wilbois, *Le Chef d'entreprise*, 93; Wilbois, *La Psychologie*, 219.
55. E. Pouget. 1914. *L'Organisation du surménage*, Paris: Marcel Rivière et Cie.
56. Frader, *Breadwinners and Citizens*, 142.
57. G. Cross. 1989. *A Quest for Time: The Reduction of Work in Britain and France, 1840–1940*, Berkeley: University of California Press, 200–214.
58. M. Fine. 1979. 'Hyacinthe Dubreuil: le témoignage d'un ouvrier sur le syndicalisme, les relations industrielles et l'évolution technologique, 1921–1940', *Mouvement social* 106, 57; Moutet, *Les Logiques de l'entreprise*, 389.
59. See H. Dubreuil. 1925. 'Au-delà du salaire', *Information sociale* 3 September, 1. For a later reiteration of this argument, see H. Dubreuil. 1935. *A chacun sa chance*, Paris: Grasset, 18.
60. H. Dubreuil. 1929. *Standards*, Paris: Grasset, 62–65.
61. Dubreuil, *Standards*, 66.
62. Dubreuil, *Standards*, 115, 422.
63. H. Dubreuil. 1931. *Nouveaux Standards: les sources de la productivité et de la joie*, Paris: Grasset, 49–51.
64. Dubreuil, *Nouveaux Standards*, 44–46.
65. Dubreuil, *Nouveaux Standards*, 218.
66. Dubreuil, *A chacun sa chance*, 100.
67. Dubreuil, *Nouveaux Standards*, 162–63, 331–32.
68. Dubreuil, *Nouveaux Standards*, 192.
69. This volume, published by the Bibliothèque d'éducation, drew on articles published in the previous year in *L'Information sociale*.
70. Dubreuil, *A chacun sa chance*, 211.
71. Dubreuil, *A chacun sa chance*, 248–53.
72. Dubreuil, *A chacun sa chance*, 254.
73. Dubreuil, *A chacun sa chance*, 262.
74. Thomas spoke on 15 November 1929 and Dubreuil on 18 December 1929. Paul Devinat, who had headed the International Management Institute in Geneva, a partner organization of Albert Thomas's International Labour Office also spoke at USIC. Unlike Dubreuil and Thomas, Devinat had not come out of the trade union movement but was an academic and a member of the Radical Party.
75. USIC. 1929. Introduction to 'Allocution du Président de l'USIC', *Echo de l'USIC* December, 528.
76. E.g. Loos. 1934. 'Les Usines Bat'a', *Echo de l'USIC* February, 104; Review of H. Dubreuil, *Les Codes Roosevelt* in *Echo de l'USIC* December, 1934, XL, which also refers back to favourable reviews given to Dubreuil's earlier works in the journal's columns; correspondence from a member in *Echo de l'USIC* November 1936, 595; J. Wilbois. 1938. 'La Joie au travail', *Echo de l'USIC* April, 246.

77. On the Human Relations School, see E. Mayo. 1933. *The Human Problems of Industrial Civilization*, New York: Macmillan; F.J. Roethlisberger and W. Dickson. 1939. *Management and the Worker*, Cambridge, MA: Harvard University Press; H.A. Landsberger. 1958. *Hawthorne Revisited:* Management and the Worker, *Its Critics and Developments in Human Relations in Industry*, Ithaca, NY: Cornell University Press; S.R. Cohen. 1983. 'From Industrial Democracy to Professional Adjustment: The Development of Industrial Sociology in the US, 1900–1955', *Theory and Society* 12(1), 47–67.

78. P. Devinat. 1930. 'Les Conditions du travail dans une entreprise rationalisée: le système Bat'a et ses conséquences sociales', *Revue internationale du travail* January-February, 48–72; H. Dubreuil. 1936. *L'Exemple de Bat'a: la libération de l'initiative individuelle dans une entreprise géante*, Paris: Grasset. The article on Bat'a published in *Echo de l'USIC* in February 1934 also testifies to the interest it attracted.

79. Dubreuil, *L'Exemple de Bat'a*, 8, 108.

80. Lt-Col E. Rimailho. 1936. *Organisation à la française*, Paris: Delmas, 34, 39. Rimailho also cited examples of the Bat'a system (Part 1, 29–30) and the application of group organization at the Delmas, Chapon and Gounouilhou printworks in Bordeaux (Part 1, 73). See also H. Dubreuil and E. Rimailho. 1939. *Deux hommes parlent du travail*, Paris: Grasset.

81. Extracts of the classes at the Ecole nationale supérieure de l'aéronautique are reproduced in Rimailho, *Organisation à la française*, Part 1, 49–72.

82. Rimailho, *Organisation à la française*, Part 1, 34–35.

83. This was the title of the first part of *Organisation à la française*, 9–76.

84. Rimailho, *Organisation à la française*, Part 1, 17.

85. Rimailho, *Organisation à la française*, Part 1, 10.

86. Bardet, 'Une expérience de collaboration ouvrière', 28.

87. Bardet, 'Une expérience de collaboration ouvrière', 36–39.

88. H. Laugier, E. Toulouse and D. Weinberg. 1932. 'La Biotypologie et l'orientation professionnelle', *Biotypologie* 1(30), 27.

89. See G. Weisz. 1998. 'A Moment of Synthesis: Medical Holism in France Between the Wars' in C. Lawrence and G. Weisz, *Greater than the Parts: Holism in Biomedicine, 1920–1950*, Oxford and New York: Oxford University Press, 68–93.

90. Laugier cited in P. Lévy. 1936. *La Sélection du personnel dans les entreprises de transport*, Paris: Hermann et Cie, 8.

91. *Le Travail humain* March 1933, 70.

92. Laugier et al., 'La Biotypologie et l'orientation professionnelle', (extracts from a talk given to an international conference of the New Education movement in Nice in July 1932); W.H. Schneider. 1991. 'The Scientific Study of Labor in Interwar France', *French Historical Studies* 17(2), 432–33.

93. AN: 468 AP 23 dossier 4 Offprint of Laugier, 'Une science nouvelle: la biotypologie. Science des types humains. Conférence donnée à la Station radiophonique de l'École Supérieure des Postes et des Télégraphes et à la Tour Eiffel le mercredi 28 novembre 1934', 55.

94. Wilbois, *La Psychologie*, 196, 206–8, 213.

95. Wilbois, *La Psychologie*, 206, 212.

96. Wilbois, *La Psychologie*, 14–15, 212.

97. Wilbois, *La Psychologie*, 210–11.

98. Coutrot spoke of morphology as an essential guide to people's psychology in AN: 468 AP 27 dr1 'Texte des Entretiens, octobre 1937', 170. Paul Planus endorsed the method in P. Planus. 1937. 'L'Organisation rationnelle et la direction des affaires', *Méthodes* April, 74 and at the CNOF study day in 1937. The report on this study day in the *Bulletin de l'INOP* 10(1–2), 16 refers to Paul Planne but the person in question appears to be Planus.

99. Mme Ch. Billard. 1942. 'Les Types humains et les stimulants psycho-physiologiques du travail', *Leçons de l'Ecole d'organisation scientifique du travail. Leçon No.162*, Paris: CNOF, 11–17, esp. 12–15; Mme Ch. Billard. 1942. 'Les Types humains: méthodes et procédés d'investigation', *Leçons de l'Ecole d'organisation scientifique du travail. Leçon No.163*, Paris:

CNOF, 1–26. Like many of the lessons in this collection, which received a *dépôt légal* only in 1942, these appear to predate the war. The fields of biotypology and occupational medicine developed significantly under Vichy but none of this material appears in the lessons which recommend readings dating from 1896 to 1938.

100.   See curriculum published in *Bulletin de l'INOP* 10(9) 1938, 206–13; C. Nony. 1938. 'L'Analyse du tempérament. Application de l'analyse factorielle à la détermination des tempéraments d'après Cyril Burt', *Bulletin de l'INOP* 10(7–8), 133–38; Anon. 1938. 'Un questionnaire permettant l'étude du caractère', *Bulletin de l'INOP* 10(9), 188–91.

101.   R. Vinen. 1991. *The Politics of French Business 1936–1945*, Cambridge: Cambridge University Press, 68.

102.   Y. Cohen. 1988. 'Mais qui sont donc ces "techniciens sociaux"? Peugeot. Sochaux. 1936–39', *Vie sociale* 2–3, 45.

103.   AN: 468 AP 16.

104.   Coutrot, *Leçons/L'Humanisme économique*, 49–50.

105.   Coutrot, *Leçons/L'Humanisme économique*, 63–66. Coutrot also endorsed Dubreuil's thinking in two talks in 1936, the first at the Journées d'études du plan français on 31 October 1936 and the second, 'Vers un humanisme économique', at the group JEUNES on 7 December 1936. See AN: 468 AP 15 dr4. E. Hijmans. 1938. 'La Psychose du machinisme et la production en masse', *Humanisme économique* May-June, 20–23 and 'L'Organisation rationnelle du travail', Un nouvel honneur ouvrier', a radio broadcast from August 1937, the text of which can be found in AN: 468 AP 19 dr 5. J. Wilbois. 1939. *Joie au travail et réformes de structure*, Paris: Bloud et Gay, especially chapters 6 and 7.

106.   H. Dubreuil. 1938. *Lettre aux travailleurs français*, Paris: Grasset, 3–8.

107.   Bardet, 'Une expérience de collaboration ouvrière', 40.

108.   In what was surely a rebuke to Coutrot, Wilbois argued that one could not speak of the mentality of the *patronat* in the same way that one could speak of the mentality of workers since the former, unlike the latter, were not a homogenous mass. See J. Wilbois. 1937. *La Nouvelle organisation du travail: réflexions sur ce qui se passe en France depuis juin 1936*, Paris: Librairie Bloud et Gay, 12–14.

109.   R. Dautry. 1937. *Métier d'homme*, Paris: Plon, preface by Paul Valéry. Rimailho's *Organisation à la française* to some extent contributed to this discussion also, though it came out just before the events of June 1936.

110.   I. Kolboom. 1982. 'Patronat et cadres: la contribution patronale à la formation du groupe des cadres (1936–1938)', *Mouvement social* 121, 75; G. Grunberg and R. Mouriaux. 1979. *L'Univers politique et syndical des cadres*, Paris: Presses de la Fondation nationale des sciences politiques, 79. See also Boltanski, *Les Cadres*, 105–6. The CGCEF included foremen as well as engineers.

111.   On the relative weakness of the employers' movement in France before 1936, see H.W. Ehrmann. 1957. *Organized Business in France*, Princeton, NJ: Princeton University Press, 15–32 and J.-P. Le Crom. 1995. *Syndicats, nous voilà! Vichy et le corporatisme*, Paris: Editions de l'Atelier, 78–79.

112.   Even Detoeuf spoke in terms of the need to arm oneself in peace time for potential crises in A. Detoeuf. 1938. 'Aperçu des services pratiques susceptibles d'être rendus par les syndicats patronaux sur le plan économique et social. Exposé introductif', *Comité central de l'organisation professionnelle. Sous-commission d'études des activités et services syndicaux. Réunion du 18 octobre 1938*, Paris: Editions du CCOP, 5–6.

113.   AN: 468 AP 4 dr1 Letter from Maurice Olivier to Coutrot 30 July 1936. This letter is cited in O. Dard. 1999. *Jean Coutrot: de l'ingénieur au prophète*, Besançon: Presses universitaires franc-comtoises, 272. See pp.271–78 in the same work for further details of Coutrot's role in the CCOP.

114.   Detoeuf was head of the educational programme at the CCOP that gave rise in 1938 to the creation of the Centre des jeunes patrons (CJP). See Le Crom, *Syndicats, nous voilà!*, 82–3 and Centre des jeunes dirigeants d'entreprise. 1988. *50 ans qui ont changé l'entreprise: 1938–1988*, Paris: Communica International; Kuisel, 'Auguste Detoeuf, Conscience

of French Industry', 166. The CJP changed its name to the Centre des jeunes dirigeants (CJD) in 1968.

115. F. Denord and O. Henry. 2007. 'La "Modernisation" avant la lettre: le patronat français et la rationalisation (1925–1940)', *Sociétés contemporaines* 68, 101–2.

116. A. Detoeuf. 1938. *Construction du syndicalisme*, Paris: Gallimard.

117. Kuisel, 'Auguste Detoeuf, Conscience of French Industry' indicates (p.156) that Detoeuf and the colleagues who formed the nucleus of the Nouveaux Cahiers group had begun to meet after the riots of 6 February 1934. The first issue of the journal was published in 1937.

118. This correspondence can be found in S. Weil. 1951. *La Condition ouvrière*, Paris: Gallimard, 181–95.

119. P. Planus. 1938. *Patrons et ouvriers en Suède*, Paris: Plon. The author of the preface is billed as André Detoeuf but appears to be Auguste Detoeuf.

120. Nicole Aubert identifies an evolution from a disciplinary model exemplified by Taylorism to one of psychological management in the twentieth century in N. Aubert. 1994. 'Du système disciplinaire au système managinaire: l'emergence du management psychique' in J.-P. Bouilloud and B.-P. Lecuyer (dir), *L'Invention de la gestion. Histoire et pratiques*, Paris: Harmattan.

121. Frader, *Breadwinners and Citizens*.

Chapter 3

ORGANIZATION GOES HOME

If women remained largely absent from the visions of a new work community discussed above, despite their presence in French workplaces, they were by no means absent from the scientific organization movement. There were a number of female psychotechnicians, for example, and women were also prominent in applying rationalization techniques to domestic work. The American, Christine Frederick, had led the way with the publication of *The New Housekeeping* in 1913.[1] By the 1920s, France had its own leader in this field in the form of Paulette Bernège, who founded the Ligue d'organisation ménagère (League for Household Organization) in 1925. The scientific organization movement exercised a considerable influence on the development of domestic science in this period, but this was not the only sphere in which domestic space was being re-imagined, and in some cases rebuilt, along industrial lines. In the world of architecture and design, the ideal and methods of rationalization shaped the way in which practitioners such as Le Corbusier, Charlotte Perriand and Robert Mallet-Stevens sought to reconfigure the home as a living space and a work space. Bernège took a keen interest in such developments, drawing on the work of architects and designers, as well as on that of engineers and psychotechnicians. This chapter examines the nature of the domestic organization project that emerged at this intersection. In doing so, it highlights the *pedagogical* project of domestic rationalization, showing how it proposed to re-educate women's (and ultimately men's) minds and bodies, by remaking the middle-class home.

Paulette Bernège and the Domestic Organization Movement

Bernège and the Ligue d'organisation ménagère sat simultaneously in the (predominantly female) world of educators and reformers that was the domestic science movement and in the (predominantly male) world of industrialists, engineers and publicists that was the scientific organization movement. As part of the former milieu, Bernège published in and edited home magazines, such as *Mon chez moi* or *art ménager*, as well as specialized journals aimed at educators such as *Education ménagère* or *Education nouvelle*.[2] She and her colleagues organized talks at local branches of the Ligue, gave classes at various *écoles ménagères* (domestic science schools) and published manuals for use by housewives and domestic science teachers, of which the best known was Bernège's *De la méthode ménagère* (1928). In 1930, Bernège set up her own Ecole de Haut Enseignement Ménager (School for Advanced Study in Domestic Science), though, like the initial attempts to educate engineers and managers in scientific organization methods, this was a modest venture. It did not have its own premises and was based at the Musée social. Nonetheless, Bernège has come to be recognised as a central figure in the history of French domestic science education. Indeed, in 1960 a special issue of *Education ménagère* was devoted to honouring the life and work of the woman whom the Director of Technical Education had once called 'notre Paulette nationale'.[3]

Formally educated in literature and philosophy, Bernège may well have been initiated into the intellectual world and professional networks of scientific organization by her relative and friend, Maurice Ponthière.[4] She published some of her first articles in Ponthière's review *Mon bureau*, before becoming the founding editor of the sister publication, *Mon chez moi*, in 1923.[5] Her professional links with the industrial milieu began at least as early as 1922, when she created an institute of domestic organization in Nancy in collaboration with a local industrialist and an engineer from the domestic appliance industry.[6] She also worked with the Salon des arts ménagers, an annual state-sponsored home exhibition launched in 1923 which provided a forum in which utility companies, appliance manufacturers and domestic science professionals operated side by side and sometimes in close collaboration, promoting new household technologies.[7] Meanwhile, national and international associations of industrial organizers were setting up domestic sections and devoting conference sessions to the home.[8] Bernège was invited to lead the domestic strand at the international conference on scientific organization in Paris in 1924 and went on to chair the domestic economy section at the Comité national d'organisation française (CNOF).

Thus, while domestic organization probably remained a secondary concern for many industrial organizers, who were more focused on factories and offices, it did occupy a certain institutional space within the movement. This was largely a space occupied by women, though there were also some vociferous male advocates of the rationalized home. Indeed, Christine Frederick's work had been introduced to a French audience in 1915 by none other than Henry Le Chatelier, who prefaced a selection of her writings in the journal that had done most to promote Taylorism in France before World War One, the *Revue de métallurgie*.[9] This was clearly a publication aimed primarily at an audience of industrial professionals and Le

Chatelier used the example of domestic organization to demonstrate the universality of the principles of scientific organization. To this extent, his early interest in this subject confirms the observation made in Chapter One: that scientific organization was conceived from the outset as a set of principles and techniques to be applied to all spheres of activity.

Like the other technician-publicists discussed in earlier chapters, Bernège not only contributed to the development and application of new techniques of organization, but was an exceptionally energetic promoter of these methods. One contributor to *Education ménagère* in 1960 estimated her output at five hundred articles in French, two hundred lectures in French, ten or so in English, and twenty-five radio broadcasts.[10] Between 1928 and 1950, she published some fourteen books and pamphlets, though *De la méthode ménagère* remained her most successful title. A second edition was published in 1934 and the book was translated into German, Dutch, Italian and Polish.[11] While Bernège appears to have been less active in domestic science education after World War Two, she was certainly regarded by postwar domestic science experts as the pioneer of an approach that continued to inform their work.[12]

Of course, the interwar generation of experts were by no means the inventors of domestic science. There was already a well-established literature on household management in nineteenth-century Europe, as those familiar with Britain's Mrs Beeton will know. In France, nineteenth-century works like Mme Pariset's *Manuel de la maîtresse de maison et de la parfaite ménagère* (Manual for the Lady of the House and the Perfect Housewife) reflected a set of bourgeois dwelling norms in which the mistress of the house was assumed to employ servants.[13] Such manuals provided advice on managing one's staff, fixing a carefully regimented timetable for their tasks and keeping records of household expenditure. By the turn of the century, there was also another kind of domestic science literature that was linked partly with the expansion of public education under the Third Republic. Among this generation of domestic science educators, the leading figure was Augusta Moll-Weiss. She and her colleagues argued for more and better domestic science education in schools, promoting a curriculum based on the teaching of tasks such as sewing and cookery. Hygienist concerns also loomed large in this period and are apparent, for example, in Moll-Weiss's emphasis on cleaning, nutrition and child health, reflecting the extent to which medical science was shaping the agenda for social intervention before the First World War.[14]

These turn-of-the-century reformers were particularly preoccupied with the state of the *working-class* home and in this respect their concerns intersected with those of promoters of social housing, who frequented centres like the Société d'économie sociale, the Société française des habitations à bon marché and the Musée social.[15] Social housing – like the company housing provided by employers in industries such as mining and the railways – was seen as a way of ensuring the health, morality and social stability of the working-class population.[16] The importance attached to housing was in part a reflection of the influence of Lamarckian social thinking in France, since Lamarck's alternative to Darwin's theory of evolution posited that biological characteristics could be acquired and inherited as a result of the action of the environment on the organism. Hence, the project of housing reformers has been summed up by Susanna Magri and Christian Topalov as 'changing housing to transform the people [peuple]'.[17]

As the Leplaysian engineer Emile Cheysson acknowledged in a study commissioned by the Musée social in 1907, domestic science education was an obvious complement to reformers' attempts to improve working-class housing. Betraying a distinct mistrust of working-class women and their homemaking standards, he suggested that there was little point in providing well-designed and hygienic accommodation, only for it to be reduced to a hovel by a 'bad housewife'.[18] Thus, at the Ecole des mères, founded by Moll-Weiss partly to train specialized domestic science teachers, students were also sent out to teach women in popular education centres in working-class neighbourhoods such as Belleville.[19] Concerns about the health of the working-class population mingled with fears that the employment of women in factories prevented them from fulfilling their assigned role as mothers. In the interwar period, this was aggravated by heightened anxiety about the low birth rate, leading some employers to organize homemaking classes for their female workers, either with the help of the *surintendante d'usine* or in conjunction with the local social insurance office.[20] In this context, domestic science was a gender-specific technique for managing 'the human factor' at a time of acute pro-natalist concern.

The movement led by Bernège took domestic science into a new phase, for it sought to establish norms for what was to be an increasingly common model of domestic organization in the twentieth century: the middle-class home without servants. One of the clearest indicators of the class profile of Bernège's target audience was the fact that students at her school were required to have passed the *baccalauréat*, an educational route not generally open to working-class girls.[21] While bourgeois women might previously have expected a home with at least some staff, a significant decline in the number of servants is visible in the census data after the First World War, with the servant population dropping by 15.3 per cent between 1911 and 1921.[22] This probably reflected not only the loss of men and the higher proportion of young women entering factories rather than domestic service during the war, but also a continuing preference for alternative forms of employment among working-class women after the war. At the same time, postwar economic and financial instability led to drastic falls in the value of investments in the 1920s, leaving many bourgeois families in reduced material circumstances. It seems likely that this was also a factor in the declining number of servants employed in this period. Bernège situated her work explicitly as a response to these changes, assuming that they were durable and that the household without servants would become the norm, at least for a significant section of the bourgeoisie.[23] Thus, in referring to Bernège's model as middle-class, I am not only excluding the most affluent homes which typically still had servants, but alluding to the changing profile of the French bourgeoisie in this period, and ultimately to the emergence of a salaried middle class that would define itself less in terms of property or *patrimoine* and more in terms of technical and professional competence. If this group was not yet clearly delineated between the wars, the discourse of the social engineer as man of action certainly contributed to its emergence, as noted in the previous chapter.[24] With its vision of homes that were well equipped, but not grand, its appeal to the values and methods of the engineer-manager, and, as we will see, its links with the professionalization of middle-class women, Bernège's domestic organization project can also be seen as part of this trend.

Bernège outlined a range of domestic arrangements that might result from the loss of servants, including a model where some work was done by external help such as a cleaning lady or laundry service, but she also accepted the possibility of middle-class women doing all their own housework.[25] One way or another, then, the women that Bernège addressed were expected to get their hands dirty, sweeping floors and washing dishes. When one considers that only a generation before, households of quite modest means, such as that of a bank cashier, could still afford a maid, one is struck by the renegotiation of notions of middle-class respectability that had to take place in order to invent the twentieth-century housewife.[26] Between the turn of the century, when the employment of one or more servants was a primary social signifier of bourgeois status, and the 1950s, when the ideal of middle-class domesticity was represented in advertising by a woman in an apron, the meanings attached to domestic work clearly changed considerably.[27] Part of what happened here was that appliances replaced servants not just functionally but symbolically, as part of an aspirational model of middle-class life. Robert L. Frost has argued that this process was already underway in the interwar years as appliances were being marketed as part of a new 'modern' lifestyle in magazines and at the Salon des arts ménagers.[28] Many rural homes were only just being connected to the electricity network between the wars and the cost of domestic appliances meant that much of what was on offer at the Salon was not immediately accessible to the average French household: a fridge, for example, cost nearly five thousand francs in 1929 and a survey in 1935 showed that there were only twenty-five thousand fridges in the whole country.[29] Only 1.2 per cent of the population owned a vacuum cleaner in 1932.[30] But even if they did not actually purchase the goods displayed, Frost contends, the interwar public attended the Salon in large numbers, participating in the lifestyle fantasy it offered. Bernège's importation of industrial management methods into the home can be read as another element in this story of the transformation of bourgeois dwelling norms in twentieth-century France. Indeed, at a time when the economic effects of the First

World War and then the Depression were being felt in many French households, Bernège promoted an ethics of efficiency that was often more productivist than consumerist and perhaps more in tune with the financial circumstances of the interwar generation.[31]

What Bernège invented was a new model of the housewife-manager. She distinguished *organisation ménagère* from the domestic science taught by the likes of Moll-Weiss. While other manuals covered task-specific knowledge and skills, with topics ranging from laundry and ironing, to basic healthcare and baby care, Bernège's lessons were devoted not to individual household chores, but to the acquisition of techniques for managing and rationalizing one's own work. The housewife was compared to the businessman in terms which drew explicitly on Henri Fayol's doctrine of management: even if she did her own housework, the rational housewife was not just a manual worker, but a manager who had to lead, plan, monitor and coordinate domestic life.[32] Indeed, Bernège adopted the organicist language of much early management theory to express the hierarchy between the woman who merely performed a series of chores and the woman who ran a scientifically organized home: in the first model, she stated, 'the housewife is like an earthworm'; in the second, she was a complex organism that had evolved to a higher level.[33] In this way, the application of scientific management to the home positioned housework as a suitable preoccupation for middle-class women, for whom it might otherwise have been regarded as menial or socially demeaning. The housewife could be a manager even if she had no staff to manage but herself.

Interwar domestic scientists tended to believe that the First World War had radically altered women's expectations of marriage and employment, making education in home-making all the more necessary. As Mary Louise Roberts has noted, the huge loss of male lives during the war brought in its wake a belief that middle-class families could no longer rely on the prospect of finding husbands for their daughters.[34] A number of educational reformers argued that women must now be more systematically educated and prepared for professional life.[35] At the same time pro-natalist and familialist movements ran vociferous campaigns insisting that women's place was in the home and that their right to paid employment should be curtailed.[36] Domestic science addressed both sets of concerns, promising simultaneously a scientific education for women and a revalidation of the domestic sphere. As one contributor to *Art ménager* put it:

> The family of 1900 raised its daughters for marriage. The postwar family has raised them for the chase to earn their daily bread. The current circumstances lead us to look for a happy medium: today's young girls and doubtless those of tomorrow must be equipped for life, but progressively they will assume once again their place in the home and take on the role that their forebears fulfilled with such sweetness and good sense.
>
> Is this a backward move? No. – The modernized home is worthy of retaining the most modern woman so long as she is fit to understand and direct it.[37]

If the emphasis here was on retaining women in the home, it was also argued by some that rationalization could help render the burden of housework compatible with a world in which women would increasingly have professional lives outside the home.[38] Indeed, Bernège sometimes used her own domestic situation, as a single professional woman with an apartment to maintain, to illustrate her arguments about the benefits of scientific organization.[39]

There may be tensions here between support for women's right to take paid work outside the home and the revalidation of feminine domesticity, but the position was less contradictory than it may at first appear. As Martine Martin has pointed out, the valorization of domestic work as a managerial task was just one way in which domestic work was 'professionalized' between the wars. Bernège also sought to extend the range of what she called 'les professions ménagères'.[40] In other words, like many of her generation, Bernège sought to mark out a space of feminine professional activity outside the home that was understood as an extension of women's domestic role. Linda Clark and Laura Lee Downs have shown how a logic that delineated a public as well as a private sphere for maternal action was instrumental in carving out professional roles for women in the nineteenth and early twentieth centuries, notably those of teacher, social worker and factory or prison inspector.[41] Bernège's vision can be situated in this context, though one of its characteristics was that it also envisaged a more commercial role for women. This was most clearly illustrated by the new type of domestic science curriculum Bernège pioneered at her school and in a proposal for a University Institute for the Domestic Sciences made in 1937. In these initiatives, 'the domestic sciences' – now in the plural – included psychotechnics, pedagogy, architecture and urban planning. The publicity for the school boasted that this broad training could help to steer women away from traditionally male professions by opening up opportunities which were at once worthy of women's intelligence and compatible with their 'feminine vocation'.[42] Bernège argued that graduates of her proposed institute would be equipped for careers not just as domestic science teachers, but in fields such as journalism, commercial research and product development, advertising and social services, which were to have an increasing role to play in shaping the organization of domestic space.[43] The domestic was not conceived here as a private space but as a space integrated into a gendered social and economic system. With the home understood as a workplace and a site of consumption, embedded in a series of relationships with external institutions, these external bodies themselves became annexes of domestic space and suitable arenas of feminine professional activity.

In exploring these developments, authors like Frost and Martin have been partly concerned with the question of how far new domestic technologies, whether in the form of appliances or organizational techniques, can be said to liberate women. This is not what the present chapter seeks to establish. Rather, it considers the domestic organizers' own construction of their project as one of adaptation, by which I mean not only the adaptation of women to perceived changes in their social and economic environment, but also the mutual adaptation of domestic space and its users. This aspect of domestic organization in turn sheds light on the whole enterprise of scientific organization, highlighting the extent to which it was conceived as a social reordering project that was to operate by moulding minds and bodies.

Scientific Organization and the Moral Economy of the Middle-class Home

One issue that concerned Bernège and her colleague at the Ecole de Haut Enseignement Ménager, Marguerite Lamy, was the education of women as consumers. Though I have described Bernège's outlook as productivist, she did believe that managing consumption was an increasingly important part of women's household responsibilities and that domestic science must respond to this.[44] Her contributions in this field included not just her lessons on household accounting in *De la méthode ménagère* but also volumes giving advice on the purchase of domestic equipment, such as *J'installe ma cuisine* and later *Le Blanchissage domestique*.[45] Lamy made her name as a specialist in consumer education, notably with the publication of *Bien acheter pour mieux vivre* in 1932.[46]

If advertising, magazines and the Salon des arts ménagers promoted new forms of domestic consumption between the wars, experts like Bernège and Lamy, who were often present in such exhibitions and publications, also attempted to teach women to be the *right kind* of consumers. It was commonplace in this period to consider women particularly vulnerable to the perceived dangers of mass consumption. Women were typically represented in anti-consumerist discourse as capricious, irrational, easily influenced by the power of the media, and sexually transgressive – a trend apparent in the conflation of consumer desire and sexual desire in representations of the *garçonne* in the 1920s or in Georges Duhamel's sexualized portraits of American women drivers and jazz club goers in *Scènes de la vie future*.[47] Bernège and Lamy articulated a more moderate version of this anxiety about women as consumers. Bernège rebuked French women for what she saw as their tendency to spend for pleasure rather than utility and suggested that their notions of what constituted good value were often simplistic.[48] Lamy was less fearful of irrational consumption than her colleague but accepted the notion that women were easily influenced and excessively susceptible to the manipulative power of advertising.[49] Both experts contrasted emotional or instinctive purchases with what they regarded as rational consumer behaviour and sought to foster the latter over the former, by training women in planning, budgeting and record-keeping techniques.[50]

Such skills had long been a part of the repertoire of domestic science manuals and the interwar experts were essentially updating the curriculum for an era in which, in their view, the labour power of housewives and servants would increasingly be replaced by external suppliers and machines, making the housewife's role as a procurer of goods and services even more important. Much was made in this context of the domestic experts' debt to industrial practices, particularly the practice of calculating the projected expenditure and savings (in time and money) that would result from a particular purchase, in order to ensure that costs would be offset. Lamy wrote admiringly of the work of the Belgian industrialist, Landauer and the military organizer, General Pierre-Roger Chayrou in this area, recommending that women adopt a similar approach in their homes.[51] This did not prevent her from accepting certain limits to the analogy between household purchases and military or industrial supplies. When all other factors had been considered, she acknowledged, some consumer choices came down to questions of taste or aesthetics, which could not be reduced to an algebraic formula.[52] The instinctive purchase was to be subjected as far as possible to rational control but could not be completely eliminated. If Lamy promoted industrial methods in spite of this qualification, it was partly as a means of forcing producers and retailers to raise their game, by training the consumer to be more exacting. A strong advocate of consumer power, she argued for a US-style customer service ethic and drew heavily on Christine Frederick's *Selling Mrs Consumer*. She even accepted that there was pleasure to be had in consumption, but located this in the 'sport' of trying to get the best deal, rather than in desire and its satisfaction.[53]

Bernège's arguments about getting good value remained centred on the economy of the home as a workplace. She insisted that before purchasing an appliance the housewife must first calculate the initial financial outlay, the interest payable on any credit taken, and the savings that might be gained in labour, time, consumables and maintenance products over the years.[54] This would allow her to work out exactly how long the appliance would take to pay for itself. Such advice reflects the fact that electrical appliances were not yet considered as standard household equipment and suggests that Bernège's imagined audience was assumed to be able to afford such goods, but not to be so wealthy as to be unconcerned by the question of value for money. Her lessons in domestic accounting illustrate just how detailed the application of these methods was supposed to be. Complete records of household transactions had to be kept and budgeting was to operate at several levels, to include a general annual budget, a monthly review process, and a range of more specific monitoring tasks.[55] Fuel consumption was to be monitored, for example, and students were asked to calculate on this basis the average cost of producing a meal (monthly and annually), as well as keeping a full monthly tally of the total expenditure per member of the household.[56]

This amounted to quite an intensive programme of financial monitoring, confirming the argument made by many feminist historians of domestic work that the rationalization of the home imposed new burdens on women, making standards of housekeeping more onerous, even if time was sometimes saved on specific tasks.[57] Ostensibly, the benefit of applying industrial methods to the home lay precisely in the time, money or energy saved and this argument may well have resonated with the concerns of women who had to use resources prudently in a period of economic instability and depression. Yet it is clear that moral and social objectives also inhabit the economic logic of Bernège's lessons. One of the first exercises in *De la méthode ménagère* asked the housewife to evaluate her overall efficiency and identify areas for improvement. Revealingly, this was referred to as 'an examination of your conscience as a housewife [un examen de conscience ménagère]'.[58] Like many members of the domestic science movement, Bernège associated a well-ordered house with a stable family unit, even claiming that rationalization could bring down the divorce rate.[59] The linkage of virtue, social stability and the material organization of the home was not new in itself, but by suggesting that the home be run on the same basis as a business, Bernège made efficiency the measure of domestic order. Thus, in her lessons on domestic accounting, it was the pursuit of efficiency that set the boundaries of appropriate consumer behaviour, for it was in these terms that any purchase had to be justified. In this way, it was productivism that promised to domesticate consumer desire.

Significantly, this operated not just at a symbolic level, but also as an attempt to inculcate rational qualities into the student. Bernège asserted that, by offering training in industrial planning and accounting techniques, she could turn the frivolous easily-led purchaser into one imbued with the qualities of 'analysis, reasoning, critical thinking [esprit critique], observation, perspicacity, and good sense'.[60] This draws our attention to a crucial aspect of domestic organization – it was an educational project that aimed not just to develop skills but also to discipline its female pupils.[61] In this context, scientific organization was, quite literally, about the *rationalization* of its human subjects.

Organization as Re-education

It was noted in the last chapter that when Joseph Wilbois educated business leaders in 'self-management', he used a combination of Fayolist principles and mental training techniques (visualization, autosuggestion etc). In the domestic organization project, however, women were aligned (functionally and to some extent psychologically) with workers as well as managers and this may be one reason why Bernège's techniques focused more on the body. Her method drew heavily on Taylorism and industrial psychophysiology, applying the concept of the human motor (which had already had a significant impact on domestic science in the field of nutrition) to the working bodies of women who performed housework.[62] The work scientist Dagmar Weinberg taught classes on domestic psychotechnics at Bernège's school, the term 'psychotechnics' being used broadly here to include fatigue study and ergonomics as well as aptitude testing.[63] Students were invited, for example, to measure the different levels of energy expended by one of their classmates while polishing a floor manually and with a machine.[64] Likewise, Bernège instructed her students on the most energy efficient series of movements required to wash dishes.[65]

Experiments and practical exercises occupied a central place in Bernège's teaching methods and it is worth examining these more closely. Each lesson in *De la méthode ménagère* was followed by exercises. These were intended not only for use in the domestic science classroom but for individual readers in their own homes. In a typical exercise, the housewife/student would be asked to carry out a household task such as making a bed and to evaluate critically her performance, perhaps with the aid of a stopwatch. She was then to experiment with changes in her technique, trying out different movements and approaches, and subjecting these to a similar process of evaluation in order to determine the most efficient way of performing the task.[66] In this way, Bernège sought to equip her students with a method for continual self-monitoring and self-improvement, making this use of Taylorism different in a crucial respect from its industrial application. In the industrial workshop, the new form of surveillance and labour discipline that Taylorist time and motion studies represented was implemented by the intervention of an engineer or some other managerial intermediary; in the middle-class home individual women were to internalize these methods for *self*-surveillance since the housewife was both worker and manager.

Moreover, these exercises did not end with the process of self-evaluation. This was followed by a second phase in which the improved technique was to be practised repeatedly. As in the Taylorized workplace, further efficiency savings were supposed to be gained as the new movements became inscribed in muscular memory. For example, having analysed her bed-making technique, the housewife was to apply a revised technique for a week, before measuring her performance again.[67] In this sense, the process of rationalization was not complete until she had gone beyond the analytical stage to a point at which the lessons gained from her analysis were embedded in her body. This belief in the value of repetition and habit-formation may also explain the gratuitous quality of some of the exercises students were asked to carry out. One exercise simply consisted of the instruction: 'Immerse yourself in all kinds of measuring [Livrez-vous à toutes sortes de mesures et contrôles]'. Suggestions for things to measure included how much water the bath held or the cost per 100 grammes of various products.[68] It was not arithmetical knowledge that was being targeted here – the lesson did not focus on methods of calculation. Rather, it seems that the habit of precision was valued in itself.

Bernège's interest in spatial organization and ergonomic design confirms the significance in her work of bodily education. In this respect her vision coincided with that of modern architects for whom functional organization and economy of movement were important design principles. We see this, for example, in the work of Le Corbusier and Mallet-Stevens in France, or Walter Gropius and Ernst May in Germany.[69] Bernège cultivated certain links with this movement: students at her school took classes on architecture and urban planning taught by the head of the Ecole spéciale d'architecture, which had helped foster the rationalist current in design, and Le Corbusier was among the patrons of the Ligue d'organisation ménagère. In her manuals, Bernège encouraged students to reflect on the spatial organization of work, exhorting them to reduce the amount of energy they spent moving between different rooms or workspaces: the distance covered in a lifetime spent running back and forth unnecessarily between the kitchen and the dining room was the equivalent to the distance from Paris to Lake Baikal in Siberia, she warned.[70] Her conception of functional organization also had a strong biologist flavour as she repeatedly compared the connection between different parts of the home to that between parts of a body. Explaining the need to organize the flow of work through space in a sequential and efficient manner, she observed that in a body, organs that combine to perform a particular task, such as the organs of the digestive system, are closely physically connected, allowing them to work efficiently. It was a basic law of organization, she concluded, that 'organs used to perform the same task must be in immediate connection and will constitute an ensemble termed a "system".'[71] In this way, she located herself explicitly within the tradition of 'organizers who take the living organism as their model'.[72]

This went hand in hand with an ergonomic approach to design. Complaining that ill-adapted work-surfaces imposed on the user movements which were abnormal, tiring and inelegant, Bernège sought to show how a rational disposition of rooms and storage spaces could have the opposite effect.[73] For example, by creating storage areas at the right height and storing items so that the most frequently used were the most easily accessible, rational design could guide the movements of the user. These principles were most clearly applied in kitchen design, a subject to which Bernège devoted a full volume in 1933.[74] One of the rules she adopted was that the key work areas – sink, cooker and preparation surface – should be arranged in a triangle allowing the user to turn easily from one to the other, a design principle still applied today.[75] Fitted kitchens – the height of functional design and spatial efficiency – featured regularly in *Art ménager* between the wars though it would be some years before they would become standard fittings in French homes.[76] Indeed, the fitted kitchen is perhaps the most visible legacy of the drive to rationalize the home in the interwar years, so much so that we might takes its convenience at face value. It is worth remembering therefore that while ergonomic design was partly about modelling the environment to fit the user, it also implied an adaptation of the individual to his or her surroundings. Le Corbusier conceived of his work in these terms, proclaiming, for example, that when he designed a chair, he was teaching a new way of sitting.[77] This explicit aspiration of functional design to shape human habits was part of what Le Corbusier invoked when he labelled his houses 'machines for living'.[78]

In his study of rehabilitation science during World War One, Matthew Price has argued that bodily re-education and habit formation were conceived as a means of rationalizing the mind as well as the body.[79] Industrial psycho-physiology and rehabilitation science were closely inter-related: scientists like Jules Amar worked in both fields and one of the main objectives of rehabilitation science was to reintegrate the war-wounded into society by turning them back into producers. It is not surprising then to find similar ideas about educating the mind through the body in Bernège's work. The benefit of constant self-monitoring was not just that it saved time but also that it instilled in the housewife 'a considered turn of mind … a logical mind … a mental discipline'.[80] This was presumed to be reinforced by physical repetition of movements. Indeed, Bernège saw particular advantages in rhythmic work. Commenting on a domestic science class she had observed, she remarked that 'by bringing into play factors … such as imitation, training, observation and rhythm, the teacher quickly notices that movements flow better, dexterity is developed, along with a taste for precision, speed and order'.[81] Pleasure in rhythmic movement was believed to enhance efficiency because it was a particularly effective means of inscribing sensations in bodily memory. But most importantly, what was cultivated through this imprinting of physical habits, according to Bernège, was not just those bodily movements themselves but a taste for precision, speed and order, a disposition of the mind and body towards efficiency.

Pedagogy as Rationalization

Taylorism and the psycho-physiology of work were not the only sources on which the re-educative project of domestic organization drew. Like Joseph Wilbois, Bernège took an interest in the pedagogical theories and practices of the New Education movement. With its criticism of theoretical learning and emphasis on learning through practical activity, this movement proposed an approach to child development that blurred the line between work and play, seeing the latter as fundamental to learning. While this outlook appears very much at odds with the regimentation of the Taylorized factory, it seems to have provided a way for some organizers to think about questions of motivation to work and adaptation to mass industrial society.[82] In the domestic branch of the scientific organization movement, where the leading figures were often professional educators, the influence of the new educational thinking is perhaps less surprising than in other areas. Indeed, domestic organization provided fertile ground for the encounter between Taylorist labour discipline and educational psychology.

Bernège's own links with the New Education movement appear to have begun in 1928, when she participated in one of the first conferences of the French branch of the movement and published an article in the review *Nouvelle éducation*.[83] The significance of this current of thinking in her work would become increasingly evident and was most explicit in her 1947 manual for domestic science teachers, *Guide d'enseignement ménager*, which was prefaced by one of the leaders of movement in France, Roger Cousinet. Several of Bernège's associates shared her interest in this field. Mme J Bernis, who taught psychology and family pedagogy at Bernège's school, was an admirer of Maria Montessori.[84] The editor-in-chief of the journal *Education ménagère*, Mme Perraud-Duban, also endorsed 'active methods', the term coined by the New Education movement.[85]

Active learning methods appealed readily to domestic scientists in part because of the emphasis they placed on practical work. As Cousinet recognised in his preface to Bernège's postwar manual, the practical component in domestic science made it an obvious terrain for the application of these methods.[86] Indeed, the New Education movement's efforts to assert the value of manual activity were very much in tune with the domestic scientists' attempts to revalorize domestic work. Bernège echoed the movement's position when she remarked that:

> We too often have the tendency in France, outside New Education circles, to think that manual and household work develop only manual skills and do not affect the superior functions of the brain. This leads frequently to contempt for these chores which are considered menial and it has also led to the dominance of a kind of education which has become increasingly distant from the practical and the real.[87]

Cousinet in turn commended the emphasis that Bernège's approach placed on learning through experimentation and on continual application of the principles studied.[88]

The convergence of the scientific organization and New Education movements may also have been facilitated by the overlap between industrial and educational psycho-physiology. Aptitude testing and biometrics (a key element in Laugier's biotypology) had developed through research and application in both fields. Researchers in these areas often worked with schools as well as with industry.[89] Aptitude testing was used by educators for diagnostic purposes, as well as in vocational guidance, which was in any case a kind of middle ground between industry and education. The New Education movement aspired to offer a scientific pedagogy, based on an understanding of the individual child and, for some pedagogues at least, aptitude testing offered a way of achieving this. Edouard Claparède and Ovide Decroly, both very much associated with the movement, were among those who developed aptitude and personality tests.[90] Indeed, this conception of scientific pedagogy was endorsed at length in 1938 in Mme Bernis's entry on 'The Family Home and the Education of the Child' in Bernège's *Encyclopédie de la vie familiale*.[91]

Claparède, Decroly and Montessori were all doctors by training and their educational theory and practice was rooted in their understanding of the biological development of the child. Montessori's method also drew on physical anthropology and especially anthropometrics, a well-established field in turn-of-the-century Italy.[92] What Montessori had in common with those who developed aptitude testing was a preoccupation with measurement and observation. Thus, according to her method, the psycho-physiological characteristics of the child were to be assessed by close observation of the subject by the teacher, who was also to take weekly measurements of the child's weight and height in school, while more detailed anthropometric data was to be collected by a doctor.[93] The importance attached to physical development was also expressed in Montessori's emphasis on the education of the senses, which was in her view a necessary prelude to the education of the intellect.[94] Here a biologized conception of education, informed by the social hygienist concerns of turn-of-the-century medicine, met the Rousseauian ideal of a pedagogy in which the child's 'natural' voyage of discovery begins with the exploration its senses and environment.[95] Children were presented with various objects to work and play with, allowing them to develop dexterity through the repetition of movements and to improve their perception of size, distance etc. For Montessori, it was important that children be allowed to carry out these activities with minimal interference and prescription by the teacher, the objects acting as a stimulus to *self-education*.[96] In this way the child was to learn self-discipline through free activity.[97] Interestingly, Montessori schools used everyday domestic tasks as one way of stimulating this process and in her 1947 guide for teachers Bernège singled out this aspect of Montessori education.[98] She recommended the use of similar exercises in the domestic science classroom, arguing that by developing skills such as physical coordination one was also developing intellectual capacities such as acuity of perception, memory and judgement.[99] In support, she cited Montessori's dictum that 'it is by training the hand that we train the mind'.[100] It is perhaps worth noting here that the skills being defined and tested by industrial psychotechnicians (in a move away from the traditional notion of skill linked to apprenticeship) were often the same psycho-motor skills that these educationalists were trying to foster.

As a volume aimed at teachers, Bernège's *Guide d'enseignement ménager* was much more explicit in its discussion of pedagogical theory than her interwar books, which had been written primarily for students and housewives. What it contained was an extended reflection on the educational practices that Bernège had developed over the previous twenty years and, as such, it offers an illuminating perspective on the interwar sources, which have been the basis of most of the observations made so far about organization as re-education. Revisiting the lessons she had offered in *De la méthode ménagère*, Bernège confirmed in the *Guide* that a number of her early exercises had 'no immediate practical purpose' but were 'above all psychological in scope', seeking as they did to instil the habit of analysis and self-evaluation. Her aim, she confirmed, was 'to train the mind'.[101] Elsewhere in the volume, she stressed that the teacher must 'seek the procedure that allows the pupil to *monitor himself constantly* [*se contrôler sans cesse lui-même*] ... [and] as far as possible put the apprentice in conditions where he is gradually led to *perfect his own* movements and equipment'.[102] Most significantly, Bernège made explicit that part of the social value of domestic work and domestic science education lay in their disciplinary action on the personality of the housewife or student:

> Learning to order and discipline one's movements is in the end nothing other than learning to control oneself by taming one's mood swings and mastering one's reflexes. Self-mastery is doubtless one of the principle aims of all education and probably one of the most difficult to achieve, yet most important for the good functioning of society.[103]

Here the idea of training the mind by training the body is articulated not simply as an argument about the intellectual value of manual work but as a belief in the power of such training to act on the affective side of the personality too. The need for this rationalization of the whole personality was expressed graphically in two diagrams. The first set out the principle characteristics of the human being in a state of moral and psycho-physiological equilibrium.[104] It was an image of order, a perfect circle divided into equal segments each of which corresponded to an attribute. The second diagram represented the dangers of allowing the personality to develop haphazardly in the absence of scientific pedagogy – it depicted an amorphous blob.[105]

New Women, New Children, New Men

In her pedagogical writings Bernège affirmed a belief in the importance of the home as an educational milieu for its inhabitants. The exercises in *De la méthode ménagère* and the effects of rational design in training the housewife's body constituted an important element of this, but the educational project of domestic organization did not end there. Bernège also sought to train women to apply similar methods to the education of their children in the home. Promotional material for the Ecole de Haut Enseignement Ménager boasted that the training it offered in medicine, child-rearing, food science, psychology and family pedagogy would equip a new generation of women as 'educators of minds and bodies'.[106] As early as 1928, Bernège had sought to demonstrate in the columns of *Nouvelle éducation* how the domestic exercises she applied in *De la méthode ménagère* could be adapted by mothers and teachers of young children in order to develop the child's taste for work, order and method.[107] Building on the already blurred distinction between work and play implicit in active learning methods, Bernège recommended that children be encouraged to undertake Taylorist task analysis, movement study and other forms of rationalizing activity in their play. In this way, she suggested, one could foster a 'spirit of organization' in the child.[108] Importantly, this was presented not just as something that was of value for the child's personal development, but also as a way of equipping children for what Bernège called 'the modern world of work'. Children should be brought up in the company of machines, she argued, allowing the new generation to develop in harmony with an increasingly mechanized environment and in tune with 'the ends towards which our era is oriented'.[109]

Bernège's enterprise dovetailed perfectly in this respect with the ambitions articulated by the 'founding fathers' of the scientific organization movement. Fayol had suggested that education in the science of administration should begin in homes and primary schools. 'Like any other business', he argued, the family required administration, 'that is, planning, organization, leadership, coordination and monitoring'. He went on: 'the family could be an excellent school of administration: principles, procedures and methods would naturally penetrate the minds of children, forming ideas that can be transmitted and perfected'.[110] Similarly, Le Chatelier believed that domestic chores provided an excellent opportunity for a practical lesson in scientific determinism, observation, experimentation, scientific method, measurement and the principles of the scientific organization of work.[111] Indeed, he argued that the spread of scientific method outside the factory was fundamental to its ultimate triumph within industry: 'To produce its full effect', he declared,

> this faith in science must spread everywhere and penetrate education which has thus far remained insufficiently scientific despite its pretensions to the contrary; *from the factories, this faith in experimental method will pass into society and from there will come back to the workshops* by providing them with leaders better prepared to use scientific methods and more convinced of their usefulness.[112]

This view was echoed by Joseph Wilbois, in his report as Chair of the Education Section at the International Congress on Scientific Organization in 1929. He argued that for scientific organization to work, everyone from unskilled workers to managing directors must not only grasp the theory but have practised the techniques 'until they become habitual'. This was to be achieved, he concluded, not just by formal teaching, but by education in the broader sense, an education which must begin in the family.[113] But nowhere was this vision of the power of domestic life to naturalize rationalization expressed more graphically than in Le Chatelier's excitement on discovering the work of Christine Frederick. 'The children raised by the readers of this domestic manual' he claimed, 'will certainly turn out as engineers later in life, and will be better prepared than the current generation for the application of the new industrial methods. They will have been suckled on the taste of science at their mother's breasts.'[114]

While it is not unusual to figure mothers as potent and crucial transmitters of social or moral values, where sons are concerned they were perhaps just as likely to be suspected of molly-coddling. It is all the more striking therefore to see women cast in this instance not as over-emotional beings, but as agents of rationalization: the rationalized woman and the rationalized home would help produce a generation with the mentality of the engineer. The idea that a well-kept home could exercise a moralizing influence on its inhabitants, notably by keeping the man of the house away from the alcoholic excesses of the café or from other temptations that might lurk outside the home, was well-established in the interwar period. But the ambitions articulated by organizers amounted to something more than this: they believed they could inculcate efficiency in France's population by changing its domestic environment.

It is perhaps in this light that we should interpret another set of remarks made by Bernège. In 1928 she published an architectural manifesto, *Si les femmes faisaient les maisons* (*If Women Made Houses*), in which the similarity between Le Corbusier's notion of the machine for living and Bernège's conception of the home as working organism is apparent. A home was not merely inert matter, she argued. Rather it must operate for the utility of 'man its creator'. It must become 'an organized body, embodying and satisfying all human needs'. She continued:

> Man is action and will. The body of the house must be able to help him in his acts, increase his power; man is sensation, sensitivity and thought: the body of the house must be able to increase his sensory capacities ... The modern house, organized in structure and designed for the needs of and on the model of the modern man, must become a living house.[115]

The material environment of the home and the minds and bodies of its inhabitants appear to be conceived here as an integrated system, an organism-machine. With the domestic environment shaped to fit the user, the material organization of space was believed to act on the behaviour of its inhabitants. What appears to be at stake in this vision is not just the emotional benefits of a happy family life, but the galvanizing effect of a well-organized home on the man's capacity for action.

The claims made for domestic organization were certainly ambitious, reflecting a remarkable faith not only in science but also in human adaptability. In itself, the belief that the domestic environment could shape its inhabitants was by no means a novelty, since it had already informed the hygienist endeavours of an earlier generation of domestic scientists and housing reformers. The Taylorization of domestic science could build quite easily on the Lamarckian assumptions of these early twentieth-century reform movements. But in targeting the bourgeois home, and reworking the ideal of the *maîtresse de maison* as manager, Bernège and her colleagues at the Ligue d'organisation ménagère did offer a new model of domesticity. This was a paired down vision of the middle-class home, without servants and with little sense of domestic space as *patrimoine*. Rather, like the factory, the home was constructed in terms of its functionality, its efficiency, and its integration into the economy as a whole. So much so that the modern home was supposed to remake its inhabitants in its image, forging rational professional housewives and men of action, rendered efficient by their surroundings and imbued with the 'spirit of organization'.

Organizers doubtless overestimated the power of their methods, not to mention women's readiness to take on some of the more onerous practices that were recommended, but the ethos of efficiency that they espoused would inform both domestic design and the models of homemaking promoted in household advice literature well into the postwar period.[116] Kristin Ross has highlighted the place of 'the new man' and 'the new housewife' in the cultural production of the 1950s and 1960s, noting that both magazine culture and literary production gave a prominent place to the *jeune cadre*, a hybrid of the bourgeois and the engineer, who embodied youth, newness, technical competence and a break with old bourgeois habits.[117] As the previous chapter indicated, a number of the features of this 'new man' discourse were already discernable in the interwar organization movement. Significantly, what we see in the domestic organization project led by Bernège, as in the industrial organizers' attachment to the embodiment of leadership in the workplace, is not just an aspirational representation of a new middle class but a kind of human engineering project that sought to reshape its bourgeois subjects. As homemakers and as educators women were called on to be both the objects and the agents of this rationalization process.

Notes

1.   On Frederick's life and work, see J.W. Rutherford. 2003. *Selling Mrs Consumer: Christine Frederick and the Rise of Household Efficiency,* Athens, Georgia: University of Georgia Press.
2.   A number of new women's magazines appeared between the wars and this developing sector provided an important outlet for disseminating homemaking ideals and expert advice. See F. Werner, 'Du ménage à l'art ménager: l'évolution du travail ménager et son écho dans la presse féminine française de 1919 à 1939', *Mouvement social* 129, 61–87.
3.   Luc's phrase was repeated by at least two contributors to this special issue. J Simonin. 1960. 'Hommage à Paulette Bernège' and M. L. Cordillot. 1960. 'Paulette Bernège et le haut enseignement ménager', *Education ménagère* 132: 6–18. Simonin was Honorary General Inspectress of Technical Education.

4.   Bernège describes Ponthière as her friend and relative (without further precision) in P. Bernège. 1943. *Explication: essai de biosociologie dirigée*, Toulouse: Didier, xvii. I discuss Ponthière's role in the organization movement in Chapter One.

5.   *Mon chez moi* became *La Joie de vivre* in 1930.

6.   M. Martin. 1984. 'Femmes et société: le travail ménager (1919–1939)', Thèse de troisième cycle, Université de Paris VII, 151.

7.   On the Salon des arts ménagers, see Martin, 'Femmes et société', 185–293; Q. Delaunay. 2003. *Société industrielle et travail domestique. L'Electroménager en France XIXe-XXe siècle*, Paris: L'Harmattan, 194–201; R.L. Frost. 1993. 'Machine Liberation: Inventing House-wives and Home Appliances in Interwar France', *French Historical Studies* 18(1), 109–30; E. Furlough. 1993. 'Selling the American Way in Interwar France: *Prix Uniques* and the Salon des Arts Ménagers', *Journal of Social History* 26(3), 491–519.

8.   On developments in the German movement and its participation in international con-ferences see M. Nolan. 1994. *Visions of Modernity: American Business and the Moderniza-tion of Germany*, Oxford: Oxford University Press, Chapter 10 and M. Nolan. 1990. '"Housework made easy": The Taylorized Housewife in Weimar Germany's Rational-ized Economy' *Feminist Studies* 16(3), 549–77.

9.   C. Frederick. 1915. 'La Tenue scientifique de la maison', *Revue de métallurgie* 12 published subsequently as C. Frederick. 1918. *La Tenue scientifique de la maison*, Paris: Dunod.

10.   Y Quintin. 1960. 'Vie et oeuvre de Paulette Bernège' *Education ménagère* 132: 8. Quintin was Honorary Inspectress of Agricultural Domestic Science Education at the Ministry of Agriculture.

11.   All citations here are from the second edition, P. Bernège. 1934 *De la méthode ménagère*, Paris: Dunod.

12.   The fact that the whole issue of *Education ménagère* 132 (September-October 1960) was devoted to Bernège testifies to this. There was even a new edition of *De la méthode ménagère* in 1969. Claire Duchen discusses the postwar influence of Bernège and the rationalization of housework in C. Duchen. 1991. 'Occupation Housewife: The Domestic Ideal in 1950s France', *French Cultural Studies* 2(4), 1–11 and in C. Duchen. 1994. *Women's Rights and Women's Lives in France 1945–1968*, London: Routledge, 69–72.

13.   Mme Pariset. 1852. *Manuel de la maîtresse de maison et de la parfaite ménagère*. Paris: Librai-rie Encyclopédique de Roret. On the history of domestic service, see T. MacBride. 1976. *The Domestic Revolution: The Modernisation of Household Service in England and France 1820–1920*, London: Croom Helm.

14.   See, for example, A. Moll-Weiss. 1907. *La Cuisine rationnelle des malades et des bien portants*, Paris: Doin and A. Moll-Weiss. 1902. *Le Foyer domestique, cours d'économie domestique, d'hygiène et de cuisine pratique*, Paris: Hachette. The influence of medical professionals in the social reform networks of this period is highlighted in several essays in C. Topalov (ed.) 1999. *Laboratoires du nouveau siècle: la nébuleuse réformatrice et ses réseaux en France, 1880–1914*, Paris: Editions de l'EHESS, notably in J. Horne, 'L'Antichambre de la Chambre: le Musée social et ses réseaux réformateurs, 1894–1914', 132–34 and in V. Claude, 'Technique sanitaire et réforme urbaine: l'Association générale des hygiénistes et techniciens municipaux, 1905–1920', 272–74.

15.   S. Magri. 1999. 'La Réforme du logement populaire: la Société française des habitations à bon marché, 1889–1914' in C. Topalov (ed.), *Laboratoires du nouveau siècle*, 239–68; P. Rabinow. 1989. *French Modern: Norms and Forms of the Social Environment*, Cambridge, MA: MIT Press, pp. 178–84 ; S. Magri and C. Topalov. 1989. *Villes ouvrières 1900–1950*, Paris: Harmattan.

16.   On company housing, see L. Murard and P. Zylberman. 1976. *Le Petit Travailleur infati-gable. Villes-usines, habitat et intimités au XIX siècle*, Paris: Recherches; Rabinow, *French Modern*, 95–103; G. Ribeill, 'Politiques et pratiques sociales du logement dans les com-pagnies de chemin de fer' in Magri and Topalov, *Villes ouvrières*, 155–70.

17.   S. Magri and C. Topalov. 1995. 'L'Habitat du salarié moderne en France, Grande Bre-
      tagne, Italie et aux Etats-Unis, 1910–1925' in Y. Cohen and R. Baudouï. 1995. *Les Chan-
      tiers de la paix sociale 1900–1940*, Fontenay/St Cloud: ENS Editions, 223.

18.   E. Cheysson, 'Preface' to Moll-Weiss et al. 1908. *Les Ecoles ménagères à l'étranger et en
      France*, Paris: A. Rousseau, I–II.

19.   B. Roussy. 1916. *Education domestique de la femme et rénovation sociale*, Paris: Delagrave,
      168–69.

20.   Employers' attempts to regulate the working-class home through the factory social
      worker are discussed in L.L. Downs. 1995. *Manufacturing Inequality: Gender Division in
      the French and British Metalworking Industries, 1914–1939*, Ithaca: Cornell University Press,
      Chapter 7, especially 259–64. The link between populationist concerns and the
      promotion of domestic science education is also illustrated very clearly in Roussy,
      Education domestique where the first hundred pages are devoted to discussion of the birth
      rate and the impact of disease, alcoholism and changing sexual mores on the population.

21.   M. Martin. 1987. 'Ménagère: une profession? Les Dilemmes de l'entre-deux-guerres'
      Mouvement social 140: 105.

22.   The highest number of servants (1,156,604) was recorded in 1881, but this dropped in
      1891 to 925,892. The numbers then fluctuated between 956, 195 (in 1901) and 929,548
      (1911), before dipping more dramatically to 787,385 in 1921. While census results tend
      to leave out workers who are part of the informal economy, and such workers may have
      been undertaking some of the work previously done by live-in servants as the numbers
      in the latter group fell, the trend away from the nineteenth-century model of domestic
      service remains clear. See MacBride, *The Domestic Revolution*, 111–12.

23.   Bernège refers to the disappearance of households with servants in *De la méthode
      ménagère*, 12. Bernège's colleague Suzanne Monin, Vice-President of the Ligue
      d'organisation ménagère and director of its Lyon bulletin, *La Maison heureuse*, also
      situated her endeavours in terms of the shift away from a domestic economy based on
      servants, notably in S. Monin. 1933. *La Maison sans domestique*, Lyon: Editions de la Mai-
      son Heureuse.

24.   See L. Boltanski. 1982. *Les Cadres: la formation d'un groupe social*, Paris: Minuit.

25.   Bernège, *De la méthode ménagère*, 16.

26.   MacBride, *The Domestic Revolution*, 18.

27.   The numbers of domestic servants also rose considerably in the nineteenth century. See
      D. Simonton. 1998. *A History of European Women's Work: 1700 to the Present*, London:
      Routledge, 96–7 and MacBride. *The Domestic Revolution*, 18–21. Examples of the aproned
      housewife of the 1950s can be found in K. Ross. 1995. *Fast Cars, Clean Bodies:
      Decolonisation and the Reordering of French Culture*, Cambridge, Massachusetts: MIT Press,
      101, 103.

28.   Frost, 'Machine Liberation', 129–30.

29.   A. Beltran. 1994. 'L'Essor de l'électrodomestique' in M. Lévy-Leboyer and H. Morsel
      (dir.) *Histoire générale de l'éléctricité en France. Tome 2. L'Interconnexion et le marché 1919–
      1946*, Paris: Fayard, 1274.

30.   This and further figures on the consumption of domestic appliances in various countries
      can be found in A. Beltran. 1991. *La Fée et la servante: la société française face à l'électricité
      XIXe-XXe siècle*, Paris: Belin, 249.

31.   I thank Richard Vinen for pressing me to think about Bernège in the context of economic
      austerity when I presented an earlier version of this chapter at the Institute of Histori-
      cal Research, London.

32.   Bernège makes reference here to Fayol's definition of the functions of administration:
      'prévoir, organiser, commander, coordonner, contrôler'. Bernège, *De la méthode ména-
      gère*, 9.

33.   Bernège, *De la méthode ménagère*, 9. The organicist roots of management theory and its
      use of biological as well as mechanical metaphors were discussed in Chapter One.

34. On the figure of the unmarried woman or *femme seule* in postwar France, see M. L. Roberts. 1994. *Civilization Without Sexes: Reconstructing Gender in Postwar France, 1917–1927*, Chicago: University of Chicago Press, 149–211.
35. Roberts, *Civilization Without Sexes*, 183–96.
36. See K. Offen. 1991. 'Body Politics: Women, Work and the Politics of Motherhood in France 1920–1950' in G. Bock and P. Thane (eds), *Maternity and Gender Policies: Women and the Rise of the European Welfare States, 1880s-1950s*, London: Routledge, especially 141–45; S. Reynolds. 1996. *France Between the Wars: Gender and Politics*, London: Routledge, 113–18; C. Bard. 1995. *Les Filles de Marianne: Histoire des féminismes 1914–1940* Paris: Fayard, 313–29; Martin, 'Femmes et société', 42–73.
37. M. Boutier. 1938. 'Évolution sociale, évolution scolaire', *Art ménager*, February, 72.
38. Bernège, *De la méthode ménagère*, 14–16.
39. See, for example, Bernège, *De la méthode ménagère*, Lesson 10.
40. Martin, 'Ménagère: une profession?'.
41. L. L. Clark. 2000. *The Rise of Professional Women in France: Gender and Public Administration since 1830*, Cambridge: Cambridge University Press, esp. Chapters 1–4 and 7; L.L. Downs, 'Les Marraines-élue de la paix sociale? Les Surintendantes d'usine et la rationalisation du travail en France, 1917–1935', *Mouvement social* 164, 45–76.
42. *La Maison heureuse* (July-August 1932), 4.
43. P. Bernège. 1937. 'Un projet de création d'un Institut des sciences domestiques' *Art ménager* 123, 248–51, 278–79.
44. P. Bernège, 1929. Report on domestic economy section of Congrès international d'organisation scientifique de Paris, *Bulletin de CNOF* October, 14.
45. P. Bernège. 1933. *J'installe ma cuisine*, Lyon: Editions de La Maison heureuse and idem. 1950 [2nd edn]. *Le Blanchissage domestique*, Paris: Editions du Salon des rts ménagers.
46. Marguerite Lamy's book was published by Dunod. A second edition followed in 1933. She also published M. Lamy. 1934. *Pour bien faire son marché. Les Secrets de la vie moins chère*, Paris: Dunod. The place of consumer education and advice in the domestic organization movement is also confirmed by a regular rubric on 'rational purchasing' in *La Maison heureuse*.
47. See, for example, G. Duhamel. 1934. *Scènes de la vie future*, Paris: Arthème, Fayard et Cie, 67, 48, 76 and Roberts, *Civilization Without Sexes*, 19–87 on the *garçonne* who was condemned not just for her hedonistic consumption of fashion and music (flapper dresses and jazz clubs) but for consuming sex rather than reserving it for the function of reproduction.
48. Bernège, *J'installe ma cuisine*, 57; P. Bernège, 1928. *Si les femmes faisaient les maisons* Paris: Editions Mon chez moi, 58.
49. Lamy, *Bien acheter*, 43.
50. This outlook could be compared to that sometimes expressed in advertising trade journals, where uncontrolled consumer desire was regarded as a risk to be avoided by appropriate scientific advertising. See M. Beale. 1999. *The Modernist Enterprise: French Elites and the Threat of Modernity, 1900–1940*, Stanford: Stanford University Press, 39–40.
51. Lamy, *Bien acheter*, 53. Chayrou's *De l'art d'acheter à l'art d'agir* was first published in 1926 with a preface by Marcel Déat but a later version in 1938 was also prefaced by Charles de Fréminville, sometime head of the CNOF and the Comité international de l'organisation scientifique. See also P.-R. Chayrou. 1938. *Achats rationnels. Caractère du plus avantageux de deux achats semblables*, Paris: Recueil Sirey, 42 and Preface.
52. Lamy, *Bien acheter*, 56.
53. Lamy, *Bien acheter*, 309–10.
54. Bernège, *J'installe ma cuisine*, 58.
55. Bernège, *De la méthode ménagère*, 94, 101.
56. Bernège, *De la méthode ménagère*, 107, 120.
57. This argument is made for example in B. Ehrenreich and D. English. 1978. *For Her Own Good: 150 Years of Experts' Advice to Women*, Garden City, NY: Anchor Press.

58. Bernège, *De la méthode ménagère*, 17.
59. P. Bernège. 1935. *Le Ménage simplifié ou la vie en rose*, Paris: Stock, 11.
60. Bernège, *De la méthode ménagère*, 112–13.
61. It will become apparent in what follows that my concept of discipline owes something to Foucault and develops themes such as the relationship between disciplining the body and disciplining the mind or the importance of self-surveillance, which are treated in M. Foucault. 1975. *Surveiller et punir*, Paris: Gallimard. However, my analysis has also been informed by work that focuses more specifically on labour discipline, including M. Perrot. 1979. 'The Three Ages of Industrial Discipline in Nineteenth-century France' in J.M. Merriman (ed.), *Consciousness and Class Experience in Nineteenth-century Europe*, New York and London: Holmes and Meier Publishers Inc., 149–68.
62. Frost, 'Machine Liberation', 110, n.2; Roussy, *Education domestique*, 215. Bernège developed at length the analogy between the human body and a motor in an article in *Art ménager* in 1935, referring to fatigue research by the physiologists Chauveau and Walther. See P. Bernège. 1935. 'Quand le moteur "cale"… ou la machine humaine', *Art ménager*, February, 58–59, 240–43.
63. P. Bernège. 1934. 'Psychotechnique ménagère' *Art ménager*, February, 470–73.
64. Bernège, 'Psychotechnique ménagère', 472.
65. Bernège, *Le Ménage simplifié*, 203.
66. Bernège, *De la méthode ménagère*, 50–52, 76, 107.
67. Bernège, *De la méthode ménagère*, 50–52.
68. Bernège, *De la méthode ménagère*, 88.
69. See L. Murard and P. Zylberman. 1983. *Recherche sur la formation et l'histoire des agencements intérieurs de l'habitat*, Paris: CERFI.
70. Bernège, *Si les femmes faisaient les maisons*, 11.
71. Bernège, *De la méthode ménagère*, 62–63.
72. Bernège, *De la méthode ménagère*, 30–31. In particular, she cited not just Taylor and Fayol but also Maurice Ponthière, who was discussed in Chapter 1.
73. Bernège, *J'installe ma cuisine*, 45.
74. See Bernège, *J'installe ma cuisine*, esp. 44.
75. Bernège, *J'installe ma cuisine*, 17.
76. Examples include 'La Cuisine de Francfort' *Art ménager* June 1931, 268–69; Robert Mallet Stevens. 1931. 'L'Esthétique de la cuisine' *Art Ménager* April, 175–77 and May, 212–13; 'Cuisine électrifiée' *Art ménager* July 1934, 439, which shows a fitted kitchen displayed at the Salon des artistes décorateurs; and 'Concours de la maison individuelle: Le Premier prix', *Art ménager*, June 1934, 388.
77. Cited in Murard and Zylberman, *Recherche sur la formation et l'histoire des agencements intérieurs de l'habitat*, 75.
78. Le Corbusier used the phrase in Le Corbusier. 1923. *Vers une architecture*. Paris: Editions Crès, 1923, though Michel Ragon points out that this idea had already been articulated by Frank Lloyd Wright and Walter Gropius. M. Ragon. 1986. *Histoire de l'architecture et de l'urbanisme modernes*, Paris: Casterman, 170.
79. M. Price, 'Bodies and Souls: The Rehabilitation of Maimed Soldiers in France and Germany during the First World War', Ph.D. Dissertation, Stanford University, 1998. Roxane Panchasi also makes a connection between domestic design and rehabilitation science in R. Panchasi. 2009. *Future Tense: The Culture of Anticipation in France Between the Wars* Ithaca and London: Cornell University Press, 24–39.
80. Bernège, *De la méthode ménagère*, 3.
81. P. Bernège. 1936. 'L'Organisation ménagère est à l'honneur', *Art ménager*, February, 90–91.
82. This will be apparent in the work of the engineer and industrial organizer Jean Coutrot in the next chapter.
83. P. Bernège. 1928. 'Le Développement de l'esprit de l'organisation chez l'enfant' *Nouvelle éducation* 67, 129–38.

84. J. Bernis. 1938. 'Le Foyer familial et l'éducation de l'enfant' in P. Bernège, *Encyclopédie de la vie familiale*, Paris: Horizons de France, 136.

85. Mme Perraud-Duban. 1938. 'Introduction à la pédagogie ménagère', *Education ménagère* 1 (July), 13–14.

86. Roger Cousinet, Preface to P. Bernège. 1947. *Guide d'enseignement ménager*. Paris: Librairie de l'Académie d'agriculture, 7.

87. Bernège, *Guide*, 24.

88. Cousinet in Bernège, *Guide*, 7.

89. Researchers such as Henri Piéron and Edouard Toulouse who had been publishing since before the First World War were reference points for both educational and industrial psychology. Henri Laugier and Dagmar Weinberg were among the interwar scientists who worked in both fields of application. On their work with school children, see H. Laugier, E. Toulouse and D. Weinberg. 1932. 'La Biotypologie et l'orientation professionnelle', *Biotypologie* 1.

90. E. Claparède. 1922. *L'Orientation professionnelle, ses problèmes et ses méthodes*, Geneva: Bureau international du travail; O. Decroly. 1928. *La Pratique des tests mentaux*, Paris: Alcan. Claparède's Institut Jean-Jacques Rousseau was actively involved in developing tests for vocational guidance as indicated in J. Fontègne. 1920. 'Le Cabinet d'orientation professionnelle de l'Institut J. J. Rousseau', *Orientation professionnelle*, March, 38–9. Decroly, like Claparède and Montessori, was interested in education through play. See O. Decroly. 1914. *Initiation à l'activité intellectuelle et motrice par les jeux éducatifs*, Neuchâtel: Delachaux et Niestlé.

91. This entry was written by Mme J Bernis, whose classes at Bernège's school were on the same subject. J. Bernis. 1938. 'Le Foyer familial et l'éducation de l'enfant' in Bernège, *Encyclopédie de la vie familiale* Paris: Horizons de France, 141–51. Bernège also endorsed testing in *Guide*, 28.

92. R. Kramer. 1976. *Maria Montessori: A Biography*, London: Basil Blackwell, 67–9.

93. M. Montessori. 1919. *The Montessori Method: Scientific Pedagogy as Applied to Child Education in 'The Children's Houses'*, London: William Heinemann, 72–80.

94. M. Montessori, *The Montessori Method*, 168–85. Kramer, *Maria Montessori*, 76. Montessori developed this approach through her early medico-educational work on children regarded as physically or mentally deficient and perpetuated it in her general theory of education.

95. On Montessori and Rousseau, see Kramer, *Maria Montessori*, 62–63.

96. M. Montessori, *The Montessori Method*, 170–73.

97. Montessori argued that true discipline was achieved in this way not through the regimented approach of mainstream education, with its rigid rows of desks and over-emphasis on correction/punishment by the teacher. See Montessori, *The Montessori Method*, 86–106.

98. For example, Montessori, *The Montessori Method*, 344–45. Bernège, *Guide*, 21.

99. Bernège, *Guide*, 29–31.

100. The phrase 'c'est par la main que l'esprit se forme' is attributed to Montessori in Bernège, *Guide*, 35.

101. Bernège, *Guide*, 60–61.

102. Bernège, *Guide*, 36. Italics (and use of the masculine) are in the original.

103. Bernège, *Guide*, 32.

104. Bernège, *Guide*, 27.

105. Bernège, *Guide*, 28.

106. Anon. 1937. 'Femmes de demain' *Bulletin du CNOF*, October, 32.

107. Bernège, 'Le Dévéloppement de l'esprit de l'organisation chez l'enfant', 131, 134–37.

108. Bernège, 'Le Dévéloppement de l'esprit de l'organisation chez l'enfant', 129.

109. Bernège, 'Le Dévéloppement de l'esprit de l'organisation chez l'enfant', 131, 136.

110. H. Fayol. 1979. *Administration générale et industrielle*, Paris: Bordas, 119.

111. F. Le Chatelier. 1968. *Henry Le Chatelier: un grand savant d'hier, un précurseur* Paris: Revue de métallurgie, 221.
112. Le Chatelier. 1914. *Le Système Taylor,* Paris: Société pour l'encouragement de l'industrie nationale, 31. My emphasis.
113. J. Wilbois. 1929. '6e section: Enseignement'. *Bulletin du CNOF,* October, 14.
114. Le Chatelier, *Le Système Taylor,* 32.
115. Bernège, *Si les femmes faisaient les maisons,*1.
116. Claire Leymonerie notes that the moralizing discourse of organization was particularly apparent in the consumer advice literature that flourished in postwar women's magazines. C. Leymonerie. 2006. 'Le Salon des arts ménagers dans les années 1950. Théâtre d'une conversion à la consommation de masse', *Vingtième siècle* 91, 46.
117. Ross finds the figure of the *jeune cadre* not just in the columns of *L'Express* but in novels like *Les Belles images* or *Roses à crédit*. See Ross, *Fast Cars, Clean Bodies,* 165–76.

Chapter 4

THE ENGINEER-ECONOMIST AND THE 'SCIENCES OF MAN' IN THE 1930S

It is the responsibility of engineers, today, to construct better societies, for it is they, and not the lawyers or politicians, who have the methods needed for the task.[1]

If the influence of scientific organization in domestic science and design illustrates one way in which the reach of the movement extended beyond industrial and administrative workplaces, then the development of economic planning provides another.[2] It was in the 1930s that *planisme* (as it was called at the time) came to the fore, though it built on the interest in economic organization and 'reform of the state' that had been developing since at least the First World War. 'Reform of the state' was a term associated particularly with the desire for a strengthening of the executive, a demand that was frequently heard between the wars, as commentators from a range of political perspectives lamented the ministerial instability of the Third Republic and criticized the parliamentary system as ineffectual. These concerns with both political and economic efficacy were linked to a particular idea of government by the 'competent' and prompted attempts by interwar governments of both the Right and the Left to apply principles of rational organization to public administration or to involve professionals deemed to have economic competence in the development of policy. It was in this context that Henri Fayol was recruited to study the rationalization of the postal and telecommunications service under the right-wing Bloc national, for example, and that the Cartel des gauches created the Conseil national économique (CNE) in 1925 in an effort to increase the representation of economic groups (labour, capital and consumers) in the institutions of the Third Republic.[3] While there were different views about who was competent and what constituted a rationally organized state – the Right was hostile to the role of organized labour in the CNE, for example – questions about economic organization often went hand-in-hand in this period with questions about the rationalization of politics. Throughout the 1920s, centres of reflection like the review *L'Etat moderne* or Redressement français, publicists such as Bertrand de Jouvenel and politicians who had frequented the scientific organization movement, such as André Tardieu, kept these issues on the agenda.[4] By the 1930s, however, the advent of the Depression gave the question of economic organization a new urgency and one of the most important indicators of this mood was the foundation of the think tank X-Crise by a group of *polytechniciens* in late 1931.[5] While there were other groups that promoted planning in various forms in the 1930s, none enjoyed the prestige and proximity to power that X-Crise did. Moreover, this centre was also the cradle of a new kind of expert with a bright future in French economic life: the engineer-economist.

Planisme

The *planiste* movement encompassed several intersecting developments. It was a response not just to the Depression but also to the rise of fascism. For some, a plan was a political strategy to mobilize electoral support for a package of counter-crisis measures. This trend began in Belgium, where the Belgian Workers' Party adopted its plan at the end of 1933, promising to nationalize credit and certain infrastructural industries such as energy and transport, in order to gain more systematic state control over the economy, while maintaining a substantial private sector. This was a form of socialist planning that was quite different from the model of the Soviet Five Year Plan. The espousal of a mixed economy (at least as a transitional stage between capitalism and socialism) was intended to rally middle-class support in a cross-class effort to beat the economic crisis and bolster democracy against fascism. By framing these proposals as a plan, the Belgian socialists were adopting what Hendrik de Man (the chief inspiration behind the plan) termed a 'voluntarist politics', which was supposed to inject social democracy with something of the mobilizing power of fascism, without giving in to authoritarianism.[6] This strategy had its roots in a revision of Marxism that owed much to de Man's interest in psychology – he had published *Zur Psychologie des Sozialismus* (*The Psychology of Socialism*) in 1926, before taking up a Chair of Social Psychology in Frankfurt in 1929.[7] Having broken with the materialist analysis of orthodox Marxism and examined the proletarian condition instead in psychological terms (rather like Dubreuil), de Man now applied social psychology to political strategy, seeking to rally the electorate to the 'mystique' of the plan with the latest propaganda methods, including everything from songs and theatre productions to mass meetings and film.[8]

Having begun in Belgium in the year of Hitler's rise to power, the idea of the plan took off in France the following year, as the Stavisky affair and the riots of 6 February intensified both criticism of the Third Republic and fear of fascism. The Confédération générale du travail (CGT), for example, devised a plan based on de Man's model and there was also interest in planism among the reformist socialists of the Révolution constructive group.[9] In contrast, the *Plan du 9 juillet* drew inspiration from more right-wing sources, though it aspired to offer a synthesis of right- and left-wing themes.[10] It was produced by a heterogeneous group which included several members of X-Crise (Jean Coutrot, Jacques Branger, Gérard Bardet and Louis Vallon), as well as an assortment of senior civil servants, journalists, politicians (notably Neo-socialists such as Paul Marion) and activists from the far-Right *ligues*, all brought together under the auspices of the novelist Jules Romains.[11] Not surprisingly, given the role of *polytechniciens* in its composition, the *Plan du 9 juillet* asserted the importance of professional and technical competence in government, proposing, for example, compulsory consultation with the Conseil national économique in the formation of economic policy, the creation of a public research and documentation service staffed by technicians and an 'Ecole polytechnique d'administration' (rather like the Ecole nationale d'administration eventually created in 1945) to train the civil service elite.[12] In relation to the economy, it attempted to steer a 'third way' between statism and laissez-faire liberalism, envisaging a dual system with a planned sector to meet people's basic living needs, and a free sector for other kinds of production.[13]

While Jean Coutrot played a significant role in drafting the economic section of the *Plan du 9 juillet*, X-Crise itself did not devise an actual plan or programme.[14] Founded more than two years before de Man's plan launched a wave of imitators, it was conceived as a centre for reflection and debate, a non-partisan space in which *polytechniciens* (and to some extent other members of the nation's political and professional elites) would study social and economic questions 'in a purely scientific spirit', providing 'objective documentation of a non-political nature'.[15] Many of the leading figures who frequented X-Crise were or had been members of other groups in what I have called the *nébuleuse organisatrice* – Coutrot, Bardet, Detoeuf and Robert Lelong all participated in both X-Crise and the Comité national de l'organisation française (CNOF), for example, Lelong being the President of the latter organization. The discussions in the new centre were wide-ranging and while economic matters were the main focus, especially in the early years, other topical issues were also discussed. Attention focused on the organization of industrial relations in 1936–37, for example, following the strikes and Popular Front reforms of June 1936, while international affairs loomed large in 1938–39, though some members had reservations about extending the work of the centre to include such explicitly political issues.[16] The review *X-Crise*, also known as the *Bulletin du Centre polytechnicien d'études économiques* (CPEE), published a monthly statistical update on economic performance ('Le Point économique') and specialized studies on particular methods and sectors, as well as contributions which reflected in fairly broad terms on economic trends, the nature of the crisis and the role of technicians in solving it.

Not all members of X-Crise were supporters of an organized or planned economy, but this was certainly the dominant current and the most significant one historically. What X-Crise provided was not so much a set of policy recommendations, but the theoretical underpinning for a new political economy and a forum for the development and dissemination of statistical and econometric techniques linked to this new economic model. Its significance must therefore be understood less in terms of immediate policy impact than in its relationship to a doctrinal and institutional evolution that took place between the 1930s and the 1950s, as part of what Michel Margairaz has called France's 'conversion' to a managed economy.[17] While there was a trend towards increased state intervention in the 1930s, evident in public works and retooling programmes, in protectionist measures or in the extension of social rights, a managed or planned economy was conceived at X-Crise as something rather different. The aim was to systematize intervention, to delineate an appropriate coordinating role for the state and for organized business, while retaining the principle of private ownership. Economic planning thus required an ability to anticipate, make provision for, and, to some extent at least, steer economic developments in a particular direction. This implied in turn a government apparatus for economic monitoring and forecasting, as well as an overview of policy areas that would generally fall within the responsibility of a number of different ministries – trade, industry, labour, finance, regional development, urbanization, and so on. After World War Two, when economic planning was at its height, the Commissariat au Plan would perform this role, while a substantial new statistical service, INSEE (Institut national de la statistique et des études économiques), was created in 1946 to provide data to policy makers. The engineering schools were a major recruiting ground for the technicians who staffed these bodies: Edmond Malinvaud at INSEE, Jean Fourastié, who was head of the Economic service at the Commissariat au Plan under Jean Monnet, and Monnet's successors, Etienne Hirsch and Pierre Massé, were all engineering graduates. Between the wars, before institutions like INSEE and the Commissariat au Plan existed, the economic thinking that would ultimately require this infrastructure and propel engineers into these roles was taking shape in the parapolitical world of technicians' groups, such as X-Crise.

But how was it that engineers came to be seen as experts in economic matters? What claim was Coutrot making when he said, in the letter quoted as an epigraph to this chapter, that engineers were better equipped than lawyers and politicians to construct a better society? And, if the science of organization had developed in a dialogue with other disciplines, how far did this manifest itself in the way that organizers envisaged the new economy? This chapter offers an answer to these questions. It shows how planning emerged partly from a process by which the 'spirit of engineering' colonized the ground traditionally occupied by political economists.[18] Classical political economists conceived of the economy as a self-regulating system, but for engineers, systems – whether mechanical or organizational – could and should be monitored, managed and perfected. This was the engineer's *raison d'être*. Drawing on their scientific training, engineers affirmed the importance of empirical observation of economic phenomena, used the laws of physics to reconceptualize economic problems, and sought to establish mathematically in what conditions the economy might function optimally in the general interest. In doing so, however, they were conscious that they were entering the realm of the 'sciences of man'. Indeed, as this chapter will show, the story of the emergence of the engineer-economist and that of the growing interest in 'human problems' in the 1930s are more closely intertwined than previous accounts have acknowledged.

Economics as Engineering

The emergence of *planisme* in interwar France was symptomatic of an international effort to rethink liberal economics in the face of the Depression, and can be compared in this respect to the development of Keynesianism in the U.K..[19] This work of rethinking liberalism involved a certain reflection on its underlying philosophy, prompting Gérard Bardet, a founder member of X-Crise, to describe the group as a response to a crisis that was moral as well as economic. The alleged moral disorder was blamed on an economic system based on excessive individualism: progress in human society came not from the unbridled pursuit of individual gain, Bardet insisted, but from the pursuit of the general good; individualism must be tempered by a commitment to collective goals.[20] In this way, X-Crise took up a theme that had already been developed in arguments about economic 'solidarity' at Redressement français in the late 1920s and one of the contributors to that discussion, Auguste Detoeuf, gave a much cited talk on 'the end of liberalism' at X-Crise in 1936. 'Liberalism has given us bad habits', he pronounced. 'It sanctified egotism.' What was now required, he concluded, was a new 'civic and social morality adapted to the new economy'.[21]

  That engineers considered themselves well placed to represent the general interest was hardly a novelty, since they had long believed that their scientific training and, in the case of *polytechniciens*, their historic role as servants of the state (traditionally seen as a defender of the general good) placed them above factional or class interests. The strong generalist ethos of the education dispensed at the Ecole polytechnique perhaps also went some way to legitimizing the intervention of its graduates in relation to any matter that could be constituted as a scientific problem. The *polytechniciens'* prestigious status was doubtless a useful asset too – the group was able to command an impressive array of guest speakers, including prominent politicians like Paul Reynaud and the former Finance Minister, Louis-Germain Martin, as well as leading economists such as Charles Rist, François Simiand and Jan Tinbergen. Finally, at a time when the world economy was in considerable disarray and critics denounced the free market as a form of anarchy, the credentials of engineers as organizers can only have helped to position them as the men of the moment. Yet none of these precious attributes explain quite how the technicians of X-Crise parlayed their mathematical and scientific expertise into a new political economy.

It is worth reminding ourselves at this point what economics looked like as a discipline in interwar France.[22] As an institutionalized university subject, it existed primarily as a branch of the law faculties and this, along with the high proportion of lawyer-politicians in France between the wars, was perhaps what Coutrot had in mind when he complained of the inadequacy of the law compared to engineering as a training for the nation's elite. It was in the law faculties that the established neo-classical economists of the older generation, such as Charles Rist (born 1874), were to be found and where most students of economics were trained. Those who challenged this predominantly liberal economics tended to come from other disciplinary backgrounds. One alternative school of thought, more concerned with the social nature of economic phenomena, could be found within the field of sociology, led by François Simiand and Maurice Halbwachs. Halbwachs, like Simiand, gave a talk at X-Crise and the sociologist's interest in empirical observation may well have appealed to the *polytechniciens*, whose preference for abstract reason over empiricism is sometimes exaggerated.[23] There was a strong interest at X-Crise in the collection of statistical data, for example, a practice that was well-established among social scientists, demographers and social reformers by the 1930s but was still a relatively new phenomenon within economics: only a small economic observatory, with a handful of staff, existed at France's national statistical agency, the Statistique générale de France (SGF).[24] *Polytechniciens*, like Alfred Sauvy, who headed the SGF economic observatory, helped to pioneer the development of economic statistics, thanks in part to their mathematical training. However, they had no training as economists: as one member put it, looking back on the early years of X-Crise, 'we were perfectly incompetent in economics'.[25] Part of what was happening in the 1930s, therefore, was that the parameters of the discipline of economics and its institutional location were being renegotiated, as engineers appropriated for themselves new areas of competence.

The economics that emerged from X-Crise can be seen in part as an extension of the systems thinking that was so central to the scientific organization movement. From its inception at the turn of the century, the field of scientific organization drew on a series of analogies between machines, bodies and businesses in an effort to articulate laws for the organization of social and economic activity. Just as Fayol had mapped out an autonomous managerial function in industry, listing its elements as planning or forecasting [*prévision*], organization, leadership, coordination and monitoring, so the planners of X-Crise mapped out an appropriate managerial role for technicians in macro-economic matters.[26] In doing so, like their turn-of-the-century antecedents who had developed the concept of the 'human motor', they turned to models from the natural sciences. The debt to physics, or more specifically mechanics, was particularly apparent, as technicians sought to establish the conditions in which the economic system would achieve a state of 'dynamic equilibrium'. Bardet set out the economic thinking of X-Crise in these terms when he summed up the first six months of the group's activities in 1932, as did the Swiss economists Georges and Edouard Guillaume, whose *Economique rationnelle* was one of a number of book-length studies to emerge from the group.[27]

Bardet's analysis drew on Le Chatelier's law on the displacement of equilibrium, first formulated with reference to physico-chemical systems, but now applied to the economy. As well as being the person who introduced Taylorism to French audiences, Le Chatelier was a distinguished chemist who used the physics of motion and energy to analyse the behaviour of chemical systems under changing conditions. His law states that when an external modification (e.g. increased temperature) disturbs the equilibrium of a physico-chemical system, it triggers a process of adaptation in which a new equilibrium is sought.[28] At X-Crise this provided a model for understanding the economic crisis and the role of the engineer in solving it: the crisis should be viewed as a crisis of adaptation, Bardet argued, and the role of the engineer was to discern what direction this adaptation was taking and work to re-establish the internal harmony of the system.[29] As this analysis illustrates, a feature of this type of thinking was that it tended to naturalize economic phenomena and promote adherence to the internal laws of the system – the law of displacement of equilibrium indicated that one should work *with* the system to find a new equilibrium, following the direction of change rather than resisting it.

This analysis is significant in several ways. For one thing, it departed from the popular contemporary view that the Depression was the result of over-production caused by rationalization or excessive technological development. Moreover, while historians have often contrasted the attachment to balance or stability in French prewar economic thinking with the more dynamic view that came to dominate after World War Two,[30] the engineer-economists' attention to the problem of equilibrium demonstrates that they saw no necessary contradiction between the pursuit of stability and a commitment to economic dynamism. One conception of the balanced economy that existed between the wars was a doctrine about the appropriate balance between agriculture and industry in France, and the engineer-economists of the 1930s certainly distanced themselves from the idea that there was a fixed set of internal conditions in which equilibrium might be achieved. However, they were really redefining rather than simply rejecting the economics of equilibrium, for, in conceiving of equilibrium as dynamic, they expressed an ideal of harmony in motion, a harmony that could be maintained, or at least re-established in changing conditions, so long as the system's ability to adapt was not inhibited – when Alfred Sauvy spoke of dynamic equilibrium, he used the analogy of a moving bicycle.[31] This was a model of economic equilibrium that was compatible with an expansionist economic policy. One thing this analysis had in common with classical economic theory was the notion that the economy had its own internal laws which must be respected, but in the engineers' version the system's capacity for self-regulation did not imply a laissez-faire attitude; rather it required intervention to enhance the functioning of the economy's natural regulatory mechanisms, which (as we will see) were not conceived only in terms of the market.

Part of what was happening in this type of thinking was that economic problems were being reconfigured as engineering or mathematical problems. This was reflected in X-Crise's contribution to the development in France of the new field of econometrics, which applied techniques of statistical analysis to economic theory. Jan Tinbergen's visit to the group was symptomatic of its interest in this field, for the Dutchman, then working for the League of Nations, was one of the pioneers of econometrics internationally.[32] At X-Crise, Jean Ullmo, Robert Gibrat and the Guillaume brothers (Georges and Edouard) were the most active in this area. They distinguished their 'rational economics' from what the Guillaumes called 'literary political economy', which they saw as little more than a series of doctrines.[33] One of the criticisms made of liberal economics at X-Crise was that it was rooted in assumptions about human psychology that were either erroneous or unverifiable: liberalism assumed that human beings were motivated by individual gain and deduced from this that the conditions which fostered the pursuit of this objective (the free market) constituted the most rational form of economic organization.[34] The X-Crise econometricians identified the question of human psychology and the motives for economic behaviour as a central problem for the construction of a rational economics but adopted different solutions in the face of this problem. Mathematically speaking, Ullmo tried to work around the unpredictability of human behaviour by constructing a model for national economic equilibrium based on more readily measurable factors. At the same time, the aim was to minimize the destabilizing effects of the 'human factor'. He defined equilibrium as 'a state (of production, distribution, exchanges and consumption) from which the system tends not to depart, under the effects of [human] motivations, assuming other given values remain fixed'.[35] The Guillaume brothers spoke of the need to quantify psychological factors so that the economic impact of human behaviour could be understood mathematically, though they did not claim to have solved this problem.[36] One study that did seek to quantify what might otherwise have been seen as a social, political or psychological issue was that of Robert Gibrat who attempted to determine mathematically what constituted a rational level of inequality in society.[37]

These mathematical theories of dynamic equilibrium were also characterized by a marked holism. Ullmo, for example, observed that liberal economics considered individuals like atomized particles, when in fact a more appropriate analogy would be to see people collectively in terms of the 'mutual potential energy' of a *system* of particles.[38] The Guillaumes distinguished the systems view of the scientific economist from the perspective of the classical economist, comparing the latter to a child who, on seeing a waterfall and an electric train passing in the distance would probably make no connection between the two. In contrast, they affirmed, 'the scientific expert [*savant*] *embraces the situation in its entirety*' (italics in original), grasping the relationship between the vapour in the atmosphere, the energy captured at the waterfall and the transformation of energy into traction by the locomotive. Similarly, while a traditional economist saw the falling price of a particular commodity simply as loss of value, they argued, one could in fact speak of a principle of conservation of value in economics, just as one could speak of the conservation of energy in physics, if only one took a more all-encompassing view of the relationship between different economic processes.[39] Classical political economists could perhaps just as easily have claimed to take a holist view of the economy, since one person's idea about what constitutes the 'whole' might be quite different from another's. Nonetheless, a concept of the system that drew on the physical sciences was central to the way in which interwar planners articulated claims that their expertise in maths and engineering equipped them to solve social and economic problems. Moreover, it was a perspective which implicitly positioned engineers above or outside the economic system, as figures whose knowledge of the laws of science (or maths) gave them an overview which others lacked.

Summing up the first six months of collective work at X-Crise, Bardet observed that an understanding of the 'evolution of the human mentality' and of human motives for economic activity was an essential starting point for the establishment of a new economic equilibrium.[40] What was emerging at X-Crise was a form of economics conceived for an age in which the rationalist ideal of the individual was in crisis. It was also an economics conceived in terms of collective or mass phenomena. If this was true even of the mathematical forms of economics being developed by econometricians, other approaches took these preoccupations even further.

La Conjoncture or Economics in the Age of the Masses

This was particularly apparent in the case made in the 1930s for *la conjoncture*, or statistical monitoring of the economic situation. This was one of the most important instruments of economic planning developed in the interwar period and X-Crise members, Jean Dessirier and Alfred Sauvy, were the leaders in this field.[41] The *conjoncturistes* sought both to extend the range of economic data being collected in France and to develop the statistical analysis of this information in order to forecast trends. This was the significance of the monthly economic updates published in the X-Crise bulletin. Although the economic observatory at the SGF had developed the study of *la conjoncture* in the 1920s under Dessirier (who was succeeded by Sauvy in 1929), this was largely the work of a few individuals. X-Crise offered a platform for wider dissemination of these techniques and the findings they produced. Sauvy, in particular, was an active promoter of *la conjoncture*, proposing that data should be collected on everything from industrial consumption of raw materials, rail freight movements and activity on the stock exchange to population trends, family budgets and numbers of nights spent by tourists in hotels.[42] He contrasted this scientific economics based on empirical observation with the theoretical approach of classical French economists trained in the law faculties: to entrust a fashion designer with the task of running an automobile factory would be less dangerous than asking jurists to run the economy, he quipped, since at least designers did not have lawyers' inflated confidence in their own capacities.[43]

It was the overview gleaned from empirical data collection that supposedly enabled the *conjoncturiste* to rise above individual or sectional interests and serve the general good. Sauvy compared forecasting (*la prévision*, literally, seeing ahead) with navigating on board ship, emphasizing that the aim was not to predict the future (which would be foolhardy) but to provide scientific data that could be used steer a safe course.[44] The role of the technician was, thus, not to govern, but to 'éclairer l'action' – to provide decision-makers with the basis for informed action.[45] This ideal of the far-sighted expert was linked with a certain vision of leadership and when Sauvy declared that 'to govern is to look ahead [*prévoir*]', he suggested an affinity between his own commitment to economic management and Fayol's vision of business leadership.[46]

Like Fayolism, Sauvy's vision of economic organization mobilized a certain idea of the economy as an organism. An example of this can be found in his discussion of work-time issues – a theme which particularly preoccupied him. Emphasizing the importance of a systems view, he argued that the test of any policy was the effect it would have on the functioning of the economy as a whole, rather than on a particular group. In giving in to the workers' demands for an eight-hour day after the First World War, he argued, French politicians had failed to take this into account. Their actions had triggered the economy's 'faculty of adaptation', 'stimulat[ing]' and 'harass[ing]' it, forcing it to adapt to an irregular set of conditions and producing unemployment as a result.[47] Here, Le Chatelier's law on the displacement of equilibrium was an implicit reference point (a change in parameters provokes an attempt by the system to adapt) but the process was envisaged as a biological one. Similarly, in a book on *la conjoncture* published under the X-Crise imprint, Sauvy remarked on the grandiose task of organization that 'man' had set himself: 'that of organizing himself and submitting to his consciousness an infinity of actions that until now merely activated reflexes'. Organizing the economy was, he argued, a process comparable to trying to master one's own circulation, digestion or glands.[48] This opposition between a body governed by reflexes and a rational mind that must master it reveals one of the ways in which arguments for planning drew on the discursive repertoire of collective psychology.

Central to Sauvy's claims for *la conjoncture* was the idea that the engineer-economist could avoid the errors of the irrational 'Malthusian' majority. This term was borrowed from demographic thinking, an area in which Sauvy was also active, producing scare-mongering statistics for the pro-natalist Alliance nationale contre la dépopulation.[49] In the economic context, Malthusianism implied a fundamentally pessimistic and conservative outlook, a resistance to economic expansion, and a fear of technical progress.[50] For Sauvy, this summed up the prevailing climate in France in the 1930s – an idea that was taken up by historians after the war.[51] It was this view of France's economic performance that led Sauvy to describe *la conjoncture* as a 'science of man'. 'I refuse to fall into a narrow economic determinism', he explained:

> I believe in the influence of personal decisions, not only those of individuals who dispose of extensive power over the course of events, but also those of groups. The former are obviously dependant on causes which are infinitesimal in comparison to their effects ... The impulsion given to economic events by the attitude of groups obeys more specific laws. ... But there are cases when collective reactions are themselves dependent on small causal factors; an incident, a tendentious presentation, a minor fact that marks people's minds can be enough to impose a different and sometimes opposing direction on the normal course of events.[52]

This conviction that economic phenomena were subject to the vagaries of individual and collective desires was rather troubling for someone who was in the business of *prévision*. Sauvy concluded that planners could ignore neither 'the opinion of individuals, nor, above all the attitude of groups, which differ markedly, as we know, from those of the individuals they comprise'.[53] This emphasis on group behaviour and on the volatility of public opinion, had already been apparent in an earlier article in which Sauvy had asserted with regard to public perceptions of economic phenomena that 'impressions are deceptive and memories fleeting. Affective preoccupations triumph resoundingly over reason.'[54] As evidence of this, he cited the French public's persistence in believing that the cost of living had increased during the Depression, despite his own statistical evidence to the contrary. He elaborated: 'the error committed is not accidental but systematic. Man feels suffering more acutely than he feels a kinder fate, he adapts much faster to an improvement in his standing than to new incidences of deprivation. In contrast his memory transmits a favourable image of the past which he of course takes for reality.'[55] The popular mind (unlike that of the *conjoncturiste*) was thus represented as duplicitous, emotional, and moved by images rather than observation and reasoned arguments – a common assumption of collective psychology since at least the late nineteenth century and one that can be found, for example, in Gustave Le Bon's *La Psychologie des foules*.[56]

This is not to say that Sauvy should simply be seen as a disciple of Le Bon. He did in fact have some contact with other currents of collective psychology in the 1930s, notably via Maurice Halbwachs, who was developing a brand of social psychology that distanced itself from the biologism of Le Bon.[57] Sauvy's preoccupation with public opinion also coincided with that of Jean Stoetzel, the pioneer of opinion polling in France, who founded the Institut français d'opinion publique (IFOP) in 1938 and would work with Sauvy at the Institut national d'études démographiques (INED) after the war. It is notable, however, that there is little trace of the encounter with Halbwachs in Sauvy's work and that on the rare occasions that he cited a theorist to support his views in later years, it was Le Bon's name that was mentioned.[58] These rather vague citations are indicative not of any close engagement with Le Bon, but of the extent to which the ideas he had codified had been appropriated in political, military and business circles by the interwar period, as those in leadership and decision-making positions reflected on their role in what they saw as the era of mass democracy.[59] Indeed, while some have seen collective psychology as an intellectual precursor of fascism, recent research has shown its significance in the thinking of the French Republican Right.[60] This was, after all, a current of thinking which saw the irrationalism of the masses as a potential threat but believed in the ability of rational elites, who had mastered their instincts, to neutralize this threat. It was as much about a cult of the rational as it was about a fearful fascination with the irrational.

For Sauvy, one of the main problems with the irrationality of public opinion was precisely that decision-makers – especially politicians who were driven by electoral popularity – were susceptible to it. Thus, for example, he complained that decisions about the regulation of work time were generally based on a false doctrine that served political rather than economic ends. He would continue to argue for decades to come that Blum's introduction of the forty-hour week rested on a mistaken belief that there was a finite amount of work in the economy which could simply be shared out differently in order to reduce unemployment.[61] Those who subscribed to such a view were seduced by the irrational attraction of round numbers, or what he later called 'la magie du chiffre'.[62] Interestingly, numbers are seen to operate here like the images and memories imprinted on the mind in the passage quoted above – round numbers, it is suggested, provoke an affective response that is not actually based on mathematical reasoning. Industrialists, like politicians, were criticized for holding on to irrational views, notably in their alleged reluctance to provide figures that would allow the *conjoncturiste* to analyse the economic situation – such secrecy was regarded as a throwback to an era of laissez-faire liberalism in which competition rather than organization had been the order of the day.[63] In this way, Sauvy echoed the views of Ernest Mercier, who had reproached French businessmen in the late 1920s for an 'individualist' attitude deemed out of sync with the age of organization.[64]

Contrasting the forward-looking temperament of the *conjoncturiste* with that of the Malthusian majority, Sauvy spoke of the 'risks' and 'dangers' involved in 'submitting oneself to the test' of formulating projections about the future.[65] This was in turn part of the wider *planiste* discourse which contrasted a generalized passivity and impotence in the face of economic events with the new voluntarism that planners sought to embody. As Jacques Branger put it, 'planning implies a belief in the possibility of forcing history …. In short it is an attitude that no longer believes in laissez-faire, or that history makes itself, but holds that history can be led.'[66] In arguing for a more managerialist approach to policy-making, planners distanced themselves from party-political positions. Their aim was to reinvigorate democratic government rather than abolish it. Nonetheless, at a time when anti-parliamentary sentiment was widespread, statements like Branger's implicitly presented planners as the opposite of parliamentarians. Kevin Passmore has noted, for example, how the politicians of the Third Republic were figured in the right-wing press as talkers, rather than doers, an attribute often linked to the alleged dominance of southerners in parliament.[67] In contrast, rather like the social engineers discussed in Chapter Two, planners represented themselves as men of action, and, in doing so, appealed to a certain idea of masculinity: for Branger, planning was about 'an attitude in the face of misfortunes, a doctrine of action …[,] almost a heroic attitude.'[68] Bardet emphasized the notion of responsibility, and fulfilling one's commitments (*respect des engagements*), linking the virtue of action with moral probity – another thing that politicians were often believed to lack.[69] Like the socialist planners in Belgium, those at X-Crise saw planning or organization as a new 'mystique' that could mobilize the public in a spirit of collective endeavour.[70] Thus, they positioned themselves as a new elite who embodied the virtues of rational action, while appealing to the power of the *ir*rational as a means of rallying the population to renewed productive effort.

The Planned Economy and the Sciences of Man

While figures like Sauvy and the econometricians at X-Crise developed techniques that were essential for economic planning and contributed to the renovation of economic theory, they did not actually provide a blueprint for a new economic order. But with the publication of *L'Humanisme économique* in 1936, Coutrot did just that. As noted in Chapter Two, this essay, provoked by the social explosion of June 1936 and the reforms that emerged from it, received considerable press attention. With the title, 'Economic Humanism', Coutrot was explicitly putting a certain idea of 'man' at the heart of his proposals for a new economic order. Like Sauvy, he believed that planners had to reckon with the non-rational dimensions of individual and collective behaviour. 'Man is not made of reason alone', he wrote 'all that he has within him in terms of sensibility also profoundly conditions his existence and obeys quite different laws.'[71] He referred repeatedly to this non-rational dimension in terms of 'instinct' and 'appetite', highlighting the urge to possess and the instinct for equilibrium as ancient forces that must be respected.[72] What he envisaged was a political economy based on a vision of 'the whole man' informed by psychoanalysis and psychobiology.

Coutrot's previous book, *De quoi vivre* (published a year before *L'Humanisme économique* but subsequently marketed as a companion volume), offers some insight into the reference points that might have shaped this thinking.[73] A wide-ranging theoretical essay, it cited not just the works of the nineteenth-century mathematician and economist Antoine Cournot, the physicist Louis de Broglie and the socialist planist Hendrik de Man, but also works by Henri Bergson, by various psychoanalysts (Sigmund Freud, Charles Baudoin, René Allendy) and by zoologists (Jean Rostand, Georges Bohn). This bibliography betrayed an eclectic interest in questions of biological adaptation, aesthetics and the unconscious.[74] Coutrot also had links with the personalist intellectuals at the review *Ordre nouveau* and endorsed their search for a third way between individualism and collectivism, even though his own conception of 'the human person' drew more on a synthesis of ideas from scientific and philosophical sources than on the Christian humanism that was influential in personalist circles.[75] Coutrot's aim in *De quoi vivre* was to identify common laws that governed phenomena not just in the physical world but also in the human sensibilities and art, as well as in the social and economic realms. In fact, for Coutrot there was no autonomous social or economic realm, but rather a universe characterized at every level by perpetual motion and hence by a constant process of displacement of equilibrium (another reference to Le Chatelier's law).[76] Everything from biological phenomena to fashion trends was believed to follow a wave pattern, forming a series of oscillations.[77] It was this energeticist view of the universe that was reflected in Coutrot's interpretation of the strikes of 1936 as a much-needed corrective to the prevailing passivity and individualism of France during the Depression, an interpretation which presented a rather more positive picture of the irrationality of the masses than that offered by Sauvy. The strikes were read as confirmation of what Coutrot saw as a fundamental law of individual and collective psychology – the 'oscillating' or 'undulating' nature of human sensibilities.[78]

This sense of 1936 as a vital moment of renewal informed the economic model that Coutrot set out in *L'Humanisme économique*. Accepting the reforms ushered in by the Matignon Agreement, he argued that the only way to maintain workers' gains in pay and reduced work time was to adopt a concerted productivity policy. The reforms adopted at Matignon clearly implied a rise in production costs and threatened the viability of businesses unless they could raise their sales prices accordingly. France therefore faced the prospect of rising unemployment or inflation, but this could be avoided, Coutrot argued, by making efficiency savings: by driving down costs other than salaries, it would be possible to prevent the whole country paying for the reforms and ensure that the workers' gains were not immediately wiped out by inflation.[79] To this end, Coutrot proposed the organization of *ententes* among businesses in each branch of industry in order to promote the rationalization of work, the standardization of goods and increased specialization of businesses.[80] This coordinated rationalization effort would also require a new openness on the part of businesses about sharing economic information. In this model of a reformed capitalism, as in Alfred Sauvy's, the culture of industrial secrecy was condemned as a throwback to the liberalism of the past.[81] As Coutrot made clear in a lecture in 1937, accounting techniques that would enable sales prices to be determined according to a calculation of production costs, rather than on the basis of the laws of supply and demand, were central to the strategy he was setting out for controlling prices.[82] To ensure that ententes would not act in a 'Malthusian' manner, Coutrot proposed the creation of an 'order' of technicians to monitor their activity. Working with organized business in each sector, these technicians would effectively regulate the economy in the general interest and act as a relay between business and the state.[83] Workers too were to be associates in the search for savings and Bardet's initiative in creating a Workers' Council before the reforms of 1936 was offered as an example of this collaborative new ethos.[84] Reasoning that the unionization of workers was now a given, Coutrot argued that labour had an interest in working with management to ensure efficiency savings in order to maintain and potentially increase wages.[85]

If psychoanalytic and biological notions infused Coutrot's interpretation of the events of June 1936, they also informed other aspects of his economic humanism. Like the socialist planists, he advocated the establishment of a mixed economy with a planned sector and a free sector (as he had already proposed in the *Plan du 9 juillet*). While the planned sector was to operate in the general interest, ensuring the provision of basic necessities such as food, clothing and housing, the free sector was envisaged as a means of delivering a kind of anti-Malthusian stimulation, allowing the maintenance of 'the race that prefers ... [the] joys and risks [of the free market] to the more mediocre peace of the planned sector'.[86] For Coutrot, the element of risk thus provided would save France from the 'ossification' which would be the fate of a nation of *fonctionnaires* (civil servants).[87] This concern with the quality of the 'race' was matched by a concern with quantity, as Coutrot argued that, in an economy organized in the interests of mankind, the state should bear part of the cost of raising children.[88] To this extent, economic humanism reflected the demographic anxiety that was expressed increasingly vociferously in the 1930s by the populationist lobby.[89] In embracing Hyacinthe Dubreuil's proposals for group organization, it also aspired to humanize 'mammoth' businesses.[90] Organizing the economy was conceived here almost as a matter of perfecting a human eco-system, one that was in harmony with the psychological as well as the physiological needs of the species. Coutrot spoke of the need for forms of organization that took account of 'the intransigence of our appetites, the rhythm of our satisfaction and disgust: in a word, the curve of our sensibilities and all the conditions of our internal and external equilibrium'.[91] 'Economic humanism' can therefore be seen as the point at which the planners' preoccupation with the psychological hurdles to a rationally organized economy intersected with the growing interest among organizers in the affective and biological dimensions of human productivity in work.

The Engineer-Economists and Government

If engineers were auto-didacts in economic matters, their claims to offer a new kind of economic expertise soon attracted the attention of politicians. Sauvy advised Paul Reynaud on economic matters from 1934 and his influence continued into the Daladier Government when he was able to get a cherished project for the creation of a new Institut de conjoncture onto the statute books as part of the decree laws of November 1938. Moreover, while Sauvy was a government employee, successive governments in the 1930s also had recourse to technicians from the private sector who had played an important part in the scientific organization and planning movements. In 1935 Laval brought in an array of organizers to head up his government's efforts to make efficiency savings in public administration – Jean Milhaud (of the CEGOS), Raoul Dautry, Jacques Branger, Jean Coutrot and Paul Planus were all part of this team.[92]

Following the election of the Popular Front Government in 1936 the influence of engineer-economists was all too apparent. One innovation of the first Blum Government was the creation of the Ministry for the National Economy (MEN), a reorganization which had been advocated by technicians' groups such as Redressement français in the 1920s. This signalled a move away from the dominance of the Ministry of Finance in economic matters, a shift that was confirmed when the new minister, Charles Spinasse, drew his policy inspiration not from the financial civil servants of the Inspection des finances, but from X-Crise engineers such as Jacques Branger and Jean Coutrot.[93] Branger was involved, for example, in drafting legislation authorizing a Public Works Plan to help reflate the economy in June 1936, while Coutrot was appointed to run a new Centre national de l'organisation scientifique du travail (National Centre for the Scientific Organization of Work, COST) in November of the same year. This was significant as it reflected the adoption by Spinasse of precisely the strategy that Coutrot set out in *L'Humanisme économique* – a coordinated effort to reduce production costs in order to pay for increased salaries and curb inflation. Spinasse was in contact with Coutrot even before the publication of *L'Humanisme économique* and in August 1936 the minister set out his vision of a productivity policy in a speech to the Senate which appears to have been drafted, at least in part, by the engineer.[94] In this way, scientific organization was envisaged by the minister not just as a means of making government more efficient, but as a central plank of economic policy.

The immediate results of this ministerial endorsement were rather limited. A proposed law on industrial ententes never materialized and when the Blum Government fell in June 1937, its successor (dominated by Radicals) did away with the independent MEN and returned to more orthodox financial analyses of the economy, though Coutrot's analysis was picked up again later in the year when the government commissioned a major study on the state of the nation's production.[95] Similarly, the COST was a modest venture with limited means at its disposal. Nonetheless, Coutrot used it to try to break down the barriers that existed between various economic and administrative actors, launching a series of inter-ministerial commissions on rationalization, bringing together employers, technicians and labour movement representatives to discuss the organization of production, and generally promoting productivity with whatever means were available to him. He liaised with educational establishments in an effort to develop the teaching of scientific organization, for example, and promoted the benefits of organization to the general public through a series of radio broadcasts.[96]

In 1938–39, Coutrot also used his position at the COST to establish contacts with populationists. He wrote to the pro-natalist campaigner Fernand Boverat on 9 February 1938, assuring him of the place of demography in 'the rational organization of the country' and suggesting that the work of the COST was likely to intersect with and reinforce that of Boverat's Alliance nationale contre la dépopulation.[97] This reflected a preoccupation that had been part of Coutrot's vision of organization since at least 1936, though it had not been a very fully developed aspect of his proposed programme. His overtures to Boverat came, however, at a time when the pronatalist lobby enjoyed unprecedented influence, culminating in a set of decrees in March 1939 (known as the Family Code) which, among other measures, reformed family allowances to offer incentives for having larger families. By 1939 the questions of immigration and assimilation were also apparent on Coutrot's agenda at the COST and this too was symptomatic of a shift in public discourse and policy-making. Anti-immigrant feeling was running high in France by the end of the 1930s, following the combined effects of the Depression and the 1938 refugee crisis. Albert Sarraut, Daladier's Interior Minister, had responded with laws that sought to restrict the rights of 'undesirables', even allowing the state to intern them on security grounds. It was against this backdrop, and as Spanish Republicans fled to France only to find themselves herded into internment camps, that Georges Montandon, the author of *L'Ethnie française*, was invited to contribute to the work of the COST on 3 March 1939. The term *ethnie* was used by French racial theorists in this period for what they considered to be hybrid racial types, such as the French, and in a COST radio broadcast on depopulation and immigration on 4 March, Coutrot cited Montandon's view that the 'anarchy' of the French spirit was due to the 'tumult of races' that had mingled to create it.[98] The focus of this brand of racist thought was on assimilability rather than racial purity, however, and what Coutrot advocated in his radio broadcast was a planned approach to immigration, requiring studies to establish which races were the best workers and could be most readily assimilated without unfavourable effects on the French people.[99] As K.H. Adler has shown, this attachment to both the quantity and 'quality' of the population would continue into the postwar period and was articulated notably in *Des Français pour la France* which was co-authored by Alfred Sauvy and the paediatrician Robert Debré in 1946.[100]

The role of the X-Crise engineers as government advisors in the 1930s was the latest example of the interactions that took place throughout the interwar period between politicians and the technicians of the organization movement. What was significant about the appointment of this particular group of organizers was that it consecrated the position of engineers as economists and economic policy advisors. But as the example of Coutrot's activities at the COST illustrates, what he and some of his fellow engineers were mapping out by the late 1930s was a very broad definition of the engineer's role in an economy conceived in terms of 'human problems'. In 1933, Coutrot had spoken of his ambition to promote 'a universal rationalization, not limited to the problem of production'.[101] While the COST provided one forum for this in the late 1930s, much of Coutrot's effort to fufil this ambition was conducted through the Centre d'études des problèmes humains.

The Centre for the Study of Human Problems and the 'New Man'

If technicians at X-Crise believed they were dealing with a crisis that had moral and psychological as well as economic dimensions, Coutrot saw all these problems as aspects of a crisis of technical civilization. The central problem in his view was that the rapid development of the material sciences, technology and industry had not been matched by a similar progression in the 'sciences of man'.[102] As Jeffrey Herf has shown, similar arguments were made by engineers in Weimar and Nazi Germany, though their analysis was shaped by a tradition of romantic irrationalism that was less present in France. When these German engineers denounced the corrosive effects of excessive mechanization and specialization, their solution was a spiritualization of technology and their vision was one that anticipated and converged with the culture of Nazism.[103] When Coutrot identified the same problems, his solution was to extend the reach of reason into the domain of intuition, instinct and emotion. The declared aim was not to eliminate these non-rational forces, but to come to terms with them through science and organize society in ways that took this dimension of human nature on board. To this end, Coutrot founded the Centre d'études des problèmes humains (Centre for the Study of Human Problems, CEPH) in 1936. The Centre developed as an extension of a study group on 'economic humanism' whose bulletin, *Humanisme économique*, became the CEPH review. It brought together not just Coutrot's associates from industry and technicians' groups (including X-Crise members such as Bardet and the Guillaume brothers), but also doctors, psychologists and educationalists, figures from the arts, such as the art historian Henri Focillon or the English novelist Aldous Huxley (with whom Coutrot maintained a correspondence) and the folkore specialist André Varagnac. In this sense, Coutrot's definition of the 'sciences of man' was a broad one. Patrons of the Centre included the left-wing work scientists Lahy and Laugier, as well as the Catholic conservative doctor and best-selling author of *L'Homme, cet inconnu* (1935), Alexis Carrel (though none of these figures was an active member).[104]

What distinguished Coutrot's enterprise from those of Carrel and the work scientists was its scope and eclecticism. Carrel shared Coutrot's view that 'technical civilization' was in crisis and that this could be resolved by the development of the sciences of man, but his was a pessimistic socio-biological analysis which posed the problem in terms of degeneration, decadence and the need to cultivate a biological elite.[105] Coutrot was less pessimistic about technology and framed his project in terms of the improvement of all mankind.[106] Moreover, while he referred to the work of figures like Carrel and Montandon, his concern was always to synthesize their concerns with other theories and approaches. He was just as likely to hold forth about the aesthetics of rhythm in cinema or modern art as he was to discuss socio-biology. As the rather esoteric synthesis he had developed in *De quoi vivre* illustrates, his project was to find common ground between science, art and religion and, in doing so, to transcend what he saw as sterile oppositions between disciplines and belief systems. This ambition brought the CEPH into contact with the unorthodox theologian and paleontologist, Pierre Teilhard de Chardin, whose efforts to bring together religious and scientific thought resonated with Coutrot's desire to develop a scientific humanism that would retain something of the mystical power of religion.[107] There were a number of the Catholics at the CEPH, but it should not be regarded as a confessional organization.[108] In many ways, as Coutrot himself acknowledged, his project was more reminiscent of that of the Saint-Simonians, who had not only proposed a model of organization for industrial society but sought to found a new scientific religion.[109]

Despite the difficulty of locating the CEPH in a political or disciplinary map, certain observations can be made about the people and currents of thinking that were most in evidence there. The Centre was composed of several study groups and one of the most active was the Psycho-biology Group. It was not the academic science of a Lahy or a Laugier that held sway here, but rather a kind of middle-brow science of doctors and applied psychologists. The declared aim of the CEPH was to foster the emergence of a 'new man' and the approach that dominated in the Psycho-biology Group was a broadly hygienist one. There was a neo-Lamarckian preoccupation with improving the quality of the population by acting on environmental factors, as members took an interest in everything from nutrition to electric cars or the banning of tobacco products.[110] Coutrot and other members repeatedly condemned the 'negative' form of eugenics espoused in Nazi Germany, with its emphasis on the elimination of those deemed unhealthy elements.[111] But this did not prevent them discussing the merits of introducing a pre-marital medical certificate, something which would become compulsory in 1942 and which was intended to discourage reproduction in couples whose offspring were deemed likely to be 'deficient' in one way or another. In a report presented by Dr Marcel Martiny and Paul Schiff (the former, a specialist in occupational medicine, member of the Société de biotypologie, and Chair of the Psycho-biology Group; the latter, a member of the Société psychanalytique de Paris who played an important role in the development of psychoanalysis and sexology in France), the Psycho-biology Group endorsed pre-marital testing as part of a 'rational' and 'human' eugenics.[112]

Martiny, who worked with apprentices in the training school of the Paris Chamber of Commerce subscribed to the theories of the Italian biotypologist Nicola Pende, whose understanding of biotypes differed in key respects from that of Laugier.[113] It was Pende who had coined the term 'biotypology' but when Laugier adopted it he explicitly distanced himself from his Italian counterpart, suggesting that the latter's work was both scientifically simplistic and driven by an ideological *parti pris*.[114] While Laugier's political affiliations lay with the Radical Party and he was interested in using biotypology for purposes such as improving educational attainment, Pende was closely linked with the Fascist regime, which funded his institute and embraced the hygienist science he espoused in its demographic policy. In 1938 he was among those who legitimized the anti-Semitic phase of Italian Fascism by signing the Manifesto of Racist Scientists.[115] Pende's method blended morpho-psychology and endocrinology, identifying the sex glands as a key determinant of temperament. It posited four biotypes and assigned subjects to a type on the basis of morphological and physiological features.[116] Both the biotypes themselves and the nature of the correlation between bodily features and psychological characteristics were therefore assumed in Pende's method. Martiny justified the use of these fixed types on the grounds that such typologies had existed since time immemorial and that four-way classifications of this kind were found in all ancient civilizations.[117] This was hardly a scientific argument and it contrasts with Laugier's efforts to subject assumptions about the correlation between physical and psychological features to the test of empirical research. However, as in the management training programmes offered at the Ecole d'administration et des affaires and the Ecole d'organisation scientifique du travail (see Chapter Two), it was the more reductive and readily applicable techniques of morphologists that were taken up at the CEPH. This shaped not only the work of the Psycho-biology group but also that of a study group on women (or 'feminine humanism' in the language of the CEPH). Here, Suzanne Brésard, who had worked with the morphologist Louis Corman, used graphology and morphology to contribute to the group's discussions on 'the conditions of woman's equilibrium' and the implications of this for women's social function.[118]

It will be apparent from this that the spirit of scientific organization infused explorations in the 'sciences of man' at the CEPH. The aspiration was to develop a form of psycho-biological organization that dealt not just with individuals in the workplace, but also with the macro-organization of social and economic activity (the sexual division of labour, population policy, eugenics and social hygiene). This was a deeply essentialist vision of organization. At the same time the process of creating a 'new man' was conceived in educational as well as biological terms. An illustration of this can be found in an initiative launched by the CEPH in 1938 as a solution to the perceived problem of the irrationality of public opinion: the Rainbow newspaper subscription. This was a deal that offered subscribers the chance to receive a different newspaper everyday—*Action française* on Mondays, *L'Humanité* on Tuesdays, *Figaro* on Wednesdays, *Le Populaire* on Thursdays and so on.[119] It was devised in collaboration with the Russian psycho-physiologist Serge Chakotin, a CEPH member, former assistant to Ivan Pavlov and author of *The Rape of the Masses: The Psychology of Totalitarian Political Propaganda*.[120] Indeed, when Coutrot explained the need for the Rainbow subscription, he did so in terms that call to mind not just Sauvy's warnings about the pernicious influence of doctrinal positions and received ideas, but also Pavlov's famous experiments with dogs: 'When you brandish before Frenchmen or Westerners a political label, whether it be Socialism, Radicalism or another' wrote Coutrot, 'the Frenchman in question salivates, he has a violent emotional reaction.'[121] If the public was reduced to an animalistic state by exposure to ideological triggers in the mass media, the multi-paper subscription was clearly intended to foster a more critical reading perspective, thereby allowing the reader to arrive at a less doctrinaire and more rational view.[122] This reflected not only Coutrot's underlying rationalist faith in the educability of the human mind but also his tendency to equate political positions with unreason.

Educational reform was another subject explored at the CEPH, which shared Joseph Wilbois's and Paulette Bernège's interest in the New Education movement. Coutrot was successful in attracting international names in this field – both Maria Montessori and Edouard Claparède were in contact with the CEPH and contributed to its deliberations.[123] Coutrot was invited to address an international Montessori convention in Copenhagen in 1937 and Annette Coutrot studied with the New Education movement in France.[124] The couple also sent their youngest child to a Montessori school.[125] With its espousal of an education based on respect for the organism's natural developmental mechanisms, the New Education movement seems to have appealed to the engineers' understanding of systems and particularly the idea that one must work *with* rather than against the internal mechanisms of a system. At a CEPH meeting in 1937, Claparède criticized mainstream schooling as excessively theoretical and 'anti-biological' in that it separated knowledge from action. One danger of this, in his view, was that it taught children to see work as an imposition rather than a source of pleasure or fulfilment. Claparède argued that true learning happens in response to a need, that this in turn stimulates action which then allows children to fulfil this need, to learn and to develop their personalities. Children educated according to this principle would learn to love work, not to hate it, he contended – a prospect that was always likely to meet with the approval of Coutrot at a time when the rationalization movement was taking a growing interest in the question of worker motivation and the social psychology of work.[126]

The New Education was also presented at the CEPH as a means of tempering excessive individualism by teaching children to work collaboratively, an outlook which dovetailed neatly with organizers' aspirations to find a third way between liberalism and collectivism.[127] In an article published in *Humanisme économique* amidst the acute international tensions of September 1938, Montessori described her approach as 'education for peace', arguing that society fuelled conflict by brutalizing the child's natural characteristics and that an education which respected the laws of psychological development could solve this problem.[128] Coutrot echoed these views. As he told the CEPH Psycho-biology Group in January 1939:

> I really have the impression that when the human race is composed of former Montessori children, we will perhaps be able to say that a psychological mutation has taken place. Men's behaviour will be modified, life and social problems will take on a completely different appearance.[129]

What characterized children educated using 'active methods', in Coutrot's eyes, was that they learned the taste for work and achieved *self*-discipline, rather than having discipline imposed on them from the outside in an authoritarian pupil-teacher relationship. There is an echo here of Hyacinthe Dubreuil's vision of the workplace as an educational space for the worker. But the CEPH was not just (indeed, not even primarily) concerned with the adaptation of the worker. Rather, in focusing on the ostensibly classless figure of the 'homme moderne' and targeting an essentially bourgeois audience, it suggested that this audience too must adapt itself to 'technical civilization'.

Educating a new elite had of course been a preoccupation of the scientific organization movement ever since Fayol. Much of this attention had focused on disseminating techniques for the organization of work and on the question of educating engineers as managers of people. The CEPH went further in two ways. Firstly, in posing the broader question of the organization and efficiency of all human activity, it set out to educate what

Coutrot called an *ingénieur ès sciences de l'homme* (an engineer trained in the sciences of man). Hence, while it drew on the expertise of doctors, psycho-biologists and educationalists, the CEPH's primary target audiences in disseminating this knowledge were engineers and organizers. Recruitment publicity was placed in reviews whose readership came from these groups, such as *X-Crise* and *Méthodes*, while CEPH memberships were awarded as prizes at the CNOF School for Scientific Organization.[130] Several members of X-Crise were among those who attended the inaugural CEPH meeting at Pontigny (Gérard Bardet, Jacques Branger, André Lochard and André Loizillon) while others attended later sessions – Sauvy participated in 1937, for example, as did Jean Milhaud of the CEGOS and the President of the CNOF, Robert Lelong.[131] There were also engineer-administrators like Gaston Traploir[132] and efficiency consultants like Paul Planus[133] and Yves Colombat.[134] Indeed, while Planus and Traploir were among the more active members, other engineers like Pierre Lévy of the recently nationalised SNCF (Société nationale des chemins de fer français) or Louis Bacqueyrisse of the Paris public transport company, the STCRP (Société des transports en commun de la region parisienne), who were closely involved with their companies' pioneering use of psychotechnics, also subscribed to the Centre.[135]

The second way in which the CEPH sought to contribute directly to the education of a new elite was by encouraging its audience to turn the tools of applied psychology on themselves. This was one of the aims of the Institute of Applied Psychology created at the CEPH in 1938, under the leadership of Dr Henri Arthus. Before joining the CEPH, Arthus had founded L'Eveil (literally The Awakening), described as a 'movement for individual and social evolution', and even as 'a kind of generalized Montessori method for adults.'[136] In fact, it was less a movement than a practical psychology course, offering techniques of self-improvement, presented as a kind of therapy that would reconcile 'man' with the nature of modern work.[137] It was aimed at a working-class and lower middle-class audience and members received monthly publications which provided exercises for improving what were termed 'the faculties of adaptation' – faculties such as memory, attention, judgement or imagination, which were also those tested by psychotechnicians. Arthus even spoke of his method as an extension of Taylorism, as a means of internalizing the process begun externally by Taylor.[138] Promoted primarily to men,[139] his method was also marketed as a means of re-conquering one's masculinity by achieving self-mastery – when the first volume of his lessons was published in 1938, it was under the title *Devenir un homme*.

Though short-lived, the Institute of Applied Psychology offered similar methods to a more bourgeois audience. According to Arthus, the aim of the Institute was to provide psychological training for those who wished to develop 'their various mental faculties, their self-control, and those diverse gifts which make a man a man of action, an efficient man'.[140] This enterprise was similar to the self-management lessons that Wilbois had proposed in *La Psychologie au service du chef d'entreprise*, though at the CEPH the project tended to be framed in terms of adapting man to the modern world, rather than purely in terms of leadership and influencing one's subordinates. One teacher at the Institute of Applied Psychology was Paul Masson-Oursel, a Professor of Oriental Philosophy at the Ecole pratique des hautes etudes, who proposed individual 'efficiency consultations' for business people and industrialists, combining elements of Western and Oriental psychology, psychotechnics and psychoanalysis.[141] This was an extension of the work Masson-Oursel had already carried out with the Pelman Institute, an international organization that had had considerable success offering psychological self-improvement courses in the U.K., particularly in the First World War period.[142] Masson-Oursel directed the Pelmanist review *La Psychologie et la vie*, which (in addition to carrying pieces by respected figures in applied psychology such as Edouard Claparède and the vocational guidance expert, Julien Fontègne) published articles on memory techniques, methods for developing the will, networking skills and the art of leadership.[143] The review *Mon bureau* (which became *L'Organisation* in September 1932) carried several articles on these methods, directing readers to *La Psychologie et la vie* for further information.[144] This type of self-improvement literature is perhaps something one more readily associates with British and U.S. culture, but it was not absent from the French context. Indeed, a similar cultivation of the self and of personal efficiency has been identified by Luc Boltanksi as a feature of the new managerial class of *cadres* that would become increasingly visible in France after World War Two.[145]

Conclusion

The array of issues discussed at the CEPH and the range of disciplines on which it drew could not be said to typify the approach of the average engineer-organizer. Yet it was part of a broader set of developments among organizers that were very much symptomatic of the impact of the economic crisis, the increasingly vociferous discontent with the political establishment that accompanied it, and the growing international tensions of the 1930s. The onslaught of the Depression led many employers to cut costs, leaving less money available to pay consultants, to introduce new methods that required up-front investment (such as production lines) or even to pay a subscription to the CNOF.[146] On the shop floor, the Depression years were characterized by a form of rationalization that was predominantly about budgetary control, the elimination of waste and the use of time and motion study to speed up production and drive down costs. But the response of technicians' groups in the face of the Depression was not to rein in their ambitions but to extend them. The development of economic planning and the turn to 'human problems' were the principal manifestations of this.

The engineer-economists of the 1930s left a number of legacies. For one thing, they provided a credible theoretical rationale for a managed economy, a rationale that was expressed in terms of an appeal to science rather than politics. The reputation of *polytechniciens* as the nation's technical *crème de la crème*, their ability to combine business experience with their historic mission of service to the state and their connections with political, administrative and business elites all enhanced the credibility of the models they proposed. Through their contributions to the emerging field of econometrics and to statistical monitoring and forecasting in France, they helped to develop tools of economic management that would soon be considered essential instruments of modern government and paved the way for France's postwar planners. Their campaigns to improve the level of economic information available in France, not just through the collation of statistical data but through the coordinated application of industrial accounting methods, were not merely technical activities but attempts to change the culture of French business. Similarly, their action as economic advisors to governments challenged not just previous economic orthodoxies but also the existing policy-making model and the conceptions of economic competence on which it rested. Moreover, in mapping out an economic model based on social partnership, in which economic equilibrium and social progress were to be assured through a coordinated productivity drive, Coutrot was among the first to articulate an analysis that would be central to the construction of the postwar economic order.

In more ways than one, the engineer-economists imagined and embodied a 'new man'. Renegotiating disciplinary boundaries, they positioned themselves as economic experts of a new kind, but also as men of action, as figures who embodied a new voluntarism in the face of crisis. In doing so, they contrasted themselves with the majority who allegedly lacked the vision and technical competence to rise above passivity or Malthusianism. In a parallel with Bernège's efforts to model a new housewife, Sauvy and Coutrot argued that the new man must cultivate his rationalism, training the mind to enhance its efficiency and bolster its defences against manipulation or irrational attachment to doctrinal positions. The engineer-economist was, to use Coutrot's phrase, an *ingénieur ès sciences de l'homme*, but this extension of engineers into the domain of the human sciences was taken even further at the CEPH, where at least two different versions of the new man intersected. On the one hand, there was a hygienist vision of the biological renewal of mankind; on the other, a vision of transformation by education or training of the mind. What they shared was the fact that their different conceptions of the 'improvement' of mankind, were rooted in psycho-biology. Indeed, what the *planisme* of X-Crise had in common with the broader project proposed by the CEPH was that both rested on a revision of the concept of the rational individual that had been the basis for liberal economic theory.

Jeffrey Herf has described the outlook of 'reactionary modernist' engineers in Germany as a 'synthesis of technics and unreason'.[147] The planist reaction among French engineers might be described as a synthesis of engineering, economics and psychology. While they conceived of human behaviour as driven in part by forces of 'unreason', framed their thinking in terms of collective psychology and believed that France could be reinvigorated by a renewal of elites, these engineers remained attached to the rational individual and suspicious of statism. It is in this sense that their search for a 'third way' might more accurately be considered, as Michel Margairaz has pointed out, as a revision of the first (liberal) way.[148] Though they distanced themselves from party-political positions they nonetheless had a politics: they hoped to avoid both socialism and fascism through managerialism. This did not prevent some of their ideas being taken up, at least briefly, by a Socialist-led government, under which Coutrot and Branger were happy to serve. Similarly, it would not prevent a number of the figures discussed in this and earlier chapters from working with the government that would shortly emerge in France in the context of Nazi occupation.

Notes

1. AN: 468 AP 6 dr7 Letter from J. Coutrot to Mr Lawrence of Manchester, 4 March 1939.
2. R. Kuisel. 1981. *Capitalism and the State in Modern France: Renovation and Economic Management in the Twentieth Century*, Cambridge: Cambridge University Press, 105–7 and O. Dard. 2002. *Le Rendez-vous manqué des relèves des années trente*, Paris: Presses Universitaires de France, 39–42 have noted the link between the scientific organization movement and planning movements.
3. On Fayol's role, see S. Rials. 1977. *Administration et organisation: de l'organisation de la bataille à la bataille de l'organisation dans l'administration française*, Paris: Editions Beauchesne, 124–27, 174–80. On the CNE, see A. Chatriot. 2002. *La Démocratie sociale à la française. L'Expérience du Conseil national économique 1924–1940*, Paris: La Découverte.
4. On what Olivier Dard terms the 'realist' circles of the 1920s, see Dard, *Le Rendez-vous manqué*, 15–91. On Tardieu, see F. Monnet. 1993. *Refaire la République. André Tardieu, une dérive réactionnaire*, Paris: Fayard, esp. 27–33, 87–94.
5. X-Crise is the better known name for the Centre polytechnicien d'études économiques or CPEE. *L'X* is another name for the Ecole polytechnique and *polytechniciens* are sometimes referred to as *les X*.
6. De Man cited in J. Jackson. 1985. *The Politics of Depression in France*, Cambridge: Cambridge University Press, 139. On de Man and the origins of planism in Belgium see P. Dodge. 1966. *The Faith and Works of Hendrik de Man*, The Hague: Martinus Nijhoff.
7. *The Psychology of Socialism* was published in French in 1927 as *Au-delà du marxisme*, Brussels: L'Eglantine. De Man's ideas were widely disseminated in France, thanks in part to André Philip. See A. Philip. 1928. *Henri de Man et la crise doctrinale du socialisme*, Paris: J. Gamber.
8. 'Le Plan, tout le Plan, rien que le Plan' was the slogan adopted by the Belgian Workers Party. On propaganda and the mystique of the Plan, see G.-R. Horn. 2001. 'From "Radical" to "Realistic": Hendrik de Man and the International Plan Conferences at Pontigny and Geneva 1934–1937', *Contemporary European History* 10(2), esp. 246. For de Man's interest in questions of psychology and motivation at work, see H. de Man. 1930. *La Joie au travail*, Paris: PUF.

9. See G. Lefranc. 1963. *Histoire d'un groupe du parti socialiste SFIO, Révolution constructive: 1930–38*, Geneva.
10. *Plan du 9 juillet*, Paris: Gallimard, 1934, 17–18. On planism in France see Jackson, *The Politics of Depression*, 137–66, and Dard, *Le Rendez-vous manqué*, esp. 192–204 on the *Plan du 9 juillet*.
11. See Dard, *Le Rendez-vous manqué*, 193–95 for further details on the backgrounds of the different signatories to this plan.
12. *Plan du 9 juillet*, 26–27, 43.
13. *Plan du 9 juillet*, 46.
14. Documents relating to the preparation and diffusion of the *Plan du 9 juillet* can be found in the Coutrot papers at AN: AP 468 11 dr 2–3. On Coutrot's influence in the drafting of the plan, see also O. Dard. 1999. *Jean Coutrot: de l'ingénieur au prophète*, Besançon: Presses universitaires franc-comtoises, 153–55.
15. This official statement of objectives from the statutes of the Association (1933) appears regularly at the beginning (p.2) of issues of *X-Crise*.
16. Centre polytechnicien d'études économiques. 1938. 'Nos préoccupations', *X-Crise* November, 3–4.
17. M. Margairaz. 1991. *L'Etat, les finances et l'économie. Histoire d'une conversion, 1932–1952*, 2 vols, Comité pour l'histoire économique et financière de la France Kuisel, *Capitalism and the State*, 93–127. Alain Desrosières also acknowledges the role of groups like X-Crise and the Société statistique de Paris as laboratories of ideas and techniques that were subsequently taken up by the French state. A. Desrosières. 1998. *The Politics of Large Numbers: A History of Statistical Reasoning*, Cambridge, Mass.: Harvard University Press, 160–62.
18. Jacques Branger referred to planning as the triumph of the 'spirit of engineering' in 1935 in 'Le Contenu économique des plans et le planisme', *X-Crise* April-May, 12. Branger was referring here to Hendrik de Man's distinction between the 'spirit of the technician' and the 'spirit of the owner or shareholder'.
19. Keynesian economics was not yet well known in France in the 1930s but there was some awareness of it among members of X-Crise, notably Georges Boris and Jean Nicoletis. Boris is also credited with introducing Pierre Mendès France to Keynesianism. See J.F. Renaud. 2000. 'J.M. Keynes et les économistes français dans l'entre-deux-guerres: quelques éléments explicatifs d'une révolution introuvable' in P. Dockès et al. (dir.). *Les traditions économiques françaises*, Paris: CNRS Editions, 925–37.
20. G. Bardet. 1981. 'Réflexions sur six mois de travaux (novembre 1931–mai 1932)' in *De la récurrence des crises économiques. Centre polyechnicien d'études économiques. Son cinquante-naire 1931–1981*, Paris: Economica, 42–43, 57.
21. A. Detoeuf. 1936. 'La Fin du libéralisme', *X-Crise* May–August, 49.
22. My portrait here draws notably on Renaud, 'J. M. Keynes et les économistes français'.
23. M. Halbwachs. 1937. 'Le Point de vue sociologique', *X-Crise* February, 23–30.
24. Desrosières, *The Politics of Large Numbers*, 163. The use of statistics in socio-economic studies is exemplified by M. Halbwachs. 1912. *La Classe ouvrière et les niveaux de vie*, Paris: Alcan and idem. 1933. *L'Evolution des besoins dans les classes ouvrières*, Paris: Alcan.
25. Centre polytechnicien d'études économiques, 'Nos préoccupations', 4. See also M. Margairaz. 1995. 'Les Autodidactes et les experts: réseaux et parcours intellectuels dans les années 1930' in B. Belhoste et al., *La France des X. Deux siècles d'histoire*, Paris: Economica, 169–84.
26. H. Fayol, 1979. *Administration industrielle et générale*, Paris: Bordas, 5.
27. Bardet, 'Réflexions sur six mois de travaux', 45; E. Guillaume and G. Guillaume. 1937. *Economique rationnelle. Des fondements aux problèmes actuels*, Paris: Editions du Centre polytechnicien d'études économiques, Hermann et Cie, 18–22. The attachment to the notion of equilibrium is also apparent in the fact that the theme for the 1938–39 lecture series at X-Crise was 'Conditions for a French Equilibrium'.

28.   On Le Chatelier and the laws of chemical mechanics, see M. Letté. 2004. *Henry Le Chatelier (1850–1936) ou la science appliqué à l'industrie*, Rennes: Presses universitaires de Rennes, 66–76.

29.   Bardet, 'Réflexions sur six mois de travaux', 45; Guillaume and Guillaume, *Economique rationnelle*, 18–20, 26–27, 70–73.

30.   E.g. Kuisel, *Capitalism and the State*, x, 15–16.

31.   A. Sauvy. 1939. *Essai sur la conjoncture*, Paris: Editions du CPEE, 189.

32.   Tinbergen's talk and the ensuing discussion were published in 1938 in *X-Crise* July, 26–41.

33.   Guillaume and Guillaume, *Economique rationnelle*, 1.

34.   J. Ullmo. 1938. 'Recherches sur l'équilibre économique', *Annales de l'Institut Henri Poincaré* 8(1), 3.

35.   Ullmo, 'Recherches sur l'équilibre économique', 1.

36.   Guillaume and Guillaume, *Economique rationnelle*, 33–34.

37.   R. Gibrat. 1931. *Les Inégalités économiques. Applications aux inégalités des richesses, à la concentration des entreprises, aux populations des villes, aux statistiques des familles etc d'une loi nouvelle: la loi de l'effet proportionnel*, Paris: Recueil Sirey. Coutrot cited Gibrat's work in J. Coutrot. 1936. *Leçons de juin 1936/L'Humanisme économique*, Paris: Editions du CPEE, 58.

38.   Ullmo, 'Recherches sur l'équilibre économique', 2–3.

39.   Guillaume and Guillaume, *Economique rationnelle*, 44.

40.   Bardet, 'Réflexions sur six mois de travaux', 47, 57–58.

41.   T. Martin (dir). 2000. *Mathémathiques et action politique: études d'histoire et de philosophie de mathématiques sociales*, Paris: INED, 120–21.

42.   A longer list can be found at Sauvy, *Essai sur la conjoncture*, 38–45.

43.   A. Sauvy. 1972. *De Paul Reynaud à Charles de Gaulle: scènes, tableaux et souvenirs. Un économiste face aux hommes politiques 1934–1967*, Paris: Casterman, 13.

44.   A. Sauvy. 1937. 'Perspectives statistiques sur la population, l'enseignement et le chômage', *Journal de la société statistique de Paris* June, 228.

45.   Sauvy, *De Paul Reynaud à Charles de Gaulle*, 11.

46.   Sauvy, 'Perspectives statistiques sur la population', 227.

47.   A. Sauvy. 1936. 'Productivité et chômage', *Journal de la société statistique de Paris* February, 98.

48.   Sauvy, *Essai sur la conjoncture*, 185.

49.   See A. Sauvy. 1932. 'Calculs démographiques sur la population française jusqu'en 1980', *Journal de la société statistique de Paris* July-September, 319–28, a study financed by the Alliance nationale.

50.   A. Sauvy. 1938. 'Le Point économique', *X-Crise* January, 7; A. Sauvy. 1939. 'Crise financière et crise demographique', *X-Crise* March, 27–29.

51.   This historiography and Sauvy's relationship to it will be discussed further in the Conclusion.

52.   Sauvy, *Essai sur la conjoncture*, 37.

53.   Sauvy, *Essai sur la conjoncture*, 37–38.

54.   A. Sauvy. 1935. 'Le Niveau d'existence depuis la guerre et depuis la crise', *Journal de société statistique de Paris*, December, 348.

55.   Sauvy, 'Le Niveau d'existence depuis la guerre', 348.

56.   Le Bon speaks of the way in which images, words and phrases or slogans (*formules*) override rational argument in the mind of the crowd. G. Le Bon. 1991. *La Psychologie des foules*, Paris: Quadrige/PUF, e.g. 32, 35, 59 (first published in 1895).

57.   Sauvy and Halbwachs co-authored the demographic section of the *Encyclopédie française*, a project led by Lucien Febvre. See M. Halbwachs and A. Sauvy (with H. Ulmer and G. Bournier). 2005. *Le Point de vue du nombre 1936. Edition critique sous la direction de Marie Jaisson et Eric Brian*, Paris: INED.

58.   Sauvy commented (1956. *L'Opinion publique*, Paris: PUF, 17) that although Le Bon's work was overly simplistic and had become discredited, it still had fundamental insights to offer. He had already cited Le Bon in 1943 in *La Prévision économique*, Paris: PUF, 106. Both books were published in the popular Que sais-je? series and went through several

editions. The latest edition of *Opinion publique* was published in 1997 (with the Le Bon references intact).

59. E.g. B. Marpeau. 2000. *Gustave Le Bon. Parcours d'un intellectuel 1841–1931*, Paris: CNRS Editions, esp. 303–36 on the appropriation of Le Bon in business circles; R. Nye. 1975. *The Origins of Crowd Psychology: Gustave Le Bon and the Crisis of Mass Democracy in the Third Republic*. London, Beverly Hills: Sage, 123–47.

60. Tracing the appropriation of Le Bon in political circles, Marpeau (*Gustave Le Bon*, 343) locates its centre of gravity in what Rémond called the Orléanist Right. In this way he takes issue with Zeev Sternhell's interpretation of collective psychology as a precursor of fascism in Z. Sternhell. 1978. *La Droite révolutionnaire. Les Origines françaises du fascisme*, Paris: Le Seuil and Z. Sternhell. 1983. *Ni Droite, ni gauche: l'idéologie fasciste en France*, Paris: Le Seuil. Kevin Passmore's extensive study *The Right in the French Republic* (forthcoming) confirms the significance of this type of thinking on the parliamentary Right.

61. E.g. A. Sauvy. 1967. *Histoire économique de la France de l'entre-deux-guerres* vol. 2, Paris: Fayard, 303, 367.

62. A. Sauvy. 1965. *Mythologies de notre temps*, Paris: Payot, 34–41.

63. Sauvy, *Essai sur la conjoncture*, 187–88.

64. Cited in Chapter Two.

65. Sauvy, *Essai sur la conjoncture*, 150–51.

66. J. Branger. 1935. 'Le Contenu économique des plans et le planisme', *X-Crise* March-April, 12 cited in Kuisel, *Capitalism and the State*, 107.

67. K. Passmore, 'Why Did People Believe that the Third Republic Was in Crisis in the 1930s? Anti-southern Prejudice, Anti-Semitism and Anti-communism', paper presented at French Historical Studies, New Brunswick, NJ, 4 April 2008.

68. Branger, 'Le Contenu économique des plans et le planisme', 12.

69. Bardet, 'Réflexions sur six mois de travaux', 43, 49.

70. See, for example, Branger, 'Le Contenu économique des plans et le planisme', 13 and R. Lelong. 1939. 'Les Facteurs du progrès économique – l'organisation scientifique du travail', *X-Crise* July, 31–32. This vocabulary was also dear to Jean Coutrot. See, for example, AN: 468 AP 11 Dr 5 'Tâtonnements' juillet 1935, a text marking one year since the *Plan du 9 juillet*.

71. Coutrot, *Leçons/L'Humanisme économique*, 60–61.

72. Coutrot, *Leçons/L'Humanisme économique*, 27, 42, 61.

73. See J. Coutrot. 1935. *De quoi vivre*, Paris: Grasset. In 1938 this and *L'Humanisme économique* were marketed along with the Guillaume brothers' *Economique rationnelle* and two other works by Coutrot (*Le Système nerveux des entreprises* and *Le Chronomètre avec ou contre l'homme*) as part of a documentation pack. AN: 468 AP 22 dr2.

74. Works cited included Freud's *Introduction to Psychoanalysis* and *Totem and Taboo*; C. Baudoin. 1929. *Psychanalyse de l'art*, Paris: Alcan; G. Bohn. 1934. *Reproduction. Sexualité. Hérédité*, Paris: Hermann, Actualités scientifiques et industrielles and G. Bohn. 1909. *La Naissance de l'intelligence*, Paris: Flammarion; J. Rostand. 1933. *Les Problèmes de l'hérédité et du sexe*, Paris: Rieder; H. Bergson. 1932. *Les Deux Sources de la morale et de la religion*, Paris: Alcan; and idem. 1907. *L'Evolution créatrice*, Paris: Alcan.

75. Coutrot discussed the personalist reaction against the inhumanities of both capitalism and communism in *Leçons/L'Humanisme économique*, 42–44. He had published in *Plans*, the forerunner of *Ordre nouveau*, in the early 1930s, and in 1938–39, when these groups appeared to have run out of steam somewhat, he was instrumental in efforts to bring together and reinvigorate the various groups identified as *non-conformistes*. See J. Coutrot. 1932. 'USA, moyen âge du nouveau monde', *Plans* July; documents relating to the inter-group meeting of 12 July 1938 in AN: 468 AP 22 dr3b; documents relating to a lunch event on 13 February 1939 in AN: 468 AP 22 dr4b. The econometrician Robert Gibrat also frequented both X-Crise and Ordre nouveau and presented at the former group some of the work being conducted in the latter. See Centre polytechnicien d'études éeconomiques. 1934. 'Compte rendu de la séance du 9 mars 1934. Conférence

de MM. Robert Gibrat et Robert Loustau: "Les Problèmes du temps présent dans la doctrine de l'Ordre nouveau. Travail humain et machinisme: l'effort constructif nécessaire"', *X-Crise* May, 6–28. The personalist philosophy that developed at *Ordre nouveau* and *Esprit* was influenced by the Catholic humanism of Emmanuel Mounier but also to some extent by Protestant thinking, notably through Denis de Rougemont, who drew on the work of the Swiss protestant theologian Karl Barth.

76.   Coutrot, *De quoi vivre*, 41–42.
77.   Coutrot, *De quoi vivre*, esp. 42, 91–95.
78.   Coutrot, *Leçons/L'Humanisme économique*, 17–19.
79.   Coutrot, *Leçons/L'Humanisme économique*, 45–46, 69–72.
80.   Coutrot, *Leçons/L'Humanisme économique*, 73.
81.   Coutrot, *Leçons/L'Humanisme économique*, 62.
82.   J. Coutrot. 1937. *Les Méthodes rationnelles, ce qu'elles peuvent apporter à l'activité économique française*, no publisher, 18.
83.   Coutrot, *Leçons/L'Humanisme économique*, 79–80.
84.   Coutrot, *Leçons/L'Humanisme économique*, 51–2, 75–6.
85.   Coutrot, *Leçons/L'Humanisme économique*, 49–51.
86.   Coutrot, *Leçons/L'Humanisme économique*, 93.
87.   Coutrot, *Leçons/L'Humanisme économique*, 93.
88.   Coutrot, *Leçons/L'Humanisme économique*, 93–94. Coutrot's commitment to pro-natalist measures was also set out in the programme which appears inside the back cover of the journal *Humanisme économique*.
89.   I use the term *populationist* rather than *pro-natalist* here following Karen Adler who highlights the extent to which concerns with qualitative as well quantitative aspects of population were present among French pro-natalists. See K. H. Adler. 2003. *Jews and Gender in Liberation France*, Cambridge: Cambridge University Press.
90.   Coutrot, *Leçons/L'Humanisme économique*, 64. On Dubreuil's proposals, see Chapter 2.
91.   Coutrot, *Leçons/L'Humanisme économique*, 60–61.
92.   O. Dard. 2000. 'Du privé au public. Des technocrates en quête d'un état rationnel et à la conquête de l'état républicain dans la France des années trente', in M.-O. Baruch and V. Duclert (dir.), *Serviteurs de l'état. Une histoire politique de l'administration française 1875–1945*, Paris: La Découverte, 491.
93.   On this shift from a financial to a truly economic conception of economic policy, I follow the interpretation of Margairaz, *L'Etat, les finances et l'économie*, esp. 245–46, 315.
94.   See Margairaz, *L'Etat, les finances et l'économie*, 348–50 on the similarities between Spinasse's speech to the senate on 13 August 1936 and a draft document apparently by Coutrot marked 'projet de déclaration au Sénat, 13 août 1936' in AN: 468 AP 15, dr 3.
95.   Margairaz, *L'Etat, les finances et l'économie*, 369–72, 394–98, 414. X-Crise continued to exercise some influence but it was the liberal current represented by Jacques Rueff rather than the planist current represented by Coutrot that was most influential in shaping the economic policy of the Chautemps Government.
96.   On the results and significance of the COST, see Margairaz, *L'Etat, les finances et l'économie*, 352–3, 359–63; For the full range of the Centre's activities see AN: 468 AP 18–20, including 468 AP 18 dr 3 for Coutrot's correspondence with educational institutions and 468 AP 19 dr 5 for the COST radio broadcasts.
97.   AN: 468 AP 20 dr4e Letter from Coutrot to Boverat, 9 February 1938.
98.   AN: 468 AP 20 dr4e Letter of invitation from Y. Henon to Montandon, 3 March 1939. On Montandon's racial theory see Adler, *Jews and Gender*, 123–26.
99.   AN: 468 AP 19 dr5 Causerie 4 March 1939 Radio PTT, 'Dénatalité et naturalisation', 2, 8–10. On interwar racial thinking and its preoccupation with assimilability, see E. Camiscioli. 2001. 'Producing Citizens, Reproducing the "French Race": Immigration, Demography and Pro-natalism in Early Twentieth-century France', *Gender and History* 13(3), 593–621.
100.   Adler, *Jews and Gender*, 85–86.

101. AN: 468 AP 3 dr5 Cutting from J. Coutrot. 1933. 'L'Organisation intégrale du travail humain', *Chantiers coopératifs* March.
102. *De quoi vivre*, 176. Here Coutrot uses the phrase 'moral sciences' but he would more commonly use the expression 'sciences of man'. E.g *Leçons/L'Humanisme économique*, 26–30.
103. J. Herf. 1986. *Reactionary Modernism: Technology, Culture and Politics in Weimar and the Third Reich*, Cambridge: Cambridge University Press, 152–88.
104. Correspondence from Carrel in August 1939 (AN: 468 AP 21 dr3d) suggests that he only took occasional interest in the group's activities and had not been in touch for about a year.
105. See A. Carrel. 1935. *L'Homme, cet inconnu*, Paris: Plon, 359–62.
106. J. Coutrot, 'Mémoire introductif à la recherche collective' in Prélot (ed.), *Entretiens sur les sciences de l'homme*, 2.
107. Teilhard de Chardin was a Jesuit who spent much of his time on scientific expeditions and had participated in Citroën's famous expedition in Central Asia, the Croisière jaune. His manuscript *L'Energie humaine* was studied at a CEPH meeting at Pontigny in 1938. See AN: 468 AP 27 dr4 'Texte des entretiens', 15 June 1938. Further evidence of Teilhard's links with the CEPH can be found in AN: 468 AP 10 dr4d Clipping from *Nouvelle revue française* 1 September 1939 and AN: 468 AP 28 dr4 'Textes des entretiens', 28 May 1939.
108. I depart here from those who have defined the CEPH as a Catholic institute, e.g. Beale, *The Modernist Enterprise*, 9) and O. Henry. 2004. 'De la sociologie comme technologie sociale: la contribution de Jean Coutrot, 1895–1941', *Actes de la recherche en sciences sociales* 3, 48–64, esp. 49, 60–61. Henry rightly notes the participation of a number of Catholic academics (Jean Baruzi, Paul Masson-Oursel and Roger du Teil), but overstates the centrality of Catholicism versus other intellectual ingredients, seeing the scientific organization inherited from Le Chatelier and Fayol simply as an attempt to provide a scientific justification for Catholic thinking.
109. AN: 468 AP 15 dr4a 'Union de la vérité, 1er février. Fin de la réponse', 4. This is the text of a talk given to the Union de la vérité in 1936.
110. AN: 468 AP 27 dr5 'Texte des entretiens', 6 June 1938, 23 and 57–58.
111. See, for example, AN: 468 AP 27 dr5 'Texte des entretiens', 6 June 1938, 18. The distinction between positive and negative eugenics is discussed in W.H. Schneider. 1982. 'Toward the Improvement of the Human Race: The History of Eugenics in France', *Journal of Modern History* 54(2), 268–91.
112. AN: 468 AP 27 dr5 'Texte des entretiens', 6 June 1938, 1–27. Schiff was a socialist and had worked with Edouard Toulouse, whose political sympathies were also on the Left. See A. Ohayon. 2003. 'L'Emergence d'un mouvement sexologique français (1929–1939), entre hygiénisme, eugénisme et psychanalyse', *Psychiatrie, sciences humaines, neurosciences* 1(4), 50–61.
113. As Secretary-General of the medical section of the Association France-Italie, Martiny was responsible for cultivating links with Italian medical institutions.
114. H. Laugier, E. Toulouse and D. Weinberg. 1932. 'La Biotypologie et l'orientation professionnelle', *Biotypologie* 1(1), 27–28.
115. See C. Ipsen. 1996. *Dictating Demography: The Problem of Population in Fascist Italy*, Cambridge: Cambridge University Press, 185–87. Like many French populationists Pende emphasized the role of environmental factors in the improvement of the 'race'.
116. M. Martiny. 1930. *La Biotypologie humaine et orthogénésique. Sa première application clinique et médico-sociale*, Paris: Masson et Cie, 6–7. In the 1930s, Pende also linked these biotypes with racial types. See N. Pende, S Gualco, F. Landogna Cassone. 1933. 'Les Variétés raciales humaines de biotypologie métrique et fonctionnelle des races blanches', *Biotypologie* 1(3), 113–34.
117. Martiny, *La Biotypologie humaine et orthogénésique*, 8–9.
118. AN: 468 AP 23 dr3a Mme Brésard, 'Conditions d'équilibre intérieur de la femme de notre temps', 5–6.

119. The remaining papers in the initial package were *L'Ordre* on Fridays, *L'Œuvre* on Saturdays and *La République* on Sundays, though the exact offering varied. See CEPH. 1938. 'L'Abonnement Arc-en-Ciel', *Humanisme économique* November-December, 57; AN: 468 AP 22 dr2b contains two other undated lists in which *Action française* is replaced by *L'Epoque* or *La Croix*.

120. Published in the U.K. by Routledge in 1940, this book was first published in French as S. Tchakotine. 1939. *Le Viol des foules par la propaganda politique*, Paris: Gallimard. The transliteration of Chakotin's name varies in both French and English.

121. AN: 468 AP 27 dr3 Coutrot, 'Texte des entretiens, 4 juin 1938', 60.

122. Coutrot hoped to recruit 100 000 subscribers to the scheme, though, not surprisingly, the task of weaning the French public from their regular paper was to prove rather more difficult than he had anticipated. On the ambitions for the scheme, see AN: 468 AP 27 dr1 'Texte des entretiens', 2 October 1937, 12 and for an indication of the problems it encountered in practice, see correspondence from subscribers at AN: 468 AP 22 dr2b especially letters from G. Bastien-Soyer, Dr B. Ballet, Dr A. Bergeret and A. Crépet. The archives contain correspondence relating to about a dozen subscribers. Even if this represents only a small proportion of those who took up the subscription, it is difficult to imagine that *Arc-en-ciel* reached a very large audience.

123. Claparède participated in the meeting at Pontigny in October 1937. See AN: 468 AP 27 'Textes des entretiens' 2 October 1937, 119–31. Montessori gave a lecture at the CEPH in late 1936 and later contributed an article to *Humanisme économique*. See J. Coutrot. 1937. 'Notre réunion du 6 juillet', *Humanisme économique* 2 October, 31–32 and M. Montessori. 1938. 'Eduquez pour la paix', *Humanisme économique* 13–14 September-October, 11–16.

124. AN: 468 AP 23 dr5d Letters from Maria Montessori to Jean Coutrot, 9 December 1936 and 10 October 1937.

125. Information on Annette Coutrot and her children's education supplied by her eldest daughter Marie Coutrot Toulouse, interviewed 2 August 1996.

126. AN: 468 AP 27 'Textes des entretiens' 2 October 1937, 120–22.

127. AN: 468 AP 27 'Textes des entretiens' 2 October 1937, 130.

128. Montessori, 'Eduquez pour la paix', 11–13. See also M. Montessori. 1932. *Peace and Education*, Geneva: International Bureau of Education.

129. AN: 468 AP 23 'Séance du 25 janvier 1939'. See also AN: 468 AP 28 dr4 'Texte des entretiens', 28 May 1939 (morning session), 52.

130. 468 AP 18 dr3c Letter from Paul Béard (Head of the Lille School) to Jean Coutrot 19 May 1938. AN: 468 AP 21dr1a contains a publicity text destined for *X-Crise* and another – 'Ne manque-t-il rien à votre documentation?' for *Méthodes*. *Méthodes* dealt mainly with questions of administrative organization and was run by Thérèse Leroy, one of the few female members of the CNOF.

131. Prélot (ed.), *Entretiens sur les sciences de l'homme*, 5. AN: 468 AP 27 dr1 'Texte des entretiens', 2 October 1937, 90; Centre d'étude des problèmes humains. 1938. 'Annexe au procès-verbal de l'Assemblée générale du 12 janvier. Exposé succinct de l'activité du CEPH durant l'année 1937', *Humanisme économique* February, 14; Sauvy participated notably in the discussion that followed a talk by fellow X-Crise member André Lochard – see A. Lochard. 1939. 'Le Problème des races et du métissage', *Humanisme économique* March-April, 123–4.

132. Centre d'étude des problèmes humains. 1938. 'Annexe au procès-verbal', *Humanisme économique* February, 14.

133. Planus made donations to CEPH funds and used his influence to try to secure contributions from industrialists. See AN: 468 AP 21 dr7c Letter from Paul Planus to Pierre Aubé 1 July 1939 and AN: 468 AP 23 dr6b Letter of 20 September 1938.

134. Yves Colombat was an *ingénieur-conseil en vente et publicité* (Sales and Advertising Consultant) who worked for the Fédération des corps de l'état et des administrations publiques and for the Confédération générale des cadres dans l'économie française. AN: 468 AP 22dr4c Letter from Colombat to CEPH 28 February 1939.

135. Bacqueyrisse did not figure prominently in the CEPH but a record of his subscription of July 1939 can be found at AN: 468 AP 21 dr3c.

136. AN: 468 AP 23 dr5d Promotional letter from Arthus, undated, 2. See also H. Arthus. 1939. *Section d'éducation active de l'Eveil, mouvement pour l'évolution individuelle et sociale*, Paris: Eveil.

137. This project was set out in H. Arthus. 1937. *Le Travail vivant*, Paris: Editions Oliven, in the Eveil *Publications mensuelles* and in a series of bulletins also bearing the title *Le Travail vivant*.

138. Arthus, *L'Eveil. Publications mensuelles* No.8, 113. Emphasis in original.

139. AN: 468 AP 27 dr3 'Texte des entretiens', 4 June 1938, 10.

140. AN: 468 AP 23 dr5d Dr H. Arthus, 'Les Sciences de l'homme et ce qu'on peut en attendre', 4.

141. AN: 468 AP 23 dr5c P. Masson-Oursel, 'Institut de psychologie appliquée. Consultations d'efficience'.

142. See M. Thomson. 2006. *Psychological Subjects: Identity, Culture and Health in Twentieth-Century Britain*, Oxford: Oxford University Press, 23–26.

143. E.g. Various articles on memory in *La Psychologie et la vie* February 1936; issue on 'L'Art de se créer des relations' January 1937, issue on 'Les Méthodes pour développer la volonté' February 1937, issue on 'Comment former de bons collaborateurs' and 'Les Conducteurs d'hommes' March-April 1938 in which Coutrot contributed an article on 'L'Art de conduire les hommes', 60–62. J. Fontègne. 1927. 'Bulletin d'orientation professionnelle. Orientation professionnelle et accidents de travail', *La Psychologie et la vie* April, 14–16; E. Claparède. 1928. 'Problèmes de psychologie pratique. Le Témoignage', *La Psychologie et la vie* June, 103–5; C. Baudouin. 1936. 'De l'observation à l'intuition', *La Psychologie et la vie* March, 59–61.

144. P. Masson-Oursel. 1932. 'Economies de temps et d'effort', *Mon Bureau* 23(NS 17), 307–8; P. Masson-Oursel. 1932. 'Le Surménage', *Mon Bureau* 23(NS 18), 351–2.

145. L. Boltanski. 1982. *Les Cadres: la formation d'un groupe social*, Paris: Minuit, esp. 186 on the example of Jean-Louis Servan-Schreiber.

146. For a detailed discussion of the contradictory effects of the Depression on the rationalization of French industry, see A. Moutet. 1997. *Les Logiques de l'entreprise: la rationalisation dans l'industrie française de l'entre-deux-guerres*, Paris: Editions de l'EHESS, 197–336. Corporate membership of the CNOF fell from 234 companies in 1929 to 103 in 1931, though it subsequently recovered (Moutet, *Les Logiques*, 206).

147. Herf, *Reactionary Modernism*, 8.

148. Margairaz, *L'Etat, les finances et l'économie*, 319.

Chapter 5

ORGANIZATION IN VICHY FRANCE

In June 1940 France was defeated by Hitler's invading army and an armistice was signed. The country was divided into several zones, the northern half and the Atlantic coast being occupied by Germany, while a southern zone was (until November 1942) left free from occupying forces. On 10 July 1940 parliament voted full powers to Marshal Philippe Pétain and the authoritarian regime known as the Vichy Government was born. The new regime drew its personnel from a variety of quarters and included military officers (General Weygand, Admiral Darlan), a few former parliamentarians (Pierre Laval, Pierre-Etienne Flandin) and a wide range of professional experts, from the agricultural economist Pierre Caziot at the Ministry of Agriculture, to the former tennis-player Jean Borotra, who served as Commissioner for Sport. Technicians from industry, engineering and the upper echelons of public administration were also prominent. Thus, for example, Yves Bouthillier, a graduate of the Ecole centrale and an Inspector of Finance, became Minister of Finance in 1940, while the *polytechnicien* and railway engineer Jean Berthelot became Minister of Communications. Another *polytechnicien*, Jean Bichelonne, served at the Ministry of Industrial Production, first as Secretary General and then, from April 1942, as Secretary of State, succeeding the Renault executive François Lehideux and Pierre Pucheu from the steel industry's Comité des forges in the latter role.[1] In the absence of elections and political parties, technical competence was arguably an even more important badge of legitimacy than it had been under the Third Republic. Certainly, in the atmosphere of crisis that followed the defeat, the Vichy Government sought to position itself as above politics and the appointment of 'experts' was one way of signalling this.[2]

While this was clearly a moment of political rupture, there were also notable elements of continuity. The appointment of figures from the world of engineering and industry to ministerial posts was not new in itself, particularly in war time or its aftermath. Louis Loucheur and Raoul Dautry had already served in such circumstances under the Third Republic (the latter having been appointed as Minister of Armaments in the Daladier Government in September 1939). Moreover, figures like Bouthillier and Bichelonne were already senior officials advising ministers when France fell. Bichelonne was brought into Dautry's armaments ministry as *Directeur de cabinet*, after working on various projects for the Ministry of Public Works in the late 1930s. Interwar organizers like Alfred Sauvy often spoke (at the time and retrospectively) as if they were largely ignored by their contemporaries, but there was less of a gap between the world of politicians and that of technicians than such accounts suggest. Technicians had access to politicians throughout the interwar period through centres like the Comité national d'organisation française (CNOF), Redressement français and X-Crise and, as previous chapters have noted, they were called on by governments at various points to rationalize public administration, advise on economic policy and promote scientific organization as a national cause. Vichy did not invent government by experts then, but it did give it a less democratic and more authoritarian form.

One feature of the Vichy Government was the proliferation of committees, consultative councils and study groups that emerged under it. Organization Committees with representatives of business and the state were set up to coordinate production within each branch of industry, while in central government bodies like the Conseil consultatif du Centre d'information inter-professionnel (Consultative Council of the Business Information Centre), the Conseil supérieur de l'économie industrielle et commerciale (Higher Council for the Industrial and Commercial Economy) and the Délégation générale de l'équipement national (General Delegation for National Infrastructure) acted as internal policy think tanks. Alexis Carrel's government-funded research institute, the Fondation française pour l'étude des problèmes humains, functioned partly as a policy-generating body and provided personnel to staff other government committees. Technicians also met in a less official capacity on the Comité d'études pour la France which was in many ways an extension of the interwar technicians' networks. Indeed, many of the figures discussed in earlier chapters participated in one or more of the above bodies. Auguste Detoeuf, for example, served as head of the Organization Committee for the electrical construction industry, as well as on the Conseil supérieur de l'économie industrielle et commerciale, the Consultative Committee of the Délégation générale de l'équipement national, and the Comité d'études pour la France. The latter committee included several of Detoeuf's colleagues from *Les Nouveaux Cahiers*, notably Jacques Barnaud (also a veteran of X-Crise), who became Delegate General for Franco-German Economic Relations in the Darlan Government formed in February 1941.[3] Similarly, several members of the Comité central de l'organisation professionnelle (CCOP), including Detoeuf, served on the board of the Ecole supérieure d'organisation professionnelle, which was built on the foundations of the school created by the CCOP in the wake of the reforms of 1936, but now had a remit to educate *cadres* for the Organization Committees.[4] Lucien Romier, who had initially refused a position at Vichy, joined the regime after the dismissal of Pierre Laval in December 1940 and became one of Pétain's most trusted advisors, acting as his liaison point with the economic ministries and coordinating policy areas such as economy, finance and agriculture within the marshal's entourage.[5] A Minister of State from August 1941, he also chaired several commissions at another Vichy advisory body, the Conseil national. Meanwhile, Gérard Bardet, who had been a member of the CNOF, X-Crise and the Centre d'études des problèmes humains (CEPH) in the 1930s, took up a series of roles on the Conseil consultatif du Centre d'information interprofessionnel, on the Conseil supérieur de l'économie industrielle et commerciale and on the Conseil supérieur du travail.

Not all the technicians discussed in earlier chapters took the same path in 1940. Sometimes it was contingency which intervened, as in the case of Jean Coutrot who died in May 1941, before he could take up the offer of a job as head of the Commission du plan comptable (National Accounting Commission).[6] Earlier, in September 1940, Coutrot had made contact with the Ministry of Industrial Production, indicating that he was prepared to serve Pétain's government.[7] But his premature death reminds us that there was nothing inevitable about the paths that individual lives took in what have become known as the 'dark years'. In contrast, some of those associated with the interwar organization movement made a conscious choice not to work with Vichy. Dautry, who had been called on to serve as Minister for Armaments in 1939, withdrew from public life after the defeat, returning only at the Liberation. It appears that, unlike his fellow Catholic engineer Georges Lamirand, who served as Minister of Youth from 1940 to 1943, he was not seduced by the opportunity to promote Catholic social thinking at Vichy.[8] For Henri Laugier, a member of the Republican scientific establishment, the choice was perhaps more clear cut. Abandoning his work science laboratory, he fled to England in June 1940 and spent time in the U.S.A. and Canada before joining de Gaulle in Algiers in 1943. In the same year, his fellow work scientist Jean-Maurice Lahy died of ill health having been removed from his post because he was a freemason.

Nonetheless, a number of organizers, particularly those from engineering and industry, did choose to work within the new regime. What was it, then, that animated these technicians at Vichy? What projects did they pursue? And how did the organization agenda that had developed between the wars evolve in the new political context of Vichy France? I do not try to provide a comprehensive answer to these questions here but address them primarily by tracing the trajectories of certain people, projects and currents of thinking that had emerged in the interwar period. Readers dipping into this chapter without having read other parts of the book may therefore find it useful to refer back to earlier chapters for further information on particular individuals or to consult the short biographical profiles provided at the end of the volume for quick reference.

Vichy and The Myth of Technocracy

The role of technicians at Vichy has generally been considered in terms of a narrative about 'modernization' and the 'rise of technocracy'. Since at least the 1970s, the historiography has emphasized the tensions between 'modernizing' and 'traditionalist' currents within the regime, identifying the technicians who staffed the economic ministries as the prime movers in the former category.[9] Modernism in this context has tended to mean rationalization, a concern with productivity and efficiency, a commitment to planning and *dirigisme*, and in more general terms a vision of France's future as an industrial one. In contrast, 'traditionalists' have been identified with social and moral objectives such as the defence of 'natural communities' (family, church, profession, region), the reassertion of the patriarchal family, the cult of the peasant and the artisan. The mythologization of the 'technocrat' – embodied notably in the emblematic figure of Jean Bichelonne – has served to reinforce this distinction, positioning technicians as above politics and distant from the regime's endeavours to create a new social order. This mythologization is most apparent in the anecdotes about Bichelonne's computer-like brain which have become a staple of historical writing about him. We are told, for example, that he reputedly had no need for a telephone book as he carried 2,500 telephone numbers in his head.[10] Another story relates Bichelonne's response to an alleged German plan to dismantle the Eiffel Tower for scrap metal: the *polytechnicien* is said to have spontaneously reassured Laval that the tower only weighed 7,175,000 kilograms.[11]

One is reminded here of Roland Barthes's analysis of the fetishization of the scientific brain in France in the 1950s in *Mythologies*. Noting how the brain of Einstein was subjected to tests and measurements, both in life and in death, in an effort to explain the nature of 'scientific genius', Barthes writes: '[P]aradoxically, the greatest intelligence of all provides an image of the most up-to-date machine, the man who is too powerful is removed from psychology, and introduced into a world of robots; as is well known, the supermen of science-fiction always have something reified about them.'[12] Something similar is surely going on in the historiographical transmission of stories about Bichelonne's prodigious head for figures. Combined with recurring remarks about his political naivety,[13] these anecdotes leave us with an impression of the technician as something close to an autistic savant, operating on a purely mathematical plain quite alien to ordinary mortals. Bichelonne may indeed have had exceptional credentials as a mathematician but what is significant about the way this image of the technician-as-machine functions in the historiography of Vichy is that it casts Bichelonne not just as an individual but as a type: the archetypal technocrat.[14] It is in this sense that such narratives constitute a mythologization.

One of the problems with the myth of the technician as an apolitical machine is that it obscures the true scope and nature of the organization projects that technicians espoused. It also distances them from Vichy's moral and social reordering projects, which are seen to be ideological rather than technical and at odds with the technicians' commitment to 'modernization'. Individuals and their actions are understood in this analysis as the embodiment of predefined models of tradition and modernity, and hence, implicitly at least, as expressions of abstract historical forces. But both the National Revolution (the name given to Pétain's domestic reordering project) and the forms of organization that came to be identified with the term 'modernization' in postwar France were products of a set of debates and experiments that took place before and during the Occupation. A host of projects for social and economic reorganization were formulated by official and unofficial bodies in Vichy France, addressing issues such as how to institutionalize class collaboration (and on whose terms), how to reconstruct the economy or how to renovate rural life. It is this Vichy – the Vichy of projects and proposals, of advisory groups and planning committees – and the technicians' place within it that is foregrounded in this chapter.

The preceding chapters have shown that while organizers were concerned with technical problems they did not see the technical as a narrowly circumscribed field that was separate from the question of what makes a good society. Rather, they tended to believe that all problems could (potentially at least) be configured as technical or scientific problems. Science in this context meant not just the disciplines of engineering and mathematics but the social and biological sciences – the 'sciences of man'. It was at the intersection of these fields that scientific organization and economic planning had developed in interwar France. This concern with what had come to be called 'human problems' continued under Vichy. It also evolved in a number of ways in response to the social, economic and political circumstances of the Occupation. In mapping these developments this chapter shows how technicians were drawn to Vichy not just by the opportunity to promote economic *dirigisme* but by their aspirations to eliminate class conflict and to cultivate productive minds and bodies. There were a number of overlapping and competing visions of a scientifically organized society in Vichy France and one of the features of the regime was the power it gave, not just to engineers, but also to doctors. This privileged position of medical science was to have significant implications for the organization of work. Moreover, a number of the initiatives that developed during the Vichy years were to have a lasting impact on the postwar order.

Organisation professionnelle and Economic *Dirigsme*

It was noted in Chapter Two that *organisation professionnelle* was a significant preoccupation within the organization movement in the late 1930s but meant different things to different people: the term was used to cover arrangements for collaboration among businesses as well as the organization of relations between capital and labour. The first incarnation of *organisation professionnelle* to emerge at Vichy was a response to the chaos caused by the invasion and defeat of summer 1940, when the first priority was to get the economy working effectively again. To this end, the law of 16 August 1940 created the Organization Committees to coordinate production, provide structures for dealing with scarcity in a context where the market could not function normally, and forestall German control of the French economy. The Committees were tasked with carrying out a census of the plant, manpower and stocks in their own branch of industry and with establishing a programme of production.[15] The law of 10 September 1940 created a government office, headed by Bichelonne, to coordinate the distribution of raw materials (Office central de répartition des produits industriels, OCRPI).[16] The Centre d'information inter-professionnel (hereafter CII) was created by decree on 30 April 1941, replacing the employers' union, the CGPF, and was assigned the role of providing economic, financial, fiscal and legal documentation to the Organization Committees.[17] In this capacity, it was one of several bodies that gathered data related to industrial production and continued the efforts of interwar planners to develop better industrial statistics.

These were crisis measures and on a day-to-day basis these institutions dealt with a host of practical and logistical problems such as shortages, recurring power cuts and poor communication across different zones.[18] But they also reflected the longer-term demand for an organized economy that had grown among a section of France's elite in the interwar years. As one of the architects of this organizational infrastructure, Bichelonne articulated his vision in terms very similar to those of the interwar movements, arguing that the 'ensemble économique' required coordination in order to operate rationally.[19] Echoing the language that had already been used at Redressement français in the late 1920s, he spoke of a 'natural' development away from individualism towards 'solidarity', the latter term covering everything from relations among businesses to the interdependence of price, salaries, income and tax as factors in economic management.[20] A significant difference between the Organization Committees and the voluntary agreements among producers that had been promoted by groups like Redressement français and the CCOP between the wars was that during the Occupation organization was imposed by the state. Moreover, for Bichelonne, the state's role in coordinating economic activity through the distribution of raw materials was not just a temporary measure but the fulfilment of an inevitable evolution towards 'a durable form of managed economy [*économie dirigée*]'.[21] But this *dirigiste* model remained distinct from a state-run economy and Bichelonne argued that private enterprise remained the true motor of economic activity.[22]

The system that emerged from the legislation passed in 1940 was one that gave considerable power to organized business. Though not entirely dominated by the *grand patronat*, the Committees did tend to be led by representatives of the larger firms in any given branch of industry and workers had no representation.[23] These structures also fostered industrial concentration, since inefficient businesses could be closed and scarce resources directed to more efficient (often larger) producers. Nonetheless, if private industry was in many ways the dominant partner in this state–business relationship, Hervé Joly has suggested that it might be more accurate to speak of an imbrication of private industry and 'state technocracy' in the Organization Committees, since a significant part of France's industrial elite shared the same educational background as its senior administrative elite, the Ecole polytechnique being a common pathway into both sectors. Indeed, some industrial leaders (like Detoeuf who was a member of the *Corps des ponts et chaussées*) had also served as state engineers. The proportion of *polytechniciens* in the leadership of the Organization Committees varied from one sector to another but was particularly significant in those industries that traditionally recruited heavily from the Ecole: 24.8 per cent of appointments to the Mining Committee, 46 per cent of those to the Steel Industry Committee and over 83 per cent of those to the Electrical Energy Committee, for example, were *polytechniciens*.[24] This shared background, along with the significance of *polytechniciens* in disseminating the organization agenda in the years prior to 1940, can only have facilitated the establishment of these new structures of economic organization.

In the context of Nazi occupation, economic organization also meant collaboration. Throughout the war, the French economy operated under increasing pressure from Germany for raw materials, goods and manpower, forcing businesses to decide how far they were prepared to work for Germany in order to survive.[25] The state sought to interpose itself in this relationship between businesses and the occupying power in the hope of coordinating and controlling the process of collaboration. This was the rationale for Barnaud's appointment as head of the Delgate General for Franco-German Relations under Darlan and then as Minister (Secrétaire d'état) for Franco-German Relations following the return of Laval in April 1942. The spirit of organization and the desire for systematization were apparent here, but this policy was also motivated by a concern to maintain French sovereignty and to make economic collaboration a matter of governmental negotiation in the hope of gaining political concessions – a hope which proved rather futile.[26]

Among the technicians who ran Organization Committees, distributed raw materials and negotiated contracts to supply Germany with goods and materials vital to its war effort, it was widely assumed, at least until 1942, that Germany was going to win the war and that France must adapt to the new economic order that this implied.[27] Serving the German economy was seen as a way of preserving French economic activity. But economic collaboration also went beyond this preservationist logic, especially under Bichelonne. In July 1943, in the face of mounting demands for workers to be deported to Germany, Bichelonne made France's most ambitious proposal to date for industrial collaboration, offering to commit a further 215,000 workers in France to armaments production for the German war effort and to increase production by a margin which exceeded Germany's own productivity targets for the French war economy.[28] This was part of a strategy to maintain and develop French industry by securing exemption from the labour draft for factories producing for the German war economy and in September 1943 Bichelonne and the German Armaments Minister, Albert Speer, formalized an agreement to this effect. Far from being just a deal to protect French workers and factories, however, this agreement articulated a shared vision of France's role at the heart of a planned European economy led by Germany.[29]

Organizers had long been interested in international economic cooperation and for this reason Bichelonne appears to have seen Nazism as an opportunity as well as a threat. This may explain in part why he remained a minister until the bitter end of the Vichy regime, though others made different choices. Barnaud resigned in November 1942, following the German occupation of the southern zone, while some interwar advocates of Franco-German economic rapprochement such as Ernest Mercier were resolutely opposed to collaboration with Hitler and kept their distance from the regime from the start.[30] These were political choices of course, despite the professed apoliticism of technicians. The technical work of the economic ministries also involved political choices, whether technicians acknowledged it or not. This has become particularly apparent as a result of recent research on the expropriation of Jews, a policy first introduced by Germany in the occupied zone, but rapidly assumed by Vichy (across both zones) with the creation of the Commissariat général aux questions Juives (CGQJ) in 1941. At the Ministry of Industrial Production 'aryanization' of Jewish property was integrated into the policy of industrial rationalization. Officials positioned themselves as advisors on the rational application of the laws and in October 1942 Bichelonne himself advocated that businesses be liquidated, where possible, under the laws on 'aryanization' rather than the law of 17 December 1941 on industrial and commercial concentration, on the grounds that this would facilitate concentration without the need to pay compensation.[31] It was this type of instrumental reasoning and disregard for human consequences that earned Bichelonne his reputation as the archetypal technocratic machine.

Organisation professionnelle and Class Collaboration

While the questions of economic *dirigisme* and collaboration have dominated accounts of the 'rise of technocracy' at Vichy, technicians were also involved in the discussions that shaped the social dimensions of *organisation professionnelle*. The case of Gérard Bardet, who worked in close partnership with Bichelonne, is particularly revealing in this respect. The organization of social relations became the object of prolonged internal debate at Vichy, following Pétain's speech at St Etienne on 1 March 1941. Written by Robert Loustau (a veteran of X-Crise and the *Plan du 9 juillet*), the speech espoused the creation of tri-partite Workplace Social Committees (composed of employers, technicians and workers) as the centrepiece of the regime's efforts to create a new work community.[32] In a series of notes written in April and May 1941 (as he began his tenure as head of the Consultative Council of the CII) Bardet also identified the business as the fundamental unit or 'elementary cell' of the new social organization and argued that workplace committees should be consulted on economic as well as social matters.[33] He proposed that skilled workers, white-collar staff and employers should be represented on these committees but unskilled workers and investors should not, on the grounds that neither possessed the sense of *métier* or shared trade that was central to this vision of class collaboration.[34] What Bardet envisaged was a work community based on technical competence – this was the most effective basis for social organization, he claimed, because technical superiority was the only form of hierarchy that would be voluntarily accepted by all.[35]

This sense that competence is an objective quality, that science is universal and that it is, or will be, the object of social consensus was typical of the organizers' worldview and gave a particularly technicist inflection to the proposal for social committees. Bardet's ostensibly meritocratic proposals reflected his self-identification, not just as an employer, but as an engineer, something that he made clear when he reviewed his first six months of service at Vichy in November 1941. Noting that as head of a machine tool manufacturing firm, he was still able to design new machines himself and would sometimes dabble in engineering tasks for pleasure, he recounted that he had been 'naturally led to the notion of solidarity which unifies all members of the same collectivity' because in his trade 'those who study, those who build and those who perfect are associated in a single *oeuvre*.'[36] There was no acknowledgement here that Bardet's proposals actually sought to divide the working class into those who were deemed fit to have a voice in the business and those were not (with women and immigrants likely to be overrepresented in the category of the 'unskilled'). As in his prewar experiments with workers' delegates in his own factory (discussed in Chapter Two), the authority of management to run the business was not questioned, but informing and consulting the personnel was seen as a means of educating them and strengthening their identification of their own interests with those of the firm. Indeed, a new edition of Bardet's account of this managerial experiment (which had anticipated the reforms of the Popular Front) appeared in 1941 in a collective volume entitled *Hommes et métiers*.[37]

Most of the currents of opinion represented at Vichy espoused some form of organization of producers as part of the new social and economic order, illustrating the centrality of organization as a rallying point for those who believed they could banish or transcend ideological conflict. Those participating in the debate about how to construct a new work community included such opposing camps as the Minister of Labour, René Belin, an anti-communist trade unionist from the Confédération générale du travail (CGT), the Minister of Justice, Raphaël Alibert (a lawyer from the anti-parliamentary Right who had been a member of Redressement français in the late 1920s), and Pierre Nicolle, a leader of the lobby for small and medium-sized businesses who had opposed the Matignon Agreement in 1936. Belin tried to promote a neo-syndicalist vision of the organized profession, proposing, for example, to give workers' representatives a consultative role on the Organization Committees, but this and Bardet's suggestion that workplace committees should consider both economic and social matters were rejected by the more conservative business leaders and ministers who sought to limit the role of workers.[38] When a Charter of Labour eventually emerged from these debates in October 1941, it made provision for an array of local, regional and national institutions including unions, corporations and 'professional families', as well as the anticipated social committees – a mix which reflected the difficulty of establishing consensus around a single model of organization.[39] But the Workplace Social Committees remained the centrepiece of the system, bringing together workers, employers and *cadres* to run social services and provide a forum for discussion of issues related to pay and conditions. The prewar trade union confederations had been dissolved by this point and the Charter made it compulsory to be a member of a single official union in each industry, while further disarming the labour movement by outlawing strikes and lock outs.

Although Bardet's proposals were not taken up in the Charter of Labour, he went on to wage a lengthy campaign within government to reform the institutions of social and economic organization, winning the support of Bichelonne in the process. This began at the Consultative Council of the CII which operated like a policy think tank, exploring a range of social and economic issues that exceeded the strict remit of the CII itself. This reflected one of Bardet's central criticisms of the institutions created by the Charter of Labour and the Law of 16 August 1940 – that they created an artificial separation between economic and social questions.[40] One of his initial solutions to this was to propose that the CII become the liaison body for both the Organization Committees and the Social Committees.[41] Later, in June 1943, as head of the Conseil supérieur de l'économie industrielle et commerciale (CSEIC), he recommended to Bichelonne that a Tripartite Council (mirroring the tripartite structure of the Social Committees) be constituted to work with the Organization Committee for each industry, giving workers the consultative role in economic matters that he had advocated since 1941. He argued that tripartite bodies such as the Social Committees were the only bodies that truly represented the profession, and that it made little sense to draw a line between social and economic questions in delineating their sphere of competence: 'How can one forbid professionals who meet in a union or in a Social Committee to envisage the economic repercussions of the problem of apprenticeship or of salary issues? How can we ask them to manage social institutions without knowledge of the economic situation?'[42] Bichelonne, who himself had made similar statements about the natural unity of the social and the economic, implemented Bardet's proposal in the brief period (November 1943 to March 1944) when he was both Minister of Labour and Minister of Industrial Production.[43] Indeed, although Bichelonne is remembered primarily as the architect of Vichy's economic *dirigisme*, he also acted as Bardet's principal sponsor as the latter promoted his vision of a new work community – it was Bichelonne who gave Bardet's schemes a new lease of life when he appointed him to the CSEIC (and later to the Conseil supérieur du travail), after his predecessor, Lehideux, had threatened to curb Bardet's ambitions by disbanding the Consultative Council of the CII.[44]

The employer-organizers who had taken an interest in the organization of class collaboration in the late 1930s also played their part in shaping the operation of Social Committees on the ground. Under the leadership of Detoeuf, the Commission générale de l'organisation scientifique du travail (CEGOS), now a semi-governmental body, partially integrated into the CII, ran training sessions for employers and managers on Social Committees and how to create them.[45] Jacques Warnier, a member of both the CCOP and the Centre des jeunes patrons (CJP) in the late 1930s, served as President of the central office created to support the Social Committees and contributed to the training offered by the CEGOS, as well as that of other organizations like the Centre de formation sociale des cadres de l'industrie et du commerce (Centre for Social Training of Industrial and Commercial Managers). Like Bardet, Warnier endorsed the workplace committees as the beginning of a new form of work community, arguing that a business was not just a moral and economic entity but a community based on technical competence in which everyone contributed their skills to a common task.[46] Recognizing that to be effective the committees needed to enjoy credibility among the workforce, he advised that delegates must be nominated or elected by their peers. Unlike some of his fellow businessmen, he was also prepared to accept that prewar delegates and union members were still recognized by their colleagues as authoritative voices and he advised employers preparing to set up a committee to liaise with them.[47]

In fact, as Jean-Claude Daumas has demonstrated, the Social Committees turned out to be one of the Vichy Government's more successful initiatives, as they were broadly accepted by employers, a few of whom had even set up their own committees ahead of the legislation. As a result, the number of Social Committees grew rapidly from 372 in January 1942 to 4,644 in January 1943, 7,807 in January 1944 and around 9,000 by

May of the same year.[48] The committees were compulsory in businesses of one hundred employees or more and by January 1944 about 60 per cent of these employers were complying with the law, while a significant number of smaller businesses had also set up Social Committees even though they were not obliged to do so.[49] After initial reticence among some employers, Warnier's arguments about the need for workers' delegates to be selected by their peers won out and elections became commonplace.[50] Thus, the Social Committees do appear to have had some success in institutionalizing consultation between management and workers, as well as establishing a social model where labour rights were codified, provision of social services was centrally coordinated and workers had a role in the management of social provision.[51] During the Occupation, the willingness of employers to accept all this was built on the defeat of organized labour, but much of it would remain in place in the Comités d'entreprise which became an established part of French labour law and business practice after the war, when trade union freedoms were restored. While figures like Bardet and Warnier cannot take credit for this, their endeavours in promoting their own version of the National Revolution did help ensure that the reformist vision of *organisation professionnelle* was not completely marginalized during the Occupation.

Dubreuil, Bernège and the Scientific Organization Movement in Vichy France

Not all the organizers who chose to work within the framework of the new regime were quite so close to the corridors of power as those discussed above. Hyacinthe Dubreuil, for example, spent the Occupation years not in the ministries of the new government but as a publicist for the values of the National Revolution. The former mechanic and trade-unionist, whose preoccupation with the organization of a new work community had taken him from the CGT to the International Labour Office before the war, now became a Commissioner of the Secours national, an official welfare organization whose campaigns resonated with the regime's politics of *travail, famille, patrie*.[52]

In *La Chevalerie du travail* (1942), Dubreuil compared Pétain to a knight who had come to protect a suffering France.[53] Like many in this period he spoke in terms of a moral crisis afflicting the nation and of a need to construct a new moral order based on work and on the values of solidarity rather than individualism. Likening industrial workers to nomads, he contrasted their purely contractual ties to their work with the peasants' attachment to the land.[54] Indeed, while the idea of recreating a lost sense of community had been accompanied in Dubreuil's earlier work by a strong commitment to decentralization and worker autonomy, a clear acceptance of hierarchy appeared in his wartime writing. This was naturalized by reference to the model of the patriarchal family: 'Given that every social organization must be constituted on the model of the family', he wrote, 'every leader must correspond to the model of the father.'[55] Moreover, while Dubreuil shared Bardet's criticism of the separation of economic and social organization under the Organization Committees and the Labour Charter,[56] he now publicly accepted the Charter's provisions on obligatory membership in a single union – a clear departure from the spirit of his earlier vision of an industrial democracy based on autonomous groups. He did argue that such top-down compulsion would be necessary only in the initial phase of organization in order to instil the appropriate fraternal spirit and, to this extent, clung to some remnants of his earlier outlook.[57] Yet the alternative social world he had once hoped to achieve by fostering worker education and responsibility in the workplace now appeared to have receded into a rather distant future, while, for the present, a more authoritarian solution had become acceptable.

Like Bardet's, therefore, Dubreuil's work with Vichy was driven by a preoccupation with the organization of non-conflictual social relations. In this respect his trajectory was similar to that of Belin or the syndicalist Hubert Lagardelle, who succeeded Belin as Minister of Labour.[58] In 1938, Dubreuil had not only denounced Marxism as a foreign doctrine but told workers that they should not rely on 'parliamentary chatter' to further their agenda.[59] In *La Fin des monstres* (also 1938), the 'monsters' Dubreuil wished to cut down to size included not just the sprawling factory, but liberal democracy and the modern state.[60] Dubreuil's rejection of Marxism and desire to foster class collaboration thus lay at the heart of all his engagements from the 1920s to the 1940s: what changed during the later 1930s was his faith in the French labour movement and his assessment of the prospect of winning the country's workers over to his point of view. As a result, he was among the most pessimistic of organizers by the late 1930s, driven by a deep sense of crisis even before the war broke out.

This did not, however, imply a retreat from the scientific organization movement. During the Occupation, Dubreuil maintained his links with the CNOF, for example, serving on the group's executive committee and teaching at its school, and he continued to cast his ideas in terms that were familiar to members of the movement, justifying corporatist structures as a form of 'rational organization of human solidarity'.[61] Addressing a meeting of the CNOF on 19 January 1942, he urged his colleagues to recognize the role that they had to play in the new order: 'since a new organization of the country is what is being prepared', he argued, 'it is important that this organization is permeated as far as possible with scientific method, as defined by the founders of the CNOF'.[62] Moreover, he was by no means the only figure to urge members of the movement to see the defeat and the advent of the National Revolution as an opportunity. In November 1940, the President of the CNOF, Robert Lelong, claimed that even those previously considered averse to the movement's message had now recognized, in the face of defeat, that 'We must organize France'.[63]

This reading of defeat as a failure of organization was clearly a key factor in the motivation of organizers to continue their work in Vichy France. The activities of the movement in this period became inflected by the priorities and ideological orientation of the regime but still embraced a range of approaches. The CEGOS, for example, ran lectures for managers and business leaders not only on the new structures of professional organization but also on topics ranging from accounting methods and the calculation of unit costs, to personnel management and industrial psychology. In 1942 the former CEPH member Marcel Martiny, who served as a *chargé de mission* at the Ministry of Labour under Lagardelle, gave a talk on 'Medicine and Psychotechnics' in which he advocated once again the methods of the Italian school of biotypology led by Pende, with its four fixed biotypes and its emphasis on morphology and the role of the sex glands in determining personality. Martiny was applying these methods during the Occupation in the medical selection of apprentices for the Paris Chamber of Commerce.[64] However, other currents, closer to Lahy's aptitude testing or to the management of human relations developed by social engineers in the 1930s, were also present in the programme, especially by 1943.[65] Laugier's Biometrics Laboratory also continued its work, now under the leadership of Henri Piéron (with whom Laugier had founded the Institut national d'orientation professionnelle in 1928). Having been converted into a state-funded facility in the late 1930s, the lab now received funds from Vichy to screen applicants for technical schools and develop selection tests and training for the personnel of Air France, using methods similar to those developed by Lahy and Laugier between the wars.[66]

At the CNOF too a variety of currents and methods were still represented but a shift towards questions which reflected government preoccupations was apparent. The Committee's wartime bulletins suggest that it often walked a difficult line, on the one hand emphasizing the extent to which its own ethos of rational organization and social peace was in tune with the official discourse and on the other implicitly acknowledging that not everyone at Vichy saw the scientific organization methods as part of this agenda. A new commission on Fayolism surely reflected the renewed interest in questions of leadership, for example, while a commission on urban planning was asked to pay particular attention to 'rural and regional planning [*urbanisme rural et régional*], always from the point of view of scientific organization', this last phrase implying an awareness of competing visions of rural and regional organization.[67]

One person who took up this challenge of considering rural life in the light of scientific organization was Paulette Bernège, who, along with Maurice Ponthière, helped to reconstitute a branch of the CNOF in Toulouse in 1940. Bernège had already done some work on rural organization before the war, publishing a series of articles on farming in the *Dépêche de Toulouse* in 1933. She had recommended the development of cooperatives as the best strategy for French agriculture, arguing that this would facilitate access to new farming technologies and improve the efficiency of agricultural production, while retaining the social benefits of the family farm.[68] She was not alone among organizers in this respect – Le Corbusier, too, had developed plans for a rationally designed farm (*la ferme radieuse*) and a cooperative village in the 1930s, displaying some of this work at the 1937 World Fair.[69] When war broke out, Bernège fled south (like many of her compatriots), returning to what she called her 'little corner of the land of her birth' in the countryside between Agen and Marmande, where she remained throughout the Occupation.[70] Here, she continued to publish studies on rural organization and domestic science, contributing both to *Produire*, the publication of the CNOF Toulouse group, and to *Éducation ménagère* which was relaunched in January 1943.[71] But her work also took on a new dimension as she became acutely concerned with what she saw as a damaging gulf between urban and rural life.[72]

In *Explication: essai de biosociologie dirigée* (1943), which Bernège would describe after the war as her 'master work', she argued that city life had become so disconnected from country life that the urban and rural populations now constituted two distinct biological types.[73] Echoing the official discourse that blamed France's defeat on the supposedly pleasure-seeking culture of prewar France, she claimed that the division of labour and the demands of mass-production had diminished men and stimulated artificial desires, replacing the true values of courage and hard work with the pursuit of materialistic satisfaction.[74] She condemned urban women for preferring the pursuit of comfort to their 'natural' function of regenerating the race and argued that the peasant family was the key to both moral and biological regeneration – regulated by the rhythms of nature, more preoccupied with subsistence than with profit, it was the healthy organ which might yet save a failing organism.[75]

Thus, rather like Dubreuil, Bernège seems to have formulated a deeply pessimistic analysis of the state of French society in the wake of defeat. Both had already professed an organicist theory of organization before the war but became more illiberal during the Occupation.[76] Bernège believed that France had been defeated at the hands of a better organized society and in this she echoed Jean Coutrot, who had assessed the defeat in 1940 as a 'striking lesson in organization'.[77] For Bernège, Germany had adapted more successfully to what was assumed to be a general evolution towards a more social or collective model of organization.[78] This was not an endorsement of Nazism as a model for France. Rather, reasoning in a way that parallels the arguments of modernization theorists, many organizers understood Nazism as one facet of an age of organization which manifested itself differently in different national cultures. Bernège's prescription for France's alleged ills was a kind of socio-biological planning that drew not just on the Fayolist organicism and work science that had informed her interwar work, but also on conceptions of biological degeneration and regeneration developed by the likes of Alexis Carrel, whose

L'Homme, cet inconnu she had already admiringly reviewed in *Art ménager* in 1936.[79]

Like the economic planners of X-Crise who had sought to systematize state intervention, Bernège attributed the aberrational development of urban-industrial society to the fact that it had been allowed to take place in an anarchic and unplanned manner.[80] She spoke of the need for government by science, insisting that leaders must learn not just the lessons of engineering or industrial organization but also those of biology, psychology and sociology.[81] After the war, she argued, reconstruction must be planned from above according to Fayolist principles, with 'tight monitoring' of everything from prices and measures to education and morals (*moeurs*).[82] In the meantime, the return to the land was conceived both as a way of growing healthier human specimens[83] and as a starting point from which to reconstruct a different relationship between rural and urban France. Bernège could also have listed geography in the disciplines that the new planning needed to take on board, for what she identified here was (in part at least) an issue of spatially uneven development. Although the details of the reconstruction she envisaged remained vague, the objective was expressed in terms of achieving a new balance between the social forms of urban and rural life.[84]

While none of this was very concrete, it does offer an insight into one kind of organizers' response to the defeat of 1940, for it highlights a reflex which sees ever greater scientific intervention as the solution to a crisis. Moreover, if Bernège was thinking partly in terms of the reconstruction that would take place after the war, the preoccupation with authority and the regulation of behaviour, as well as the ruralism that informed this vision of planning, resonated strongly with the priorities of the regime already in place. In fact, Bernège's turn to a more medicalized and a more geographical conception of organization was also symptomatic of broader trends in planning and the scientific organization of work during the Occupation.

The Biological Organization of Work

The role of Carrel's Fondation française pour l'étude des problèmes humains, founded in 1941, was significant in relation to this process of medicalization. Unlike Coutrot's CEPH, the Carrel Foundation (as it is also known) was a large state funded institute, whose membership reached as many as four hundred. Moreover, it differed from the CEPH, not only in the resources at its disposal, but in the relative balance of power between medicine and engineering. While the CEPH drew significantly on engineers and industrialists and was an eclectic grouping (in which public health issues, eugenics and biotypology were explored alongside art, aesthetics, psychoanalysis and folklore) at the Carrel Foundation, the medical profession was dominant, particularly at a senior level where Carrel was supported by his fellow doctors André Gros, Jacques Ménétrier and Jean-Jacques Gillon.[85] Nonetheless, questions about work and the economy figured prominently among the concerns of the Foundation's research teams and a team dedicated to the study of work (composed of six doctors, one engineer, a lawyer and a social worker) was one of the first to be set up in early 1942.[86]

The research carried out at the Foundation was wide-ranging but much of it was conceived in terms of an effort to measure and/or improve the physical quality of the population. This reflected not just a preoccupation with the reproduction of the French 'race' but a concern with the productive capacities of the population and the organization of work. Young people in particular were the objects of the Foundation's attentions, as research projects subjected tens of thousands of children and adolescents to a battery of biotypological tests.[87] The methods used encompassed various medical examinations (notably of the examination of the glandular system, perhaps reflecting the influence of Pende's constitutionalist biotypology), as well as psychotechnics, intelligence tests, anthropometrics and graphology. However, the published report on the work of the Biotypology Research Team emphasized the insights into psychological types provided by morphology, an area that was developed at the Foundation by Dr Louis Corman (whose method had also been adopted by some interwar organizers).[88] In addition, there was a strong hygienist dimension to the Foundation's work and this was particularly apparent in the Work Research Team, which drew heavily on the field of occupational medicine, announcing a new 'biological phase' in the organization of work.[89]

One of the clearest indicators of the medicalization of the organization of work in Vichy France was the institutionalization of occupational medicine. The influence of the Carrel Foundation in this development was all too visible. In October 1941 a Medical Labour Inspectorate was created, functioning alongside the main Labour Inspectorate which had monitored compliance with French labour legislation since 1874. Three Medical Inspectors General headed the new service, among them Carrel's right-hand men, Jacques Ménétrier and André Gros, both of whom were specialists in occupational medicine.[90] Ménétrier was later replaced by another member of the Carrel Foundation, Dr Pierre Winter (who had been an associate of Le Corbusier and Hubert Lagardelle at the review *Plans* in the early 1930s). In July 1942 it became compulsory to appoint a doctor to every Organization Committee and to provide social and medical services in all firms with fifty or more employees. The role of these workplace doctors was a preventive, hygienist one: they were not there to treat injuries (though they were allowed to do so in certain circumstances), but to provide what André Gros called, 'a maintenance service for *the thinking machine that is man*'.[91] Their tasks included carrying out workshop hygiene inspections and examining job applicants in order to establish a medical profile that would inform decisions about hiring and assignment of workers.[92] In this respect, they acted as medical consultants in the organization of work, their title (*médécin-conseil*) mirroring that of the engineer-organizers (*ingénieurs-conseils*) who had emerged between the wars.

The emergence of an increasingly medicalized conception of the capacity to work had already been apparent in the development of biotypology in the 1930s. Occupational medicine had also acquired greater recognition as an area of professional specialism in this period and the careers of doctors like Gros and Martiny highlight the extent to which the practice of occupational medicine had already developed through a variety of institutions between the wars.[93] Indeed, having been appointed Head of a Medico-social service at the Mutualite de la Seine in 1938, Gros had been recruited by Dautry to organize medical services in the armaments sector in 1939.[94] By 1942, however, occupational medicine was enshrined in a set of legal obligations. Moreover, the creation of a Permanent Committee on Occupational Medicine allowed doctors (rather than one of the relevant ministries) to define the doctrine and scope of French occupational medicine. The result was an approach which infused the psychotechnician's ideal of 'the right man in the right place' with general hygienist and pronatalist objectives. Workplace doctors were to carry out regular medical examinations of all workers in order to detect illnesses such as tuberculosis, while, in the case of women, examinations were to focus especially on 'the state of the genital organs' in order to ensure that their work did not interfere with their primordial child-bearing function.[95] Such preoccupations doubtless reflected the fact that over half the doctors on the Permanent Committee were members of the Carrel Foundation.[96] The human motor discourse that had established itself in interwar work science also took on a more explicitly anti-liberal dimension in the literature on occupational medicine under Vichy as the biological organization of work was contrasted with a liberal organization of work which sought to drive up production with little regard for the psycho-physiological needs of the worker.[97] In this way, the medico-social services created by Vichy legislation (like the Workplace Social Committees that oversaw them) were conceived in terms of the regime's vision of a new work community, a community in which a rational organization of work based on an understanding of 'human problems' would transcend class conflict.[98]

Planning and the Rebalancing of Urban and Rural Development

The mingling of scientific organization, ruralism and socio-biology that characterized Paulette Bernège's work in Vichy France also found a parallel in aspects of the reconstruction plans drawn up by the government. The body responsible for drawing up a reconstruction and development plan for after the war was the Délégation générale de l'équipement national (DGEN), created in February 1941. Made up of six sections – agriculture, industry, communications, urban planning, scientific and technical infra-structure, overseas territories – as well as a planning service and a Consul-tative Committee, it produced a ten-year plan (*Plan d'équipement*) in 1942 and another more short-term plan known as *Tranche de démarrage* (Start Up Phase) in 1944. The leadership of the Delegation came from the worlds of industry, engineering and town planning: the first Director, Lehideux (who combined this portfolio with his post as Minister of Industrial Production between July 1941 and April 1942) was succeeded by the Paris Director of Public Works, Henri Giraud, and then by the engineer Frédéric Surleau, who had collaborated with Dautry on housing projects at the SNCF before the war. Representatives of industry and agriculture (including the heads of several Organization Committees) also had a voice in the Delegation by virtue of their role on its Consultative Committee.[99]

At the DGEN, as at the Ministry of Industrial Production, planners con-ceived of their role in terms that echoed those of the interwar movement. They spoke of the need to establish a 'vue d'ensemble' and their aim to 'coordinate' and 'make choices', ensuring that the action of the state had a 'directive' function.[100] It was regarded as essential, therefore, that policies in areas such as industry, agriculture and rural and urban planning should be considered together, not simply left to individual ministries. To consider these matters in isolation from each other would have been, in the words used in *Tranche de démarrage*, 'to chop into inert pieces something that is in reality a living organism'.[101] Building on interwar attempts to develop inter-ministerial services, this holist outlook led (initially at least) to an organi-zational innovation: since the DGEN's task cut across areas overseen by a number of ministries, it was decided that its Director would have ministe-rial rank and would report directly to the Head of Government. Although Laval later rowed back from this position, placing the Delegation under the Ministry of Economy and Finance, the principle of a planning agency with autonomy from individual ministries was reinscribed after the war, when Monnet insisted that the Commissariat au Plan must have control of the planning process and report directly to Matignon.[102]

Though the two plans drawn up by the DGEN focused heavily on investment in infrastructure, they also exhibited a certain concern for the state of the nation's *human* resources. A meeting of the Consultative Com-mittee in July 1942 which focused on proposals tabled by Guillaume de Tarde (an associate of Detoeuf and co-founder of *Les Nouveaux Cahiers*) stressed the importance of population policy: such a policy must address both quantity and quality, it was noted, encompassing not only the long-standing struggle against the 'social scourges' of alcoholism and tuberc-ulosis, but the issues of the birth rate and immigration.[103] Similarly, in the *Plan d'équipement* itself, economic performance was seen as dependent on a number of factors, including not just infrastructure and methods, but also 'the value of the race and the adaptation of its qualities to its productive activity.'[104] Indeed, one reason given for investing in *équipement* – housing, sports facilities, schools, food production – was that it would improve the quality of the population.[105] Particular attention was paid here to the problem of rural depopulation which was seen to pose a dual threat: firstly, it had implications for the country's ability to meet food production targets, and, secondly, it threatened to undermine the strength of the French 'race' which was believed to owe its greatness to the simple and disciplined life of its peasant stock.[106]

This concern with rural depopulation is one of the aspects of Vichy often identified with traditionalists and the plans drawn up by the DGEN have been seen to encapsulate the tensions between traditionalism and modernity within the regime. Richard Kuisel's pioneering work contrasted the plans' modernizing focus on productivity with their 'glorification of the family, of social solidarity, of elites, of peasant virtues, of a spartan ethic and of physical fitness', features which he attributed to the influence of traditionalists.[107] Other historians have nuanced this interpretation somewhat, but have not challenged the fundamental interpretive framework.[108] However, since the first plan in particular is a composite document, based in part on proposals from ministries and in part on input from the DGEN itself, it is often difficult to identify who contributed what. The *Plan d'équipement* proposed to invest over 130 million francs to improve agricultural land, equipment and rural housing and although one aim of such investment was to encourage people to stay in or return to the countryside, the ideal of a mass return to the land was described at one point as 'probably utopian'.[109] The plan also spoke of: 'a rural France, no longer enslaved to the past, but turned to the future, open to all new ideas.'[110] What was envisaged was not a 'return' to a rural life that was imagined as unchanging, but a renovation of rural living and working conditions that would make country life better organized and more viable. Since interwar studies by the likes of Bernège and Le Corbusier had had similar aims, one cannot assume that such preoccupations were alien to technicians.

Importantly, it was anticipated that this renovated agriculture would live 'in symbiosis with the nation's industry'.[111] This logic of 'symbiosis' (rather than opposition) between urban and rural was central to the work being done by engineer-urbanists at the DGEN. Indeed, this is one area where we do know the origin of the proposals that emerged from the Delegation. In September 1942, Gabriel Dessus, an engineer with the Paris electricity distribution company and member of the CNOF, was asked by Henri Giraud to investigate the question of urban and industrial decentralization. A series of studies ensued which not only informed the plans drawn up during the Occupation but led to a brief period of collaboration between Dessus and the Ministries of National Economy and of Reconstruction and Urban Planning at the Liberation.[112] The *Plan d'équipement* included a proposal for *cités-satellite*, or rural residential centres for industrial workers, linked to urban workplaces by rapid transportation networks, but it also proposed to bring small factories to the countryside where peasants could have access to industrial work without migrating.[113] This was part of a wider agenda for industrial decentralization, which sought to move industry and people out of congested urban areas, especially the Paris region.[114] It was an agenda maintained in *Tranche de démarrage* in 1944, which was drawn up by the DGEN team with little or no input from ministries in anticipation of the Liberation. The attachment in this document to 'agriculture–industry liaison' was not the product of political influences elsewhere in the regime, therefore, and was framed in terms that had become well-established between the wars: planning, it was argued, must consider problems in 'human' rather than purely economic terms.[115]

It is notable that these projects, and indeed much of the work on town and country planning at the DGEN, emanated from engineers. Town planning or *urbanisme* had initially been the domain of architects, though the public works departments in cities like Paris were led by engineers who also used the term. Nationally, it was the powerful state engineers of the *Corps des Ponts et chaussées* who were charged with major infrastructure projects. But the planners of the DGEN developed a new practice of *regional* planning which was enshrined in the law of 15 June 1943. This law created Regional Planning Constituencies (Circonscriptions régionales d'urbanisme) with responsibility for developing a *Plan d'aménagement* for the area and approving any construction projects. In doing so, it extended the logic of urban planning beyond the unit of the town, provided an important part of the organizational infrastructure for France's postwar reconstruction and contributed to the development of what has become known since the war as *l'aménagement du territoire*.[116]

The 'spirit of organization' which inhabited this new regional planning was apparent in the reports on industrial decentralization published by the Dessus group.[117] For Dessus, the task was to identify the 'optimum location' for industry by examining the impact of location on the cost price of products and the social state of the worker.[118] Calculating the cost price meant factoring in not just transport and building costs but also human productivity and the impact on training and recruitment – Dessus looked to the CEGOS to help provide data on these problems.[119] The condition of workers was discussed in terms of exposure to 'social scourges' such as tuberculosis but also in terms of fatigue study – what would be the impact on fatigue levels of reduced commuting time and of exposure to a rural or small-town environment, for example? What was the optimum size of garden (i.e. energy to be spent on gardening) for workers? Illustrating once again the planners' interest in cross-disciplinary collaboration, as well as the influence of doctors at Vichy, Dessus commissioned a study from André Gros at the Carrel Foundation on these questions.[120] But if the likely benefits of decentralization were to be the subject of scientific research, some provisional conclusions were offered at the end of the collection of reports published by the DGEN in 1944. Not only was it anticipated that decentralization would increase the birth rate, provide better housing than in the cities, and foster greater social cohesion (since rather than migrating to the city workers would retain links with their family and the land), but such a planned approach to industrial development would also, it was claimed, allow better coordination of supply and demand in the labour market.[121] In other words, the convergence of so many migrants from the provinces on Paris in search of work was seen as both economically and socially irrational, resulting in poor living conditions and unemployment: decentralization promised a rational solution.

Far from being a product of the influence of a group of Vichy 'traditionalists', the idea of industrial decentralization had a pedigree in the interwar scientific organization movement. Its appearance on the agenda was informed by strategic as well as social and economic considerations, as the geographical concentration of industry was seen as particularly vulnerable to aerial bombardment. Plans for the relocation of factories were drawn up by the Ministry of Defence and by major companies such as Renault in the 1930s – indeed it was the first head of the DGEN, Lehideux, who had drawn up the Renault plan in 1938–39. Much of the French aeronautical industry had been decentralized in the 1930s and the Dessus group studied this and other interwar experiments closely.[122] The *Plan d'équipement* cited the decentralization of defence industries in the 1930s as a starting point for future projects.[123] But decentralization was never conceived in purely strategic terms. At a meeting of X-Crise in 1935, for example, Roland Ziegel had proposed a system of decentralized production units which would take the form of small workshops grouped around towns, where skilled workers would live on the land and work independently. Imagining the France of 1960, he argued that, in an economy with a high division of labour and highly developed communications networks, components could be manufactured in these small workshops and brought together in larger centres only for the assembly of the final product. Similarly, specialist service providers like engineers could travel the area, visiting individual producers. Like Dessus, Ziegel saw economic and social benefits in such an arrangement. By re-rooting workers in the countryside it would help increase the birth rate and reduce class conflict.[124] At the same time, he reasoned, the system would prove cheaper for industry since taxes and the cost of living were cheaper in the countryside.[125] Ernst Hijmans, a close collaborator of Jean Coutrot, made similar arguments in *Humanisme économique* in 1938, linking decentralization with Coutrot and Dubreuil's agenda for the 'humanization' of mass industry and presenting a federal, decentralized mode of production as the next stage of industrial development.[126] What both men appeared to envisage was a future in which technological progress would begin to work in favour of decentralization rather than ever greater geographical concentration.

It is also worth noting that such schemes were not the product of a peculiarly French attachment to rural life. A further example of decentralization cited in the *Plan d'équipement* was Henry Ford's Village Industries.

Though known primarily for his massive plant at Dearborn on the river Rouge, Ford also created nineteen small town factories in his native rural Michigan between 1921 and 1944, with the explicit aim of reconciling industrial production with country living. The Village Industries scheme focused not so much on resettling city-dwellers but on providing an alternative pattern of development to the continual expansion of cities and large factory complexes.[127] Ford was quite happy to see farming industrialized on a large scale, but workers in the Village Industries were still expected to keep a plot of land on which to produce their own food.[128] To this extent, Ford's scheme was inhabited by the same aspiration to reconnect and rebalance urban and rural life that animated Hijmans' and Ziegel's proposals. Moreover, according to Howard P. Segal, the idea of decentralization commanded significant support in interwar America, filling the columns of leading business and engineering journals.[129]

Population and Planning

It was noted earlier that planning at Vichy was marked by a hygienist concern for the quality of the 'race', but it also reflected the technicians' concern with 'economic Malthusianism' discussed in Chapter Four.[130] Alfred Sauvy, who had campaigned for better economic statistics and forecasting between the wars as a means of overcoming 'Malthusianism' continued to make this case during the Occupation. Indeed, Sauvy's career provides a good illustration of the continuities that existed in the French administration in the period from the Third to the Fourth and even the Fifth Republic. Having worked as a government statistician since the 1920s (and having advised Paul Reynaud on economic matters in the 1930s), he remained in post during the Occupation before going on to serve as head of the newly created Institut national d'études démographiques (National Institute of Demographic Studies, INED) from 1945 to 1962. Sauvy saw his role as an apolitical one and, unlike Bichelonne or Barnaud, never occupied a ministerial post. During the Occupation he headed the Institut de conjoncture and produced regular bulletins on economic performance for the government.[131] He also taught at the Ecole supérieure d'organisation professionnelle, had links with other advisory groups, such as the Comité d'études pour la France and the Carrel Foundation, and published *Richesse et population* (1943), a work which made significant recommendations about economic and demographic policy.[132] In this sense, while he claimed to be above politics, Sauvy, like other technicians, can certainly be seen as part of the political culture of Vichy.

Sauvy may have had some direct input into the *Plans d'équipement* or it may be that the wide dissemination of his conception of 'Malthusianism' was sufficient to ensure that it was adopted without direct influence. In any case, what was articulated in both the 1942 plan and in *Tranche de démarrage* was a linkage between economic and demographic 'Malthusianism' that was an increasingly central tenet of Sauvy's thinking. In much of his prewar work, he had discussed 'Malthusianism' either in terms of demographic attitudes (reluctance to have children) or in terms of economic attitudes (the desire to limit production) and if he articulated a relationship between the two it was one of analogy. His key contribution to the evolution of French demographic thinking had been to constitute the age profile of the population as a central problem, focusing attention not just on depopulation or *dénatalité* but on *vieillissement*, a term that has stronger connotations of decline than the English equivalent, 'ageing'.[133] This idea had been present in Sauvy's thinking since the late 1920s but at X-Crise in 1939 he used it explicitly to establish a causal relationship between demographic and economic 'Malthusianism'. Not only did he assert that it was the same fear of excess that lay at the root of both phenomena, but, taking the example of the nineteenth century, he claimed there was historical evidence of a correlation between periods of demographic expansion and economic expansion. Malthusian attitudes were particularly strong in an ageing population, he alleged, thus creating a vicious circle, where low birth and mortality rates reinforced and perpetuated the mentality that was responsible for both demographic and economic weakness.[134] In *Richesse et population* he set out this theory more systematically and argued that an organized economy required not just engineer-economists who could monitor and forecast economic developments, but a 'demographic plan'.[135]

Although the interwar pro-natalist movement had often emphasized moral and military arguments for population increase, it was not new to see depopulation as an economic problem.[136] Adolphe Landry, one of France's leading demographers between the wars, was also an economist and Jacques Bertillon, founder of the Alliance nationale contre la dépopulation, had argued in the 1890s that the German economy was overtaking France because the number of workers in Germany was growing faster.[137] What was distinctive about the population economics that Sauvy set out in *Richesse et population* was the way the concept of *vieillissement* defined economic performance as a psychological problem and proposed population policy as a means of transforming mentalities. He argued, for example, that having more children would incite people to greater economic effort and that in larger families younger children would be less able to rely on following their father's footsteps and hence more motivated to create their own place in society.[138] In this sense, demographic change was seen as a way of breaking the mental logjam of Malthusianism by providing incentives to work. Sauvy also argued that increasing quantity or 'demographic pressure' had a positive impact on 'quality', citing the success of growing nations such as Germany, Italy and Japan in the 1936 Olympic Games as evidence.[139] Like the doctors who took a hygienist view of population questions, he saw alcoholism as a threat to the 'quality' of the French population.[140] But if he saw the 'improvement of man' as a kind of technical progress,[141] age remained the primary qualitative category which interested Sauvy. While France's decreasing mortality rate might appear to compensate quantitatively for the low birth-rate, he argued, in qualitative terms it was an aggravating factor because of its implications for the collective mentality.[142] The presence of an excessive proportion of *'vieillards'* (old people) in France was blamed for the country's alleged lack of inventiveness and contrasted with the more youthful and therefore more 'enterprising' populations of other countries.[143] It was precisely this argument that was taken up in the *Plans d'équipement,* which evoked the threat of *'vieillissement',* claiming that an ageing population 'strips a country of all dynamism'.[144]

What had emerged in Sauvy's work by 1943 and found its way into the plans produced at the DGEN was a form of populationist economic planning that was to be extremely influential after the war. Because it defined the rejuvenation of the population (through pro-natalist measures and immigration) not just as a prerequisite for economic growth but as a means of breaking with the mentalities that had allegedly dominated the prewar order, this current of populationist planism could be readily adopted at the Liberation, when 'rupture' was the order of the day (at least rhetorically). *Vieillissement* became a staple theme of general works on demography between 1945 and 1950 and in a context of cross-party support for measures to increase and rejuvenate the population, the creation of INED under Sauvy's leadership in 1945 marked the elevation of demography into a state science in France.[145] This is not to say that Sauvy won his place in postwar France because he was (by some objective criteria) a 'modernizer', but rather that he was one of the chief inventors of and ideologues for a project that came to call itself modernization after the war. A state technician whose arguments constantly invoked technical competence and rested on mathematical demonstrations, Sauvy might appear to conform all too well to the caricature of the apolitical 'technocrat'. At the same time, the assumptions that shaped his reasoning were those of many members of the French establishment in this period. Throughout the 1930s, his arguments about the benefits of statistical forecasting and the role of the technician in economic organization were cast in terms of collective psychology and the need for rational elites to overcome the irrationalities of public opinion.[146] When he and the planners of the DGEN identified the age composition of the population as a psychological and economic problem they followed a similar logic. Despite their appeals to empiricism, it should be noted that at no point did they cite any attitudinal data to support claims about the mentality of different age groups. Rather, this vision relied, as Hervé Le Bras has pointed out, on a notion of *vieillissement* that derived from organicist and biologist theories about the life cycle of civilizations, transposing onto the social body ideas about decline and decay which were modelled on the life cycle of individual organisms.[147]

Historiographically speaking, one could be forgiven for thinking there were at least two Alfred Sauvys. The scholarly interest in pro-natalism and population science since the 1990s, along with Sauvy's visibility as a commentator on population issues in postwar France, have marked him out as a demographer, while in the history of economic planning he is remembered for his contribution as an economist and statistician. Here, I have brought the two Sauvys and their respective fields together, as one surely must if one is to make sense not only of Sauvy's biography, but also of the way planning emerged in France at the intersection of engineering and the 'sciences of man'. Populationism was one aspect of this quest on the part of technicians to find a new 'dynamic equilibrium' for the socio-economic system. The biological organization of work, the institutionalization of class collaboration and the rebalancing of urban and rural life were other aspects. All these trends had roots in the interwar period, for throughout the history of the organization movement, organization had been seen as a problem of how to adapt minds and bodies. This embodied organization project was envisaged in a variety of ways by organizers who sometimes had significant political divergences. But scientific organization and economic planning certainly did not wait for the Occupation to become human engineering projects.

This is not to say that nothing changed in 1940. If anything, the sense of national crisis that marked the Occupation years accentuated the concern with what interwar organizers had begun to call 'human problems'. Bardet, for example, mounted a veritable crusade for his vision of a new work community at Vichy, while populationist elements in the planning agenda appeared in a much more developed form. As the cases of Dubreuil and Bernège demonstrate, a sense of crisis led some organizers to propose or accept more coercive, hierarchical or socio-biologist solutions than those they had envisaged between the wars. While left-wing research scientists who had been central to the development of work science were purged or went into exile, doctors enjoyed unprecedented influence in Vichy France and were able to promote a more conservative form of biological organization of work through institutions like the Carrel Foundation. They also entrenched the role of the medical profession in the workplace through the legislation on occupational medicine. The Liberation would bring further changes, of course, but it was not just populationism that remained firmly on the agenda after the war. The Vichy legislation on occupational medicine would be only slightly revised, while the law on regional planning would be incorporated into the postwar *Code d'urbanisme*. Even the practice of class collaboration in the management of social policy that was established under the Charter of Labour provided an inheritance for the postwar Comités d'entreprises. The technicians of the organization and planning movement were by no means the only group that shaped this legacy. But they certainly played their part in Vichy's efforts to reshape France socially, psychologically and biologically, as well as economically.

Notes

1. The first Minister of Industrial Production and Labour was René Belin but the Industrial Production portfolio went to Pucheu in February 1941 and to Lehideux in July 1941, before Bichelonne was appointed following the return of Laval.
2. The importance of experts has also been noted in studies of 'race' and gender at Vichy, notably in G. Noiriel. 1999. *Les Origines républicaines de Vichy*, Paris: Hachette, 211–72 and F. Muel-Dreyfus. 1996. *Vichy et l'éternel féminin. Contribution à une sociologie politique de l'ordre des corps*. Paris: Seuil, Chapter 8, esp. 327–33.
3. A full list of members of the Comité d'études pour la France is given in P. Mioche. 1987. *Le Plan Monnet: genèse et élaboration, 1941–1947*, Paris: Publications de la Sorbonne, 1987, 16–18. See also M-O. Baruch. 1997. *Servir l'Etat français. L'Administration en France de 1940 à 1944*, Paris: Fayard, 174–76.
4. Prewar members of the CCOP who remained involved with the School in its new incarnation included Antoine de Tavernost, Jean Lobstein and Roger-Jean Gaulon. Lists of board members, teaching staff and courses taught at the School can be found in *Ecole supérieure d'organisation professionnelle. Réglement et programme d'enseignement, année scolaire 1941–1942* and *Ecole supérieure d'organisation professionnelle. Réglement et programme d'enseignement, année scolaire 1942–43*, produced by the Centre d'information interprofessionnel. The school was headed by the law and economics professor and former CGT planiste Achille Dauphin-Meunier.
5. C. Roussel. 1979. *Lucien Romier*, Paris: Editions France Empire, 208.
6. O. Dard. 1999. *Jean Coutrot: De l'ingénieur au prophète*, Besançon: Presses universitaires franc-comtoises, 396.
7. Dard, *Jean Coutrot*, 394–95.
8. Lamirand was one of a number of Vichy officials and ministers who developed contacts with the Resistance and he entered full resistance following his dismissal in 1943.
9. See, for example, J. Jackson. 2001. *France: The Dark Years 1940–1944*, Oxford: Oxford University Press, 148–65; H. Rousso. 1987. 'Les Paradoxes de Vichy et de l'Occupation. Contraintes, archaïsmes et modernités' in P. Fridenson and A. Straus (eds), *Le Capitalisme français, 19e-20e siècle. Blocages et dynamismes d'une croissance*, Paris: Fayard; R. Paxton. 1982 [1st edn 1972]. *Vichy France: Old Guard and New Order*, New York: Columbia University Press, 210–20, 259–73; R. Kuisel, 'The Legend of Vichy Synarchy', *French Historical Studies*, 6(3), 365–98.
10. This anecdote from J. Sabin, *Jean Bichelonne*, 54 is cited in Jackson, *France: The Dark Years*, 163.
11. R. Kuisel, *Capitalism and the State in Modern France: Renovation and Economic Management in the Twentieth Century*, Cambridge: Cambridge University Press, 132.
12. R. Barthes. 2000. *Mythologies*, trans. Annette Lavers, London: Vintage, 67.
13. Jackson, *France: The Dark Years*, 163; Paxton, *Vichy France: Old Guard and New Order*, 220.
14. E.g. Kuisel sees Bichelonne as 'the model technocrat' in *Capitalism and the State*, 132, while for Jackson (*France: The Dark Years*, 163), he 'epitomized the caste of technocrats who rose to prominence at Vichy'.
15. H. Rousso. 1979. 'L'Organisation industrielle de Vichy (Perspectives de recherches)', *Revue d'histoire de la deuxième guerre mondiale* 116, 29.
16. Kuisel, *Capitalism and the State*, 136.
17. Decree of 30 April 1941, reproduced in Sabin, *Jean Bichelonne*, 171. The CII even took over the premises and staff of the CGPF.
18. A flavour of the difficulties can be gleaned from the bulletin *Courrier du CII*, AN: 68 AJ 90–91.
19. J. Bichelonne. 1943. *Conférence de M Bichelonne. Hôtel de Ville de Paris 5 août 1943*, Paris: Imprimerie Municipale, 21.
20. J. Bichelonne. 1942. *L'Etat actuel de l'organisation économique*, Paris: Ecole libre des sciences politiques, 24–5 and *Conférence de M Bichelonne*, 20.

21. Quoted in M. Margairaz. 1991. *L'Etat, les finances et l'économie. Histoire d'une conversion, 1932–1952*, 2 vols, Paris: Comité pour l'histoire économique et financière de la France, 538.

22. Bichelonne, *L'Etat actuel de l'organisation économique*, 40.

23. See H. Joly. 2000. 'Prosopographie des dirigeants des Comités d'organisation' in O. Dard, J.-C. Daumas and F. Marcot (dir.), *L'Occupation, l'Etat français et les entreprises*, Paris: Association pour le développement de l'histoire économique, 251.

24. Joly, 'Prosopographie', 254–55. These figures are based on appointments announced in the *Journal officiel*.

25. There is now a growing literature on French business during the Occupation and on economic collaboration, thanks in part to the work of a CNRS research group led by Hervé Joly and the government-initiated Commission pour l'indemnisation des victimes de spoliations, which investigates compensation claims relating to the expropriation of Jews. See, for example, Dard, Daumas and Marcot (dir.), *L'Occupation, l'Etat français et les entreprises*; J.-C. Daumas and C. Chevandier. 2007. *Travailler dans les entreprises sous l'Occupation*, Besançon: Presses universitaires de Franche-Comté; H. Joly. 2004. *Les Comités d'organisation et l'économie dirigée du régime de Vichy*, Caen: Centre de recherche d'histoire quantitative; A.Callu, P. Eveno and H. Joly. 2009. *Culture et médias sous l'Occupation: des entreprises dans la France de Vichy*, Paris: Editions du Comité des travaux historiques et scientifiques; A. Beltran, R. Frank and H. Rousso (dir.). 1994. *La Vie des entreprises sous l'Occupation. Une enquête à l'échelle locale*, Paris: Belin; D. Rousselier-Fraboulet. 1998. *Les Entreprises sous l'Occupation: le monde de la métallurgie à Saint-Denis*, Paris: CNRS Editions; R. de Rochebrune and J.-C. Hazéra. 1995. *Les Patrons sous l'Occupation*, Paris: Odile Jacob; A. Lacroix-Riz. 1999. *Industriels et banquiers français sous l'Occupation: la collaboration économique avec le Reich et Vichy*, Paris: Armand Colin; Mission d'étude sur la spoliation des Juifs de France. 2000. *Aryanisation économique et restitutions*, Paris: La Documentation française; P. Verheyde. 1999. *Les Mauvais Comptes de Vichy: l'aryanisation des entreprises juives*, Paris: Perrin.

26. Rousso, 'Vichy et les entreprises', 43.

27. See Margairaz, *L'Etat, les finances et l'économie*, Chapters Seventeen and Eighteen.

28. A. Radtke-Delacor. 2001. 'Produire pour le Reich. Les Commandes allemandes à l'industrie française (1940–1944)', *Vingtième siècle* 70, 110–11.

29. Radtke-Delacor, 'Produire pour le Reich', 112.

30. R. Kuisel. 1967. *Ernest Mercier, French Technocrat*, Berkeley: University of California Press, 72–73, 143–51.

31. P. Verheyde. 2000. 'L'Aryanisation des grandes entreprises juives' in Dard, Daumas and Marcot (dir.), *L'Occupation, l'état français et les entreprises*, 132, 123.

32. Loustau had also been a member of Jacques Doriot's Parti populaire français in the late 1930s.

33. See Margairaz, *L'Etat, les finances et l'économie*, 566–68 and AN: F 37 20 Dossier on *Organisation professionnelle. Le statut des professions*, Notes 1–4 dated 8 April to 5 May. The notion of the business as cell appears in *Note 1*, pp.3, 6. In the negotiations about the Labour Charter, representatives of the Centre des jeunes patrons also defended a vision of professional organization in which the individual business was privileged as the basic organizing unit. J.-P. Le Crom. 1995. *Syndicats, nous voilà! Vichy et le corporatisme*, Paris: Editions de l'Atelier, 135.

34. AN: F 37 20 Bardet, *Le Statut des professions, Note 1*, 4–6.

35. AN: F 37 20 Bardet, *Le Statut des professions, Note 1*, 5.

36. AN: F37 77 Bardet, 'Réflexions sur six mois d'activité publique', November 1941. The title of this document echoes that of Bardet's 'Réflexions sur six mois de travaux' written at X-Crise in 1932.

37. H. Théallier, J.-F. Buchmann, G. Bardet, Dr R. Merle d'Aubigné, J.-B. Barrère and J. Bérard. 1941. *Hommes et métiers*, Paris: Editions 'Je Sers'.

38. Le Crom, *Syndicats, nous voilà!*, 130. Bardet had also proposed the creation of a Council of Professional Representatives that would liaise with the relevant CO.

39. Le Crom, *Syndicats, nous voilà!*, 151–57.
40. This criticism was also made by the Catholic economist François Perroux. See J. Jackson. 2005. '"Mal embarqué bien arrivé": The Strange Story of François Perroux' in H. Diamond and S. Kitson, *Vichy, Resistance, Liberation: New Perspectives on Wartime France*, Oxford: Berg, 155–69 (163).
41. Région économique de l'est. 1942. *Réunion régionale tenu à Nancy, le 20 janvier 1942. Exposés de M. Gérard Bardet, Président du Centre d'information interprofessionnel et de M. de Tavernost, délégué général de ce centre*, 19–20.
42. CSEIC. 1943. *Projet de réforme de l'organisation économique sur le plan national. Rapport de la première session des travaux de la Commission No.1 adopté en séance plénière du Conseil de 6 juillet 1943*, Paris: CSEIC, 7.
43. 'The necessary harmony between economic organization and social organization is born of the unity of nature. There are few questions that are truly economic and few questions that are truly social.' *Conférence de M. Bichelonne*, 14.
44. See AN: F37 77 Letter from Bardet to Lehideux 31 March 1942 about the decision to disband the Council. This document indicates that Bardet believed he was being reproached (unfairly) for exceeding his brief by addressing doctrinal matters. This may have reflected an awareness of the growing anxieties about the power of business interests at Vichy and the allegations that the Synarchy was trying to impose its own vision of a new order. Lehideux may also have seen Bardet's ambitions as a potential threat to his own role in planning a new economic order as head of the Délégation générale de l'équipement national, which will be discussed shortly. As part of his proposed rationalization of the structures of economic organization Bardet had recommended not only grouping the proliferation of COs into a more streamlined set of professional groups, but also the creation of a National Economic Directorate for the Professional Family which would work in liaison with a new Bureau du Plan at the Ministry of Industrial Production – a proposal which implicitly questioned the DGEN's role in drawing up a *Plan d'équipement*.
45. As a sub-section of the CGPF, the CEGOS might well have been dismantled when the employers' organization was dissolved to make way for the Organizing Committees and the CII, but Bichelonne was keen that it should be maintained. A new dual status was invented therefore, with one branch being integrated into the CII as a technical service for the Organizing Committees, while the other became an autonomous consultancy and training bureau offering its services to businesses. See A. Weeksteen. 2000. 'La Commission générale d'organisation scientifique du travail (Cégos) sous l'Occupation, 1940–1944' in Dard, Daumas and Marcot (dir.), *L'Occupation, l'état français et les entreprises*, 200.
46. J. Warnier. 1943. *Comment constituer un Comité social d'entreprise*, Paris: Edition sociale française, no page numbers. This was the text of a lecture given on 8 December 1942 at the Centre de formation sociale des cadres de l'industrie et du commerce. See also J. Warnier. 1943. 'Attributions, fonctionnement et financement du comité social d'entreprise' in G. Scelle (ed.), *Les Comités sociaux d'établissement. Etat présent et vues d'avenir. Collection Droit Social No. 20*, 19
47. Warnier, *Comment constituer un Comité social d'entreprise*, no page numbers.
48. J.-C. Daumas. 2000. 'La Révolution Nationale à l'usine. Les Politiques sociales des entreprises sous l'Occupation', in Dard, Daumas and Marcot (dir.), *L'Occupation, l'Etat français et les entreprises*, 183–84. Daumas notes that in the Parisian metals industry and the industrial regions of Reims, St Etienne and Lyon as well as in businesses such as the Blin et Blin textile company in Elbeuf, workplace committees of various kinds preceded the Labour Charter.
49. By October 1943, 35 per cent of committees had been established in businesses where they were not compulsory. Daumas, 'La Révolution Nationale à l'usine', 183–84.
50. Daumas, 'La Révolution Nationale à l'usine', 186–87.
51. Daumas, 'La Révolution Nationale à l'usine', 187, 189–190.

52. The Secours national began as an organization reliant on private philanthropy but soon became an instrument of the regime. See J.-P. Le Crom. 2001. 'De la philanthropie à l'action humanitaire' in P.-J. Hesse and J.-P. Le Crom, *La Protection sociale sous le régime de Vichy*, Rennes: Presses universitaires de Rennes, 183–236. Le Crom notes (196) that Dubreuil was one of several former associates of Raoul Dautry to work for the organization, Robert Garric being one of the others.

53. H. Dubreuil. 1942. *La Chevalerie du travail*, Paris: Grasset, dedication at beginning of book.

54. Dubreuil, *La Chevalerie*, 43–45.

55. Dubreuil, *La Chevalerie*, 93–137 on leadership, quotation from p.97.

56. Dubreuil, *La Chevalerie*, 141–42.

57. H. Dubreuil. 1942. *L'Organisation de la solidarité nationale*, Paris: Centre communautaire, 26–27.

58. A former revolutionary syndicalist, Lagardelle had links with a number of interwar nonconformist reviews including *Plans* and *L'Homme réel* and worked as a *chargé de mission* for the French embassy in Rome in the 1930s. He sat on the constitutional commission of Vichy's Conseil national and was a *chargé de mission* for Pétain in 1941, before being appointed Minister of Labour in April 1942.

59. H. Dubreuil. 1938. *Lettre aux travailleurs français*, Paris: Grasset, 3–8, 10, 25. The evolution of Dubreuil's thinking from 1938 is also noted by L. Van-Lemesle. 2004. 'La "République industrielle" de Hyacinthe Dubreuil (1883–1971), ou la dérive corporatiste' in S.L. Kaplan and P. Minard (eds), *La France, malade du corporatisme? XVIII–XXe siècles*, Paris: Belin, 397–99.

60. H. Dubreuil. 1938. *La Fin des monstres*, Paris: Grasset, 27–55.

61. Dubreuil, *L'Organisation de la solidarité nationale*, 25.

62. H. Dubreuil. 1942. 'Le Rôle social de l'organisation scientifique du travail dans les problèmes du jour. Compte rendu de la conférence du 19 janvier 1942', *Comité national de l'organisation française. Feuilles d'informations et comptes rendus* 13, 2.

63. R. Lelong. 1941. 'Allocution du Président Robert Lelong', *Comité national de l'organisation française. Feuilles d'informations et comptes rendus* 2 (January), 4.

64. M. Martiny. 1942. 'Médecine et psychotechnique' in *2e Cycle de perfectionnement des techniques de direction du personnel, 16–20 février 1942*, Paris: CEGOS, 35–47.

65. Weexsteen, 'La CEGOS sous l'Occupation', 208–11.

66. W.H. Schneider. 1991. 'The Scientific Study of Labor in Interwar France', *French Historical Studies* 17(2), 443.

67. *Comité national de l'organisation française. Feuilles d'informations et comptes rendus* 1 December 1940, 2.

68. Cooperatives in Denmark and the Netherlands provided the model for these recommendations. P. Bernège. 1933. 'L'Agriculture dans les pays du nord', *Dépêche de Toulouse* 7 June, 1–2; idem. 1933. 'L'Aide de l'état à l'agriculture', *Dépêche de Toulouse* 8 June, 1–2; idem. 1933. 'Le Mouvement coopératif agricole. L'Aide qu'il apporte aux paysans du nord', *Dépêche de Toulouse* 9 June, 1–2; idem. 1933. 'L'Enseignement agricole dans les pays du nord', *Dépêche de Toulouse* 10 June, 1–2.

69. The Rural Centre exhibited at the 1937 World Fair also emphasized cooperative organization and technical innovation. See S. Peer. 1998. *France on Display: Peasants, Provincials and Folklore in the 1937 Paris World's Fair*, Albany: SUNY Press, 112–17, 128–29 and M. Macleod. 1985. 'Urbanism and Utopia: Le Corbusier from Regional Syndicalism to Vichy', Ph.D. Thesis, Princeton University, Chapter 5.

70. P. Bernège. 1943. *Explication: essai de biosociologie dirigée*, Toulouse: Didier, xi.

71. The review was relaunched in the wake of Vichy legislation, setting out a compulsory programme of domestic science education for all girls, in March 1942. Although this programme was based on conventional teaching of skills like sewing and cooking, rather than Bernège's methods, this did not prevent her from contributing articles such as P. Bernège. 1943. 'Postulats de base', *Education ménagère* June-July, 2–3; idem. 1943.

'Les Deux enseignements', *Education ménagère* November, 2–4; idem. 1944. 'L'Assiette', *Education ménagère* January, 3–4.

72.   Bernège, 'Postulats de base', 2.
73.   Bernège, *Explication*, 36. Bernège described *Explication* as her masterwork and reiterated a number of her wartime themes in P. Bernège. 1950. *J'organise ma petite ferme*, Paris: Editions du Salon des arts ménagers, 99–109.
74.   Bernège, *Explication*, 7–18, 203.
75.   Bernège, *Explication*, 85, 4–5, 20.
76.   In *Explication*, xiii, she observed that this work took to a new level the rudimentary organicist theory she had developed in her interwar work on domestic organization.
77.   J. Coutrot. 1940. 'Commandes de paix après commandes de guerre', *L'Oeuvre* 15 July cited in Dard, *Jean Coutrot*, 394.
78.   Bernège, *Explication*, xiv and 171.
79.   P. Bernège. 1936. 'L'Education biologique', *Art ménager*, 1 November, 570–74, 600–601.
80.   Bernège, *Explication*, 217–19.
81.   Bernège, *Explication*, 217.
82.   Bernège, *Explication*, 217–19.
83.   Bernège, *Explication*, 206, 204, 56.
84.   Bernège, *Explication*, 204.
85.   Moreover, although the Foundation was an interdisciplinary institute, it has been calculated that there were at least fifty doctors among the two to three hundred *chargés de mission* who worked for it and this is likely to be a conservative estimate. S. Buzzi, J.-C. Devinck and P.-A. Rosental. 2000. *La Santé au travail 1880–2006*, Paris: La Decouverte, 46.
86.   Fondation française pour l'étude des problèmes humains. 1943. 'Ce qu'est la Fondation. Ce qu'elle fait', *Cahiers de la Fondation française pour l'étude des problèmes humains* 1, 17; Dr A. Gros. 1943. 'Avant-Propos' to Degas, *La Mutualité française*, Paris: Bernard Frères, 3. The Foundation's broad concern with work related problems is also highlighted in A. Reggiani. 2007. *God's Eugenicist: Alexis Carrel and the Sociobiology of Decline*, Oxford: Berghahn, 128, 149–50.
87.   A study of the physical condition of twenty thousand adolescents was carried out in May 1943, for example, and followed by a further study of sports students in Paris. This was followed by a major study of children with special needs which aimed to examine a sample of one hundred thousand subjects and had collected forty-five thousand sets of test results by spring 1945. See Reggiani, *God's Eugenicist*, 143–47.
88.   Fondation française pour l'étude des problèmes humains. 1944. 'Compte rendu pour l'année 1943', *Cahiers de la Fondation française pour l'étude des problèmes humains* 2 (October), 54–56.
89.   Fondation française pour l'étude des problèmes humains, 'Compte rendu pour l'année 1943', 63–75; Jean Daric (an engineer and member of the Foundation's Work Research Team) cited in Reggiani, *God's Eugenicist*, 149.
90.   V. Viet and M. Ruffat. 1999. *Le Choix de la prévention*, Paris: Economica, 71; Buzzi, Devinck and Rosental, *La Santé au travail*, 45.
91.   Dr A. Gros. 1941. *Le Service médico-social d'une usine de métallurgie. Installation et fonctionnement*, Paris: Bernard Frères, 9 (italicized in the original). A copy of the law of 28 July 1942 which created compulsory medico-social services can be found in *Archives des maladies professionnelles de médecine du travail* 4(5–6) 1942, 225–27.
92.   Dr P. Winter. 1943–44. 'Cours d'hygiène professionnelle. Introduction. 1. Les services médicaux du travail' in *Préparation au concours pour l'emploi d'Inspecteur du travail. Cahier No.5*, Paris: Ministère du travail, 5.
93.   Buzzi, Devinck and Rosental, *La Santé au travail*, 24–40.
94.   Buzzi, Devinck and Rosental, *La Santé au travail*, 42, 45.
95.   Winter, 'Cours d'hygiène professionnelle', 6; Dr A. Gros and Dr J. Ménétrier. 1941. *La Médecine du travail*, Paris: Bernard Frères, 14
96.   Buzzi, Devinck and Rosental, *La Santé au travail*, 49.

97. Winter, 'Cours d'hygiène professionnelle', 4–5.
98. Viet and Ruffat, *Le Choix*, 74–75.
99. AN: F60 658 Comité consultatif de l'équipement national. Procès Verbal No.15, Meetings of 16 June and 21 July 1942.
100. AN: F60 658 Plan d'équipement national. Préambule et remarques préliminaires. Première Partie, 29–30.
101. AN: F60 659 Tranche de démarrage. Première Partie: Buts généraux, 27.
102. Margairaz, *L'Etat, les finances et l'économie*, 855.
103. F60 658 Comité consultatif de l'équipement national, Procès Verbal No.15, Meetings of 16 June and 21 July 1942, 4.
104. AN: F60 658 Plan d'équipement. Deuxième Partie. Les Buts du Plan, 156.
105. AN: F60 658 Plan d'équipement. Deuxième Partie Les Buts du Plan, 66
106. AN: F60 658 Plan d'équipement. Deuxième Partie Les Buts du Plan, 67–74.
107. R. Kuisel. 1977. 'Vichy et les origines de la planification économique 1940–1946', *Mouvement social* 98, 82–83.
108. Julian Jackson, for example, notes that even *Tranche de démarrage*, drafted in spring/summer 1944, and generally seen as more modernist, retained the assumption that France required a strong agricultural sector and spoke more in terms of 'balance' than 'modernization'. He concludes that this is a case where 'it would be wrong to exaggerate the dichotomy between modernizers and traditionalists', but retains the polarity as an interpretive framework nonetheless. See *France: The Dark Years*, 163. In this respect, Jackson follows A. Shennan. 1989. *Rethinking France: Plans for Renewal 1940–46*, Oxford: Clarendon Press, 231. Similarly, having previously written of the 'paradox' of traditionalist and modernizing elements at Vichy, Henry Rousso (1991. 'Vichy et la "modernisation"' in Anon., *Reconstructions et modernisation: la France après les ruines 1918...1945*, Archives nationales, 77–78) observes that the boundary the 'archaic' and 'technocratic' tendencies was not impermeable, but he does not pursue this insight. Philippe Mioche argues that Kuisel overstates the modernist elements in the Vichy plan but in doing so accepts a debate framed in terms of degrees of modernism and '*passéisme*'. See Mioche, *Le Plan Monnet*, 22–3, 29, 33 n.42.
109. AN: F60 658 Plan d'équipement. Deuxième Partie. Les Buts du Plan, 84.
110. AN: F60 658 Plan d'équipement. Troisième Partie. Chapitre 2. Agriculture, no page numbers.
111. AN: F60 658 Troisième Partie. Chapitre 2, no page numbers.
112. I. Couzon. 1997. 'La Place de la ville dans le discours des aménageurs du début des années 1920 à la fin des années 1960', *Cybergéo: European Journal of Geography* document 37, 9–14. http://www.cybergeo.eu/index1979.html accessed 16 February 2010.
113. Couzon, 'La Place de la ville', 7; Lehideux's testimony in Hoover Institution on War, Revolution and Peace. 1959. *France during the German Occupation 1940–1944. A Collection of 292 Statements on the Government of Maréchal Petain and Pierre Laval*, Stanford, California: Hoover Institution, 37.
114. AN: F60 658 Deuxième Partie. Les Buts du Plan, 76–77.
115. AN: F60 659 Plan d'équipement national. Tranche de démarrage. Première partie: Buts généraux et moyens de réalisation, 13, 27.
116. Couzon, 'La Place de la ville', 9. The achievements of the law of 15 June 1943 and the role envisaged for these structures in reconstruction are outlined in AN: F60 659 Plan d'équipement national. Tranche de démarrage, Les principaux secteurs d'équipement (buts particuliers et programmes), 145–48.
117. I use the term 'regional planning' here to indicate the move beyond the unit of the city, but it should be noted that the region was not the only unit of analysis for the DGEN planners, who discussed industrial decentralization within the framework of the locality, the region and the nation.
118. G. Dessus. 1944. *Introduction à l'étude de la localisation de l'industrie. Rapports et travaux sur la décongestion des centres industriels, No. 1*, Paris: DGEN, 7–23.

119. Dessus, *Introduction à l'étude de la localisation de l'industrie*, 13.
120. Dessus, *Introduction à l'étude de la localisation de l'industrie*, 17.
121. G. Dessus. 1944. 'Conclusions provisoires' in DGEN, *Rapports et travaux sur la décongestion des centres industriels, No.4*, Paris: DGEN, 62.
122. See G. Bohn. 1944. 'Etudes sur la décentralisation de l'industrie aéronautique' (5–44) and other contributions to *Rapports et travaux sur la décongestion des centres industriels, No.3*, Paris: DGEN.
123. AN: F60 658 Deuxième Partie. Les Buts du Plan, 77.
124. R. Ziegel. 1935. 'Une tâche nationale: la dissemination de l'industrie française. Sa necessité - mesures d'exécution', *X-Crise* 18–19, 26.
125. Ziegel, 'Une tâche nationale', 27.
126. E. Hijmans. 1938. 'La Psychose du machinisme et la production en masse', *Humanisme économique* May-June, 10–23; 1938. 'Un facteur d'équilibre économique et social. La décentralisation industrielle', *Humanisme économique* November-December, 31. The latter is a report on a discussion about industrial decentralization held at the Dutch Institute for Efficiency, to which Hijmans contributed. See also P. Heurteaux. 1939. 'Une solution immédiate pour rénover la vie rurale', *Humanisme économique* March-April, 105–11.
127. H.P. Segal. 2005. *Recasting the Machine Age: Henry Ford's Village Industries*, Amherst and Boston: University of Massachusetts Press, 27.
128. Segal, *Recasting the Machine Age*, 27–28.
129. Segal, *Recasting the Machine Age*, 108–20.
130. AN: F60 658 Plan d'équipement. Deuxième Partie. Les Buts du Plan, 65; AN: F60 658 Plan d'équipement. Troisième Partie. Chapitre 2. Agriculture, no page numbers; AN: F60 659 Plan d'équipement. Tranche de démarrage. Première Partie. Buts généraux et moyens de réalisation, 12.
131. On this and other studies Sauvy carried out during the Occupation, including an investigation of Occupation costs, see A. Sauvy. 1972. *De Paul Reynaud à Charles de Gaulle: scènes, tableaux et souvenirs. Un économiste face aux hommes politiques 1934–1967*, Paris: Casterman, 160–64.
132. A. Sauvy. 1943. *Richesse et population*, Paris: Payot.
133. Hervé Le Bras notes the distinction between ageing and *vieillissement* in H. Le Bras. 1991. *Marianne et les lapins*, Paris: Olivier Orban, 123. On the invention of *vieillissement* in French demography and Sauvy's role in it see P. Bourdelais. 1997 [1st edn 1994]. *L'Age de la vieillesse: histoire du vieillissement de la population*, Paris: Odile Jacob, Chapter Three.
134. A. Sauvy. 1939. 'Crise financière et crise de population', *X-Crise* 55, 26–28.
135. Sauvy, *Richesse et population*, 290.
136. Reggiani contrasts the emphasis on moral and military arguments between the wars with the emphasis on economics in postwar demography in A. Reggiani. 2002. 'Alexis Carrel, the Unknown: Eugenics and Population Research under Vichy', *French Historical Studies* 25(2), 355.
137. See, for example, J. Bertillon. 1897. *Le Problème de la dépopulation*, Paris: Armand Colin, 17. Landry was the author of A. Landry. 1934. *La Révolution démographique*, Paris: Sirey.
138. Sauvy, *Richesse et population*, 241.
139. Sauvy, *Richesse et population*, 77. Sauvy observed (p.78) that 'a more systematic quest for value' in authoritarian countries was doubtless responsible for this Olympic success but noted that it provided counter evidence against those who believed that having fewer children was the way to improve quality.
140. Sauvy, *Richesse et population*, 77.
141. Sauvy, *Richesse et population*, 75.
142. Sauvy, *Richesse et population*, 214.
143. Sauvy, *Richesse et population*, 209.
144. AN: F60 658 Plan d'équipement. Deuxième Partie. Les Buts du Plan, 65.

145. On the place of *vieillissement* in the postwar literature see Bourdelais, *L'Age de la vieillesse*, 127–8. On postwar populationism and the institutionalization of demography as a state science, see P.-A. Rosental. 2003. *L'Intelligence démographique: sciences et politiques des populations en France 1930–1960*, Paris: Odile Jacob and K.H. Adler. 2003. *Jews and Gender in Liberation France*, Cambridge: Cambridge University Press, esp. Chapter Four. Sauvy's focus on ageing and rejuvenation also contributed to a cult of youth in postwar France. On this theme see R.I. Jobs. 2007. *Riding the New Wave: Youth and the Rejuvenation of France after the Second World War*, Stanford: Stanford University Press.
146. See Chapter Four.
147. Le Bras, *Marianne et les lapins*, 125–27.

Conclusion

From the earliest days of the reception of Taylorism in France, certain features were apparent in the development of the scientific organization movement. One was that that the science of organization would be shaped by a dialogue between engineering and the 'sciences of man'. Another was that organizers believed the science of organization was universal and that all human activity could be scientifically organized. Initially this was little more than an aspiration but within twenty years, other professionals, such as architects and domestic scientists, had turned to scientific organization as a model and engineers were addressing new problems such as economic planning. Following the institutionalization of the movement in France from the mid-1920s, this extension of what was now often called rationalization became increasingly apparent. If rationalization was conceived in the late 1920s as a process to be applied not just within the workplace but in the economy as a whole (through industrial concentration and more coordinated relations among businesses), the advent of the Depression in the 1930s brought macroeconomic issues into even sharper focus. At the same time, the 1930s were marked by a renewal of thinking about the social and psychological organization of work, as the 'human factor' came to be conceived of not just in terms of aptitude and bodily discipline, but also in terms of the organization of relationships, personalities and motivation. This heightened interest in the non-rational aspects of human behaviour also manifested itself among economic planners who sought to overcome France's alleged Malthusianism and elevate organization into a mystique.

While the agenda of organizers shifted in response to changing circumstances and influences, it is nonetheless possible to identify a certain coherence of outlook. What dominated was a tendency to apprehend problems through a form of systems thinking which conceived of systems in terms that drew on both mechanics and biology. Holism, dynamism, equilibrium and symbiosis were the recurring tropes of these technicians' efforts to map the social and economic world. At a time when the boundaries of many disciplines were less institutionalized in France than they are today, when the fields of management and organizational science were just taking shape, when biotypologists aspired to synthesize existing biological sub-fields into a total science, and when economics was being reconfigured as a discipline in the face of the Depression, holism often implied borrowing from or appropriating the terrain of other disciplines. It was by this process that technicians defined all problems as problems of organization, and problems of organization as primarily 'human problems'. They tended to believe that they were living in a civilization defined by technological change and a period in which a new order – a new age of organization – was emerging whether people liked it or not. Indeed in this vision of a society in evolution and a universe permeated by work, where equilibrium could be increasingly identified with economic and demographic expansion, human habits and mindsets were among the few things figured as too static or resistant to change. Certainly, technological improvements in equipment had their part to play in rationalizing French production. But the central problematic of organization was increasingly seen between the wars as one of human adaptation – the psychological and physiological adaptation of the worker to the task, the elimination of social conflict, the (re-)education of the middle class, the transformation of Malthusian attitudes.

The key figure embodying this possibility of adaptation was the 'new man', or rather, several different 'new men' – the social engineer or reforming *patron*, the planner, engineer-economist or *ingénieur ès sciences de l'homme*. These were models which linked technical competence and leadership. In the workplace, this vision of leadership required a social and psychological competence and, for some at least, an ethos of consultation and communication with workers. The social engineer and the reforming *patron* did not challenge the principle of managerial authority, but rather provided new models for how it might be exercised, in a context where the prevailing managerial culture in many companies before the reforms of 1936 was distinctly authoritarian.[1] At the same time, planners represented themselves as men of action and foresight in the face of crisis, able to manage processes of adaptation through their understanding of systems and 'human problems', able to provide the state with the technical means to direct change in a way that was rational, systematic and effective, rather than the result of doctrine or political compromise. There was certainly a new woman in all this too – a middle-class housewife-manager without servants, who exercised her own kind of technical competence and might even have a profession – but in a period when attempts to enfranchise women were consistently blocked, it was symptomatic that political and economic renewal should be conceived so much in terms of the reconstruction of masculinities and (by implication at least) the revirilization of the state.

After the war planism morphed into *planification*, a term which reflected its growing institutionalization. It was no longer a movement but part of the apparatus of the state. It also became explicitly aligned with a project that was now called modernization. At a conference on regional planning in September 1947, a representative of Jean Monnet (head of the Commissariat général du Plan) explained to an audience of technicians that modernization was 'a state of mind opposed to an excessive concern only with security and immediate profitability.' He continued:

In an old nation in particular, routine too often results, as a distortion of the spirit of tradition: the public authorities must therefore intervene to stimulate and encourage creative initiatives which would otherwise be slow to manifest themselves. Indeed, is this not simply to observe that the Nation requires the same coordination of effort that scientific organization advocates for businesses.[2]

Before the war, the term 'modernization' had been used sparingly, primarily to describe material or technological change, usually with reference to a particular sector – one could speak of the modernization of farming equipment, industrial plant or administrative methods, for example. In contrast, at the Liberation, modernization became a central category in public discourse, thanks in no small part to the abundant government output on planning, but its meaning also shifted as it became identified with a wider societal project which implied not only social, political and economic change but also a new culture or mentality.[3] Again and again, postwar planners and productivity experts would repeat the mantra that what France required was not just new machinery but a new state of mind. Etienne Hirsch, another member of Monnet's team at the Plan, even suggested that one would engender the other, arguing for the modernization of farm equipment on the grounds that 'a farmer on a tractor will no longer think like a farmer behind a horse.'[4]

This discourse about planning as modernization was, of course, a language of rupture, signalling a break with old habits that were now widely believed to have contributed to France's defeat. At the same time, the parallel drawn above between modernizing France and organizing a business highlights the extent to which the national 'modernization' project had its roots in an organization movement that can be traced back to the turn of the century. To condemn an alleged preoccupation with security and short term profit was to echo the interwar organizers who had denounced the culture of French business as Malthusian and individualist. But this critique of individualism (which was really a form of self-critique since it came in part from a section of France's business leadership) had taken on a new resonance by the Liberation, as prewar elites were blamed for France's fall and the business community was discredited not just by collaboration but by accusations of profiteering. All the main political currents emerging from the Resistance converged on the planned economy as a solution, and as Andrew Shennan has pointed out, in doing so, they contrasted an economic order based on activism with one based on passivity: what was demanded was a break with an order that had been overwhelmed by international events, an order in which the worker was merely a cog in the machine and (in the eyes of the Left at least) the bourgeois was a parasite. Shennan argues that this activist economic model drew on the Resisters' model of political *engagement*, but it would perhaps be more accurate to say that this Resistance language grafted itself onto the mystique of planning as action which had already taken shape in the interwar planist movement.[5]

Clearly, not all the currents that fed into the postwar project of 'modernization' can be found within the technicians' networks discussed in this book. My study has not extended to the role of Resistance elites or political parties and has had relatively little to say about the Left, focusing only on those elements of organized labour which became most embedded in the rationalization movement. Socialists and Communists played an important role in shaping the Resistance vision of a new economic order and a social Republic at the end of the war, when there was significant demand not just for a renewal of managerial elites, but for a greater involvement of workers in running the economy.[6] This was linked to demands for nationalization and was not only taken up in Resistance circles during the Occupation, but also enacted on the ground at the Liberation, through wildcat nationalizations by miners in the northern coalfields and the creation of patriotic workers' committees in factories like Berliet in Lyon.[7] This attachment to democratization of the economy went hand in hand with a commitment to planning that was inflected with anti-capitalism. In terms of interwar antecedents, such proposals owed less to the technicians' groups per se than to the Socialist *planisme* that had flourished in centres like Révolution constructive and parts of the CGT in the 1930s. The leading Socialist planners of the Resistance, Jules Moch, André Philip and Robert Marjolin had all been associated with this current between the wars.[8] Marjolin became Monnet's Assistant Commissioner at the Commissariat au Plan in 1946, while Philip and Moch headed ministries with a significant role in postwar reconstruction – respectively, the Ministry for the National Economy (1946–1947) and the Ministry of Public Works and Transport (1945–1947).[9]

Nonetheless, other currents within Resistance thinking and Liberation politics were closer to the outlook of interwar Catholic organizers or reforming engineer-employers like Bardet and Coutrot, particularly on the question of class collaboration. The years 1944 to 1946 saw a flurry of schemes aimed at social reconciliation and organizations linked to social Catholicism made an important contribution to these debates. The Mouvement républicain populaire (MRP, the new Christian democratic party which emerged as a major political force at the Liberation) and the Centre des Jeunes Patrons (CJP), which had its roots in the 1930s trend towards social management and class collaboration discussed in Chapter Two, were among those who proposed schemes to encourage worker participation (even profit sharing in some cases), while maintaining the basic principles of capitalist ownership and managerial authority.[10] This was close to the position adopted by de Gaulle's provisional government, which soon acted to rein in the radical experiments of the de facto workers' committees that sprang up in 1944. Building on the precedent of Vichy's social committees, an ordinance of 22 February 1945 required firms employing more than one hundred people to have a committee on which all categories of employees would be represented, and which would run the workplace social services.

Importantly, these committees had only a consultative function in relation to economic matters – a model rather reminiscent of Bardet's proposals and one that was welcomed enthusiastically by another veteran of the interwar debates, Auguste Detoeuf.[11] Likewise, while the debate about these issues certainly moved to the Left at Liberation, the Communists' departure from the governing coalition in 1947 left the Socialists and the MRP in need of support from conservatives and Radicals, which in turn ushered in a retreat from some of the more radical steps towards industrial democracy that had been introduced in newly nationalized companies.[12] What ultimately emerged at the Liberation then was a kind of cross-party compromise around the themes of planning, nationalization of key industries, renewal of elites, social rights, and a drive for efficiency and productivity.

Although the war changed the political balance of power and partially discredited existing political elites, recent studies have suggested there was less renewal of personnel than received opinion once maintained.[13] Continuities can also be observed between the prewar and postwar organization movements. While some of the figures discussed in previous chapters had died during the war (Coutrot, Ponthière), and others remained but had had the highpoints of their careers before 1945 (Dubreuil, Bernège), still others went on to occupy major roles in the postwar order. Raoul Dautry served not just in the crucial post of Minister for Reconstruction and Urban Planning in the Provisional Government, but subsequently as head of France's Atomic Energy Commission. Dautry's interest in housing and urbanism dated back to the 1920s and his return to a ministerial post at the Liberation was possible in part because he had withdrawn from public life during the Occupation and was untarnished by association with Vichy. At the same time, like many who occupied administrative rather than political positions, Alfred Sauvy's links with Vichy did not disqualify him from heading a major government agency (INED) after the war. Substantial parts of the administration of OCRPI and the DGEN were also absorbed directly into the Directorates for Programmes and Equipment at the new Ministry of National Economy (MEN), where Frédéric Surleau, the last Director of the DGEN, became Director of Equipement national in September 1944. Other organizers continued their work through the key institutions of the interwar movement – the CNOF, CEGOS, INOP, *Le Travail humain* – which remained in place.

Indeed, not surprisingly, the organization movement enjoyed something of a resurgence at the Liberation. The pages of the CNOF bulletin in the late 1940s are filled with adverts for consultancy firms vying for work as the postwar productivity drive got underway and a number of the figures I have discussed in relation to the interwar movement were among those offering their services: the well-established Planus firm was now one of the larger consultancy companies, for example, while the Compagnie d'ingénieurs en organisation brought the veteran First-World-War organizer Emile Rimailho (now in his eighties) together with Coutrot's erstwhile colleague, the doctor and psychologist Henri Arthus.[14] Other firms too boasted the services of experts in applied psycho-biology who had established their credentials in the interwar years – the Organisation des conseils en organisation scientifique brought together psychotechnicians such as Léone Bourdel, who had taught at the School of Scientific Organization with former CEPH members Pierre Lévy and Jacques Lobstein. The School of Scientific Organization continued to educate a new generation of organizers, while the CEGOS developed further its wartime role as a provider of training and consultancy services.[15] Its first Secretary-General, Jean Milhaud, who was only in his late forties at the Liberation, maintained the interest in the rationalization of public administration that he had developed between the wars and founded the Institut technique des administrations publiques (Technical Institute of Public Administration) in 1947.[16] He also became the first Director of a new review, *Hommes et techniques*, whose title was symptomatic of the ongoing interest in the 'human' dimensions of what would increasingly be known as *le management* or *la gestion*. Founded in 1945 in association with the CNOF and the CEGOS, *Hommes et techniques* was absorbed in 1975 by the *Revue française de gestion*.[17]

As the durable role of many of these organizations, reviews and individuals suggests, the developments discussed in this book can be situated in terms of a number of broader historical trends. Firstly, the story I have told is in part about the development of management as a discipline, the emergence of the professional manager and the growth of management education. The technicians' interest in 'human problems' might also be seen as a chapter in the history of the applied social sciences. The growth of applied psychology and sociology was an important trend in the postwar period as the social sciences were increasingly expected to serve the needs of an expanding economy – a model which proved controversial and would be one of the targets of the 1968 student movement.[18] This approach was quite alien to the Durkheimian theoretical tradition which had dominated the academic discipline of sociology in France before the war. Arguably, then, it was in the sphere of technicians' networks, in work science and early management education, and in multi-disciplinary institutes like the CEPH and the Carrel Foundation that an alternative model began to take shape before 1945. If these developments straddled the social and biological sciences, psychotechnicians and biotypologists, as well as figures such as Coutrot and Wilbois, who built bridges between the academic and business worlds, could be seen to have created a favourable environment for the development of a new role for the social scientist in the 1950s as a technician or 'social engineer', as well as contributing to the ongoing importance of fields like psychotechnics and occupational medicine.[19] Certainly, Georges Friedmann, a central figure in the new sociology of work in France after the war, identified Bardet's experiments with workers' delegates and the interwar vogue for group organization as the beginnings of a move beyond psycho-biological approaches towards a more sociological view of industrial organization. His observation of these interwar experiments, discussed in his thesis on the 'human problems' of industrial society, served to map out the terrain of his own postwar sociological project.[20]

The technician-publicists of the interwar years, among whom Jean Coutrot remains the emblematic figure, can also be seen in a longer term perspective. Though Coutrot's taste for the world of writing, study groups and reviews has been regarded as something that separates him from much of the interwar business community, it could also be seen as something that links him to postwar technician-publicists such as Jean Fourastié, Louis Armand or Gaston Berger. Fourastié, an engineer-economist who shared Coutrot's refusal to abide by conventional disciplinary boundaries (having studied in the law faculty and the Ecole libre des Sciences politiques as well as at the Ecole centrale), combined a series of roles at the Commissariat au Plan with a prolific publishing career in which he tirelessly proclaimed the social and economic benefits of technical progress.[21] Armand, the Chair of Euratom and former head of the SNCF, and Berger, an industrialist turned philosopher, were among the founder-members of Prospective, a think tank and review created in 1958. In an unusually varied career Berger was also an expert in 'characterology' and the founder of an Institute of Biometrics and Vocational Guidance in Marseille.

Prospective shared something of the CEPH's aspiration to study human problems in an interdisciplinary framework. The group, which also included the senior financial civil servant François Bloch-Lainé and Dr André Gros (who had been one of the major figures in the institutionalization of occupational medicine at Vichy) sought to examine 'the technical, scientific, economic and social causes which accelerate the evolution of the modern world' and to forecast their consequences.[22] Berger spoke of the need for 'the prospective attitude' which he linked closely to a systems view and a concern for 'human problems', because:

> Far from becoming mechanized, as some seem to think, the human world is becoming more and more like an organism, in which no one function is the end goal of all the others, but in which each works with the others to ensure the life and development of the whole …. The 'human world' is becoming a veritable reality rather than simply a word which designates largely independent systems.[23]

In a further echo of interwar themes and personalities, Louis Armand's contribution to the first issue of the review *Prospective* – an article on questions of transport – even began in Coutrot-esque fashion with references to Teilhard de Chardin and Aldous Huxley.[24] A few years later Armand published *Plaidoyer pour l'avenir* in which he argued, much as Coutrot had done, that rapid technological advance was the defining feature of the age, that this rapid transformation brought problems of adaptation but also solutions, and that 'organization' was vital to orient material progress towards human ends – an agenda he summed up as a call for 'technological humanism'.[25]

Although the issues discussed had evolved since the 1930s – this was now the era of nuclear power and the emergence of the 'third world' – the persistence of this ideal of the engineer as humanist and of the aspiration to solve the problems posed by technological progress through a dialogue with the 'sciences of man' suggests that the agenda mapped out between the wars was by no means an ephemeral one. Indeed, other projects like the decentralization of industry also had a postwar existence in government policy and in industrial practice, particularly in western France, where major companies like Citroën established rural factories in the 1950s and 1960s and tried to foster a model of the 'peasant-worker', which was not so far from the ambitions of some of those who had supported decentralization in the 1930s and 1940s.[26]

So how might all these findings help us to rethink the period from the 1920s to the 1940s in terms that move beyond the historiography of crisis and 'modernization' that was outlined in the Introduction? Firstly, to provide a fuller account of the range of organizational problems examined by technicians before 1945 and to challenge the mythologization of the technocrat raises the question of why this myth has been so resilient, particularly in relation to Vichy. Like many myths, this one does some important ideological work, for in divorcing the technical from the political, it positions technicians as being *at* Vichy but not *of* it, members of the government yet untainted by its politics. In this way, the construction of Bichelonne as the archetypal technocrat confers a certain purity on those who are seen as France's modernizers (even if they are reproached for their naivety or poor judgement). My own contention is that there is no ideologically pure pedigree for the project that came to be called modernization. The origins of this project can be located at least in part in the history of interwar interactions between engineering and the 'sciences of man', including those elements that we have come to regard as retrograde (such as collective psychology, eugenics or socio-biology). This is not to demonize the organizers' projects, nor to dismiss them as reactionary, but simply to explore them in their historical complexity and to integrate them into a history which resists mythologization. Thus, unlike other historians who have addressed this impurity of French 'modernization' projects, I do not see it in terms of a 'reactionary modernism', that is, as a special French variant of modernism that was somehow a compromise between 'tradition' and 'modernity'. Rather I am suggesting that the pure modernism against which France is measured in such implicitly comparative statements is itself a mythical construction.

This also has implications for how we think about gender and the construction of 'modernity'. Studies such as those of Robert Frost, Ellen Furlough and more recently Adam Stanley have argued that an appeal to traditional gender roles served as a means of domesticating a 'modernity' that is seen to emerge as an autonomous force from outside France. These studies ostensibly take a constructionist and anti-essentialist view of gender but do not carry this over to their thinking about the 'modern'.[27] Yet if the economic and social order identified with 'modernity' in these studies – a mass consumer society – is understood instead as a historical product, shaped by human actions, and if 'modernization' is conceived of as a project rather than a historical force, we can begin to see efforts to produce a new man and a new woman in the interwar period as an integral part of the making of this new order. Hence, for example, it seems to me that the model of middle-class domesticity offered by Bernège and her colleagues did not just serve to make an inevitable external force of 'modernity' less threatening by harnessing it to an updated version of traditional ideas about feminine domesticity, but was conceived of as a means of furthering a rationalization project in which 'human problems', 'mentalities' and psycho-biological types (including gender difference) occupied a central place.

If the historiography of twentieth-century France has remained so infused with modernization narratives it is perhaps in part because this discourse has become so widespread both in the world of work and in the world of politics since the 1980s, especially in the Anglophone world. But these narratives first took hold in historical writing on interwar France just after World War Two, reflecting certain affinities between the outlook of the postwar generation of political and social scientists and that of technicians themselves. The preoccupation with mentalities as an obstacle to progress or (subsequently) a driver of change was certainly taken up by the likes of David Landes, Charles Kindleberger and Stanley Hoffmann.[28] These classic Cold War analyses were produced at a time when a liberal functionalism reigned supreme in the American social sciences, propagating a view of societies as systems which tended to towards equilibrium, consensus and evolution, while conflict and revolutionary change were regarded as pathological – a systems view that squared rather well with that developed by interwar technicians.[29] This view was apparent, for example, in Hoffmann's stalemate society thesis, with its attempt to construct a model that integrated the social, the political, the economic and the question of mentalities, as well as its preoccupation with locating systemic *dys*functions in the prewar period. At the same time, the postwar technician-publicists cited above were themselves active in promoting a popular historical narrative that contrasted a troubled prewar history in which France struggled to adapt to technical civilization with a present defined not just by rapid technological change but by a new 'modern' attitude and mode of organization.[30]

One of the clearest intersections between the academic analyses and the popular historical narratives of technicians can be found in the work of Alfred Sauvy. From the late 1920s to Vichy, Sauvy had used history to legitimize the role of the engineer-economist as an expert and to argue for his particular blend of planism and populationism. His arguments constantly appealed to historical evidence, whether recent (work time reforms, decisions about monetary policy) or more distant (patterns of economic and demographic expansion/contraction in the nineteenth century). A constant harking back to the interwar period (as evidence of his own foresight and the errors of politicians and public opinion) was also a feature of his postwar writings.[31] Historians have often consulted his memoirs (which constitute one of the sources for anecdotes about Bichelonne's extraordinary brain).[32] But Sauvy was not only a frequently cited commentator and memoirist; he contributed directly to the historiography of the interwar period with his monumental four-volume *Histoire économique de la France de l'entre-deux-guerres*, published between 1965 and 1975.

This study was reissued in a new edition in 1984 and continues to be used by researchers today, particularly as a source of statistical information about the period. In interpretive terms, however, its major contribution was to promote a vision of interwar France as backward and, more specifically, in Sauvy's terms, Malthusian. This version of the backwardness thesis, which fused the preoccupation with collective mentalities together with a demographic analysis, did receive some dissemination in English, notably in the *Journal of Contemporary History* in 1969, but it was particularly influential in the French historiography.[33] Even as revisionists moved away from this interpretation in the 1990s, they defined their positions in relation Sauvy's analysis, testifying to its classic status. In a special issue of *Mouvement social* in 1991, for example, contributor after contributor cited Sauvy's as the orthodox interpretation which they sought to test and reevaluate.[34] Moreover, others have continued to adhere to the old orthodoxy, as works such as Eugen Weber's *The Hollow Years* (1994), Christophe Charles, *La Crise des sociétés impériales* (2001) or Jean-Pierre Dormois' textbook, *The French Economy in the Twentieth Century* (2004) have demonstrated.[35]

By pathologizing the interwar period, Sauvy's interpretation played into narratives of rupture which served the postwar modernization project well. Yet his own life history tells a rather different story: a story about the breadth and versatility of engineers' plans for a new order before 1945, about their preoccupation with 'human problems', with the renewal of elites and with the construction of a mystique of organization embodied by the new man; a story about the ways in which these projects converged with other attempts to remodel France and its population, under Vichy, as well as under Republican governments; a story about some of the ways in which both the postwar order and the historiography of twentieth-century France that we have inherited have been directly shaped by the interwar encounter between engineering and the 'sciences of man.' Although explicit use of terms like Malthusianism and backwardness has declined, the survival of this type of analysis in the new cultural histories of 'reactionary modernism', with their emphasis on what is now understood as cultural rather than psychological resistance to 'modernity', suggests that we have by no means managed to gain a critical historical distance on these developments. But this book has at least begun to map out an alternative approach.

Notes

1. See J. Jackson. 1990. *The Popular Front in France: Defending Democracy* Cambridge: Cambridge University Press, 98–9 on the culture of the French workplace before 1936.
2. J.-R. Rabier. 1947. 'La Deuxième Séance plénière. Planification locale et régionale' *Bulletin du CNOF* September, 32.
3. A quick indication of the explosion of the term and its prevalence in the planning literature in particular can be gained from the entries in the catalogue of the Bibliothèque nationale de France.
4. Cited in R. Kuisel. 1981. *Capitalism and the State in Modern France: Renovation and Economic Management in the Twentieth Century*, Cambridge: Cambridge University Press, 226. Those who participated in the productivity missions under the Marshall Plan reasoned in a similar way, identifying attitudes and 'the human factor' as the key to productivity. See R. Kuisel. 1993. *Seducing the French: The Dilemma of Americanization*, Berkeley: University of California Press, 83–84.
5. A. Shennan. 1989. *Rethinking France: Plans for Renewal 1940–1946*, Oxford: Clarendon Press, 45.
6. The Charter of the Conseil national de la Résistance spoke of the need for a 'démocratie sociale'.
7. See Shennan, *Rethinking France*, 192–93; H. Chapman. 2007. 'France's Liberation Era, 1944–47: A Social and Economic Settlement', in A. Knapp (ed). *The Uncertain Foundation: France at Liberation, 1944–47*, Basingstoke: Palgrave MacMillan, 104, 107; and for more detail C. Andrieu, L. Le Van, A. Prost (dir.). 1987. *Les Nationalisations de la Libération: de l'utopie au compromis*, Paris: Presses de la FNSP.
8. See Kuisel, *Capitalism and the State*, 160–61, 173–79. Moch, a *polytechnicien* provided a link between the technicians who gathered at X-Crise and the socialist planners at Révolution constructive.
9. Philip served under the Gouin government (January-June 1946) and the Blum Government (December 1946– January 1947) when his portfolio included Finance as well as the economy and then under the Ramadier government (January–October 1947). Moch continued as a minister until 1951, heading the Ministries of Defence and the Interior and was recalled to the Ministry of Interior in 1958.
10. Shennan, *Rethinking France*, 198–99.
11. Shennan, *Rethinking France*, 194–95
12. At EDF, for example, the function of personnel boards was reduced from a decision-making one to a purely consultative one. Chapman, 'France's Liberation Era', 110.
13. O. Wieviorka, 2007. 'Replacement or Renewal? The French Political Elite at the Liberation', in A. Knapp (ed.), *The Uncertain Foundation: France at Liberation, 1944–1947*, Basingstoke: Palgrave MacMillan, 75–86.
14. See especially *Bulletin du CNOF* 1947. On the Compagnie d'ingénieurs en organisation, see *Organisation à la française. Cahiers de la Compagnie d'ingénieurs en organisation* 1–8 1945–1949.
15. See http://www.cegos.com/en/groupe/histoire/Pages/histoire-cegos.aspx. Last accessed 20 December 2010.
16. See J. Siwek-Pouydesseau. 2006. 'L'Institut technique des administrations publiques, entrepreneur militant de la productivité administrative (1947–1968)', *Revue française d'administration publique* 120, 711–719.
17. A third organization established between the wars, the Bureau des temps élémentaires, also participated in the establishment of *Hommes et techniques*. The Bureau des temps élémentaires, which specialized in time and motion study, had begun within the CNOF in 1938 before becoming an autonomous association in 1942.
18. Nationalized industries like Renault and EDF were among the most active in bringing in social scientists to research their businesses and a Research service was established at Renault as an institutionalized part of the Department of Personnel and Social Rela-

tions. It carried out studies on the ergonomics of work at Renault, as well as on the question of housing which was a major issue at a time when the firm was expanding and accommodation was in short supply, especially in the Paris region. See A-S Perrault.1999. *Renault et les sciences sociales 1948–1991*, Paris: Seli Arslan, 17, 35–40, 63.

19. Here I follow in part the argument of O. Henry. 2004.'De la sociologie comme technologie sociale: la contribution de Jean Coutrot, 1895–1941' *Actes de la Recherche en sciences sociales* 153, 48–64. Historians of the Carrel Foundation have also noted its significance in the development of the population science and applied social research. See A Reggiani. 2007. *God's Eugenicist: Alexis Carrel and the Sociobiology of Decline*, Oxford: Berghahn, 167 and A. Drouard. 1992. *Une inconnue des sciences sociales: la Fondation Alexis Carrel, 1941–1945*, Paris: Editions de la Maison des sciences de l'homme/INED.

20. G. Friedmann. 1977. *Industrial Society*, New York: Arno Press, 304–338 which is a translation of Friedmann's 1946 study *Problèmes humains du machinisme industriel*.

21. See, for example, J. Fourastié. 1947. *La Civilisation de 1960*, Paris: Presses universitaires de France; J. Fourastié with the collaboration of F. Fourastié. 1950. *Histoire du confort*, Paris: Presses universitaires de France; J. Fourastié. 1951. *Machinisme et bien-être*, Paris: Minuit, as well as his best-known work, J. Fourastié. 1979. *Les Trente Glorieuses où la révolution invisible de 1946 à 1975*, Paris: Fayard. Fourastié's work is perpetuated today by the Comité Jean Fourastié. See http://www.jean-fourastie.org/ and its website aimed at educating young people in his economic thought http://www.kezeco.fr/. Last accessed 20 December 2010.

22. Declaration on cover page of *Prospective*, 1, 1958.

23. G. Berger. 1958. 'Préface' *Prospective*, 1, 1, 5, 7.

24. L. Armand. 1958.'Vues prospectives sur les transports' *Prospective*, 1, 38.

25. L. Armand and M. Drancourt. 1961. *Plaidoyer pour l'avenir*, Paris: Calmann-Lévy, esp. 147–59.

26. I am grateful to Matthew Wendeln, who is completing doctoral research on this topic at New York University and the Ecole des hautes études en sciences sociales, for drawing these continuities and the example of Citroën to my attention.

27. For example, gender discourse is seen by Adams as hinging on 'a push-and-pull between the forces of tradition and the advance of modernity'. A. C. Stanley. 2008. *Modernizing Tradition: Gender and Consumerism in Interwar France and Germany*, Baton Rouge: Louisiana State University Press, 9.

28. D. Landes. 1951. 'French Business and the Businessman: A Social and Cultural Analysis', in E. M. Earle (ed.), *Modern France: Problems of the Third and Fourth Republics*, Princeton: Princeton University Press, 334–53; S. Hoffmann. 1963. 'Paradoxes of the French Political Community' in Hoffman et al., *In Search of France: The Economy, Society and Political System in the Twentieth Century*, New York: Harper and Row, 1–117; C. Kindleberger, 'The Postwar Resurgence of the French Economy', in Hoffmann et al., *In Search of France*, 118–58.

29. This view has been particularly associated with Talcott Parsons, who taught at Harvard from 1927 to 1979 and was the author of Talcott Parsons. 1937. *The Structure of Social Action*, New York: MacGraw Hill and Talcott Parsons. 1951. *The Social System*, New York: Free Press. David Landes cited Parsons as one of those who had helped to define the problem of 'the human factor' in social systems in 'French Business and the Businessman', 335.

30. E.g. Armand and Drancourt, *Plaidoyer pour l'avenir*, 29–41.

31. E.g. A. Sauvy. 1965. *Mythologies de notre temps*, Paris: Payot, 20–22 and A.Sauvy. 1985. *De la rumeur à l'histoire*, Paris: Bordas, 101–284.

32. A. Sauvy. 1972. *De Paul Reynaud à Charles de Gaulle: scènes, tableaux et souvenirs. Un économiste face aux hommes politiques 1934–1967*, Paris: Casterman.

33. A. Sauvy. 1969. 'The Economic Crisis of the 1930s in France' *Journal of Contemporary History* 4(4), 21–35.

34.   'Paradoxes français de la crise des années 30', special issue of *Mouvement social* 154, 1991; Michel Margairaz also defines his position against Sauvy's in Margairaz. 1991. *L'Etat, les finances et l'économie. Histoire d'une conversion, 1932–1952*, 2 vols., Paris: Comité pour l'histoire économique et financière de la France.

35.   Volumes published respectively by W W Norton and Co, Seuil and Cambridge University Press.

Biographical Profiles

Bardet, Gérard

Engineer and industrialist. Born in 1903, Bardet was the son of a self-made man who had built up a business manufacturing machine tools (Machines Automatiques Bardet). He graduated from the Ecole polytechnique before entering the family firm in 1925. Between 1927 and 1935 he implemented a series of reforms in the company including the introduction of paid holidays, a forty-hour week and a consultative Workers' Council. He was also one of several interwar engineers to experiment with team-working. A close associate of Jean Coutrot, he was a member of the Comité national d'organisation française (CNOF), the economic think tank X-Crise and the Centre d'études des problems humains (CEPH). During the Occupation he served as head of the Conseil consultatif du centre d'information inter-professionnel, the Conseil supérieur de l'économie industrielle et commerciale and the Conseil supérieur du travail, and campaigned with the support of Bichelonne to give workers a consultative role in economic as well as social matters in Vichy's business committees.

Bernège, Paulette

Paulette Bernège led the movement for the application of scientific organization to the home in France. Her publishing career spanned three decades from 1920 to 1950. She studied literature and philosophy before embarking on a career as a writer and teacher in what she termed 'the domestic sciences'. Her association with the organization movement appears to date from 1920 when she started writing for the review *Mon bureau*. She also developed close links with the Salon des arts ménagers, an annual government sponsored exhibition which promoted new domestic technologies and had its own monthly review, *Art ménager*, to which Bernège contributed. In

1925 she founded the Ligue d'organisation menagère and in 1928 she published *De la méthode ménagère* which offered lessons and practical exercises for improving one's efficiency in domestic work. Bernège's approach was informed not just by Fayolism, Taylorism and applied psycho-physiology, but reflected her strong interests in architecture, design and the pedagogical methods of the New Education movement. She also wrote on farm organization in the 1930s and on socio-biology and rural life during the Occupation. She maintained her interest in rural organization after the war when she published *J'Organise ma petite ferme* (1950).

Bichelonne, Jean

Born in 1904, Bichelonne entered the Ecole polytechnique in 1923 with the highest score ever recorded in the entrance exam. Having graduated at the top of his class he entered the *Corps des mines* and studied at the Ecole des mines before being appointed to a post in the Lorraine mining region. He returned to Paris in 1935 to teach at the Ecole des mines and take up a series of posts at the Ministry of Public Works before being appointed *Directeur de cabinet* in Raoul Dautry's Ministry of Armaments in September 1939. According to his associate and biographer Guy Sabin, he frequented X-Crise in the 1930s, but he was not one of the more active members. With the creation of the Vichy government he was appointed *Secrétaire général* at the Ministry of Industrial Production, was involved in the creation of the Organization committees and headed the Office central de répartition des produits industriels which coordinated the distribution of raw materials to industry. In April 1942 he was promoted to Secretary of State for Industrial Production. A proponent of economic collaboration, he established a good working relationship with the Nazi armaments minister Albert Speer and through the Speer-Bichelonne Accords in September 1943 he sought to establish a position for French industry in an organized European economy under Germany leadership. He died in a German hospital in 1944 before he could be tried for collaboration.

Coutrot, Jean

Born in 1895, Coutrot became active in the scientific organization movement in the 1920s and rose to prominence in the 1930s, before dying in controversial circumstances in 1941. A war veteran who had lost a leg in 1915, he married Annette Gaut in 1917 and became head of the Gaut-Blancan paper company before going on to found one of France's first management consultancy firms, the Bureau des ingénieurs-conseils en rationalisation in 1931. He was notable for the wide range of his interests and contacts which included artists, intellectuals, industrialists and politicians. He was a leading member of a host of interwar technicians' groups including the CNOF, the economic think tank X-Crise and the Plan du 9 juillet group. Having embraced the social explosion of May-June 1936, he was at his most prominent in the late 1930s. In 1936 he was appointed head of the Centre national de l'organisation scientifique du travail, created by the Popular Front Government. In the same year he laid the foundations of the CEPH which brought technicians and industrialists together with specialists in a range of fields including psychology, biology and aesthetics. Though he was prepared to serve the Vichy Government he died before he could take up a post. His body was found outside his Paris apartment, the cause of death uncertain. This became the pretext for a wave of conspiracy rumours in the collaborationist press linking Coutrot to an alleged plot by a network of technicians and financial interests known as the Synarchy.

Dautry, Raoul

Dautry was born in 1880. He studied at the Ecole polytechnique and spent much of his career in the railway industry (Chemins de fer du nord, Chemins de fer de l'Etat) where he became known for his social action, notably in providing housing and medical services for workers. At the Chemins de Fer de l'Etat, he built over 5000 homes between 1929 and 1932. He was a member of Redressement français in the late 1920s along with Detoeuf, Romier and Mercier. He was also a member of the CNOF and the Union sociale des ingénieurs catholiques. Inspired by Marshal Hubert Lyautey and by the Catholic social movement the Equipes sociales, one of his favourite topics was the social role of the engineer. In September 1939 he was appointed Minister of Armaments and, as well as overseeing France's arms policy, he set about developing social services in the armaments industry. Having kept his distance from the Vichy Government, he was appointed Minister of Reconstruction and Urban Planning by de Gaulle in September 1944 and Head of the French Atomic Energy Commission in January 1946. He died in 1951.

Detoeuf, Auguste

Born in 1883 Detoeuf studied at the Ecole polytechnique and began his career as a state engineer (*Pont et chaussées*) before moving into private industry. He was appointed managing director of Thomson-Houston in 1922 and went on to be a director at Alsthom and President of the Syndicat général de la construction électrique. He was a central figure in technicians' networks between the wars participating in a number of committees and think tanks including Redressement français, the CNOF, X-Crise, the Commission générale d'organisation scientifique du travail (CEGOS) and the Comité central de l'organisation professionnelle. He was the founder of the review *Les Nouveaux Cahiers*. The strikes and reforms of 1936 led him in *Construction du syndicalisme* (1938) to propose a model of industrial relations built on negotiation between single obligatory unions for labour and employers in each branch of economic activity. During the Occupation he served as head of the Organization Committee for the electrical construction industry and was a member of the Conseil supérieur de l'économie industrielle et commerciale, the Comité consultatif de la Délégation générale de l'équipement français and the Comité d'études pour la France, as well as maintaining his role as President of the CEGOS. He continued to be active in the organization movement (at the CNOF, for example) until his death in 1947.

Dubreuil, Hyacinthe

Mechanic, trade unionist and writer. Born in 1883, Dubreuil rose to a position on the executive committee of the Metalworkers Federation of the CGT before the First World War. Having rallied to a reformist position in 1919 he wrote for labour movement publications such as *La Voix du Peuple*, *L'Atelier* and *L'Information ouvrière et sociale* and was close to Albert Thomas. In 1927–28 he spent 15 months working in the U.S., sponsored by the Council for Industrial Relations (financed by the Rockefeller Foundation). His account of his experience, *Standards* (1929), became a bestseller. A member of the CNOF, he was well known and widely read in technicians' networks. He broke with the CGT in March 1931 and worked for the International Labour Office from 1931 to 1938, during which time he published several books including *Nouveaux Standards* (1931) and *A chacun sa chance* (1935). In *Lettre aux travailleurs français* in 1938 he chastised the French labour movement for being taken in by the 'foreign' doctrine of class conflict and during the Occupation he published books and pamphlets which supported Pétain's National Revolution including *La Chevalerie du travail* (1942). He worked for the national welfare organization the Secours national, and continued as a member of the CNOF, serving on its executive committee. After the war he was a social advisor to the independent socialist mayor of Kremlin-Bicêtre, Antoine Lacroix, and had contacts with Dautry (to whom he had been close since the late 1930s) and Louis Armand (head of the SNCF) as well as writers such as Daniel Halévy and Paul Claudel. In 1968 he opposed the May movement in the columns of *Le Figaro*. He died in 1971.

Fayol, Henri

Born 1841. A graduate of the Ecole de mines de Saint-Etienne, Fayol worked in the mining industry from 1866 to 1918. He rose to become Director General of the Commentry-Fourchambault company in 1888. He began developing and disseminating his management theory from around 1900 and published *Administration industrielle et générale* in 1916. This book codified a social organicist theory of management which emphasized the coordinating and planning role of the leader at the head of a business. Between 1920 and 1923 Fayol was appointed by the Bloc national government to rationalize the postal and telecommunications service and the public monopoly of tobacco. He died in 1925 but his management theory continued to be disseminated within the organization movement.

Lahy, Jean-Maurice

Born in 1872, J-M Lahy was the son of a stonemason and a hatmaker who went on to become one of France's most important researchers in applied psychology. He was one of the pioneers of psychotechnics, a form of aptitude testing which had applications in vocational guidance and the recruitment and assignment of workers. Having begun his research before the First World War, he went on to carry out studies on transport workers in the early 1920s, which led to the creation of a psychotechnic laboratory at the Paris transport company the STCRP in 1924 and a similar facility at the Chemins de fer du Nord in 1931. Lahy also held posts at the Institute of Psychology at the Ecole pratique des hautes études where he became Director in 1927. He was co-founder of the *Revue de la science du travail* (1929–30) and *Le Travail humain* (1933 to present) and in 1932 he joined the Société de biotypologie. A *dreyfusard* and member of the Ligue des droits de l'homme, he was close to the Communist Party in the interwar period and was a member from 1920 to 1923. He also became a member of the Comité de vigilance des intellectuels anti-fascistes (created in 1934). In 1941 he was forced out of his job because he was a freemason and he died from ill health in 1943.

Laugier, Henri

Born in 1888, Laugier was a physiologist who played an important role in work science and in the organization of scientific research in France. After being mobilized in the First World War he worked at the Hôpital Henri Rousselle with Edouard Toulouse. In 1928 he founded the Institut national d'orientation professionnelle (INOP) along with Henri Piéron and Julien Fontègne, and was appointed Professor of the Physiology of Work at the Conservatoire national des arts et metiers, a post he held until 1937. From 1933 he headed a work science laboratory at the Chemins de fer de l'Etat, which became a national facility for biometric research. Close to the Radical Party, he served as *Chef de cabinet* for Yvon Delbos in 1925 and in 1936. In 1937 he founded the Palais de la découverte along with Jean Perrin. He was involved in developing the law that created the CNRS (Centre national de la recherche scientifique) in 1939 and was appointed its first director. During the Occupation he worked at the University of Montreal and was active in the Free French in the U.S. before joining de Gaulle in Algiers in 1943. In 1946 he was appointed Assistant Secretary General to the United Nations with responsibility for social and economic affairs. From 1952 he was the French representative on the Executive council of UNESCO. He died in 1973.

Le Chatelier, Henry

Born in 1850 to a bourgeois Catholic family, Le Chatelier studied at the Ecole polytechnique and the Ecole des mines and worked briefly in industry before taking up a teaching post at the Ecole des mines in 1877. Here he began research in chemical engineering and formulated a law on the displacement of equilibrium in chemical systems which bears his name. From 1903 he was the founding editor of the *Revue de métallurgie* and in 1904 he was elected President of the Société d'encouragement pour l'industrie nationale. In these positions he was the leading promoter of Taylorism in France before the First World War. By the 1920s and 1930s he was an elder statesman of the scientific organization movement, regarded by the interwar generation as a 'founding father'. He died in 1936.

Martiny, Marcel (Dr)

A doctor and specialist in occupational medicine. In the 1930s Martiny worked with apprentices at the training school run by the Chambre de commerce de Paris, was a member of Société de biotypologie and Secretary-general of the medical section of the Association France-Italie. He cultivated links with the Italian biotypologist Nicola Pende and publicized the latter's work in France. He headed the Psycho-biology group at Jean Coutrot's Centre d'études des problèmes humains (1937–39) and was part of the networks of occupational medicine that became influential in Vichy France, serving as a chargé de mission in Hubert Lagardelle's Ministry of Labour. By 1948, he was running biotypology consultations at the Hôpital Foch in Paris and was President of the Société de Morphophysiologie humaine. In 1954 he was the founding director of the review *Connaissance de l'homme. Revue des sciences de l'homme et de leurs applications pratiques*, which provided an intellectual home for a number of figures who, like Martiny, were veterans of the holist current in interwar medicine or the Carrel Foundation (J. Sutter, Louis Corman, J. Ménétrier, A. Missenard).

Mercier, Ernest

Born to a protestant family in 1878, Mercier graduated from the Ecole poly-technique and the Ecole supérieure de l'électricité and worked as a naval engineer before beginning a career in the electrical distribution industry in 1913. He fought in the First World War and in 1917 was appointed to a post on the technical staff of Louis Loucheur who was then Minister of Arma-ments. In 1919 he became Managing Director of the Union d'électricité and between 1920 and 1940 he went on to head a number of other companies including the Compagnie française des pétroles. He founded Redressement français (with Lucien Romier and Auguste Detoeuf) in 1925, and was a strong advocate of rationalization, industrial concentration and the Pan-Europe movement. He disbanded Redressement français in November 1935 and from December 1933 to March 1936 he was a member of the far Right Croix de Feu. During the Occupation he opposed collaboration. His career as a manager in the electricity industry was brought to an end by national-ization in 1946. He died in 1955.

Ponthière, Maurice

A law graduate who became a journalist, Ponthière was active in the Catholic nationalist Right before the First World War. He was critical of Action française and accepted the Ralliement, arguing for the creation of a large popular conservative party to defend the values of the Church. In 1921 he was one of the founders of the Conférence de l'organisation française. He became editor of *Mon bureau* in 1925 and was a member of the CNOF from its creation in 1926. He published *Le Nouvel Esprit des affaires* (1931) and *Le Bureau moteur* (1935) and from 1934 was director of the Ecole d'or-ganisation scientifique du travail created by the CNOF. He promoted a ver-sion of scientific organization which drew heavily on Fayolism and on social organicist thinking. During the Occupation he founded a branch of the CNOF in the Toulouse region in association with his friend and relative Paulette Bernège. He died in 1942.

Rimailho, Emile

Born in 1864, Rimailho studied at the Ecole polytechnique and became a military engineer. In 1900 he designed a piece of mobile heavy artillery equipment to which he gave his name. In 1913 he left the army for the arma-ments industry, where he was involved in the application of scientific organ-ization methods. After the war he continued to work as an industrial organizer and taught at Ecole nationale supérieure de l'aéronautique. He was one of several interwar engineers to experiment with team working methods as a means of motivating workers and involving them in the organization of work. He published on his experience of applying this method in *Organisation à la française* (1936) and went on to publish a book with Hyacinthe Dubreuil (*Deux hommes parlent du travail*) in 1939. He was a member of the Catholic engineers union USIC, as well as the key groups dedicated to promoting scientific organization (CNOF, CEGOS). He was still promoting his methods at the Liberation despite being in his eighties. He died in 1954.

Romier, Lucien

Born in 1885, Romier was a historian and paleographer who became a prominent journalist and publicist in the 1920s. He was Editor-in-chief of the business newspaper *La Journée industrielle* and of the *Figaro* (from 1925 to 1927 and again from 1934). In 1924 Herriot offered him the post of Treasury Minister but he declined. A close associate of Ernest Mercier, he was a founder member of Redressement français (founded 1925). Among his publications were *Qui sera le maître? L'Europe ou L'Amérique?* (1927) and *Explication de notre temps: idées très simples pour les Français*, which served to popularize the Redressement programme. In 1940 he initially refused to join the Vichy Government, but (following the dismissal of Pierre Laval), he accepted a position as *chargé de mission* in February 1941 and became Minister of State with responsibility for developing a new constitution in August 1941. A close advisor to Pétain, he acted as a link between the Marshal's entourage and the technicians of the economic ministries. He also chaired several commissions of the Conseil national. In November 1943 he encouraged Pétain to attempt to create a constituent assembly and establish a new constitution, but this was blocked by the Germans who demanded his departure from the government. He died of a heart attack in 1944.

Sauvy, Alfred

Born in 1898. After graduating from the Ecole polytechnique, Sauvy entered the Statistique générale de France (the national statistical service) in 1922. He campaigned for the extension of economic monitoring and forecasting and was active in the Société statistique de Paris and in X-Crise. He also wrote on demographic issues and supplied statistics for the pro-natalist Alliance nationale contre la dépopulation. From 1934 he was an advisor to Paul Reynaud and in 1938 the Daladier government created an Institut de Conjoncture (economic observatory) under his leadership. He continued to serve as head of this institute during the Occupation and in 1943 published *Richesse et population*, the culmination of his reflection on economic and demographic questions since the late 1920s. One of Sauvy's chief contributions to French demographic thinking was the notion of population ageing (*vieillissement*) and his argument that the proportion of older people in France led to a 'Malthusian' collective mentality which acted as a brake on both economic and demographic growth. In 1945 he was appointed head of the newly created Institut national d'études démographiques, a post he held until 1962. He also directed the journal *Population,* was appointed to a Chair in Social Demography at the Collège de France in 1959 and remained a prolific publicist even into the 1980s. His theory about French 'Malthusianism' became influential in the historiography of the interwar period in part through the publication of his four-volume *Histoire économique de la France entre les deux guerres* (1965–1975). He died in 1990.

Wilbois, Joseph

Born in 1874, Catholic educator and admirer of Henri Fayol and Frédéric Le Play. Wilbois taught at the private boarding school, the Ecole de Roches (from 1904 to 1906) and the Ecole française in Moscow (from 1906 to 1912) before founding the Ecole d'administration et des affaires in 1919 to educate business leaders. He was an adept of the New Education movement, led by figures such as Maria Montessori and Ovide Decroly, and believed in a form of education for leadership that gave an important place to the social sciences. When the CNOF was created in 1926 he joined and served for a period as its secretary. He defended a paternalist conception of management, and between 1923 and 1930 published a series of manuals based on classes taught at the Ecole d'administration et des affaires. He remained active in the CNOF during the Occupation, chairing commissions on Fayolism and education. Throughout his life he also published on religious issues. He died in 1952.

Sources

AN: 468 AP 32 Biographical notes on Jean Coutrot

Baudouï, R. 1992. *Raoul Dautry 1880–1951: le technocrate de la République,* Paris: Balland.

Cointet, M. and J.-P. 2000. *Dictionnaire historique de la France sous l'Occupation,* Paris: Tallandier.

Connaissance de l'homme. Revue des sciences de l'homme et de leurs applications pratiques 1, July 1954.

de Rochebrune, R. and J.-C. Hazéra. 1995. *Les Patrons sous l'Occupation,* Paris: Odile Jacob.

Education ménagère 132, 1960, special issue on Paulette Bernège.

Entreprises et histoire, 34, 2003, special issue on Henri Fayol.

Fine, M. 1979. 'Hyacinthe Dubreuil: le témoignage d'un ouvrier sur le syndicalisme, les relations industrielles et l'évolution technologique, 1921–1940', *Mouvement social* 106, 45–63.

Kalaora, B. 1995. 'Le Mysticisme technique de Joseph Wilbois', in Y. Cohen and R Baudouï, *Les Chantiers de la paix sociale 1900–1940*, Fontenay/St Cloud: ENS Editions, 185–94.

Kuisel, R. 1967. *Ernest Mercier, French Technocrat*, Berkeley: University of California Press.

Kuisel, R. 1975. 'Auguste Detoeuf, Conscience of French Industry: 1926–1947', *International Review of Social History* 20, 149–74.

Letté, M. 2004. *Henry Le Chatelier (1850–1936) ou la science appliquée à l'industrie*, Rennes: Presses Universitaires de Rennes.

Lévy-Leboyer. M. and Henri Morsel (dir.). 1994. *Histoire de l'Electricité en France (vol.2 1919–1946)*, Paris: Fayard.

Maîtron, J. 1986. *Dictionnaire biographique du mouvement ouvrier. Vol 26*, Paris: Editions ouvrières.

Maîtron, J. 1988. *Dictionnaire biographique du mouvement ouvrier. Vol 33*, Paris: Editions ouvrières.

Martiny, M. 1948. *Essai de biotypologie humaine*, Paris: Peyronnet.

Moutet, A. 1997. *Les Logiques de l'entreprise. La rationalisation dans l'industrie française de l'entre-deux-guerres*, Paris: Editions de l'EHESS.

Ponthiere, M. 1914. *Les Partis de droite*, Paris: Librairie de documentation politique.

Roussel, C. 1979. *Lucien Romier*, Paris: Editions France Empire.

Sabin, G. 1991. *Jean Bichelonne: ministre sous l'Occupation 1942–44*, Paris: Editions France-Empire.

Sauvy, A. 1972. *De Paul Reynaud à Charles de Gaulle: scènes, tableaux et souvenirs. Un économiste face aux hommes politiques 1934–1967*, Paris: Casterman.

Schneider, W. H. 1991. 'The Scientific Study of Labor in Interwar France', *French Historical Studies*, 17(2), 410–46.

Bibliography

Primary Sources

Archives Nationales, Paris (AN)
468 AP 1–33 Jean Coutrot Papers
68 AJ 90–91 Centre d'information interprofessionnel
F37 77 Délégation des relations franco-allemandes
F22 1837–8 Conseil supérieur du Travail
F12 10144 Conseil supérieur de l'économie industrielle et commerciale
F60 658–9 Délégation générale de l'équipement national

Periodicals
Art ménager
Biotypologie
Bulletin du CNOF
Bulletin de l'INOP
Cahiers de la Fondation française pour l'étude des problèmes humains
Cahiers du Redressement français
Comité national de l'organisation française. Feuilles d'informations et comptes rendus
Echo de l'USIC
Education ménagère
Esprit
L'Eveil. Publications mensuelles
Humanisme économique
Journal de la société statistique de Paris
Mon chez moi
La Nouvelle Education
Méthodes
Les Nouveaux Cahiers
Ordre nouveau
Organisation
Plans
Le Travail humain
X-Crise (aka *Bulletin du CPEE*)

Other Published Primary Sources

Amar, J. 1914. *Le Moteur humain*, Paris: H. Dunod et E. Pinat.

Amar, J. 1920. *L'Orientation professionnelle*, Paris: Dunod.

Armand, L. 1958. 'Vues prospectives sur les transports', *Prospective* 1, 37–43.

Armand, L. and M. Drancourt. 1961. *Plaidoyer pour l'avenir*, Paris: Calmann-Lévy.

Arthus, H. 1937. *Le Travail vivant*, Paris: Editions Oliven.

Arthus, H. 1939. *Section d'éducation active de l'Eveil, mouvement pour l'évolution individuelle et sociale*, Paris: Eveil.

Bardet, G. 1936. 'Une expérience de la collaboration ouvrière à la direction d'une usine', in J. Coutrot. *Leçons de juin 1936. L'Humanisme économique*, Paris: Editions du CPEE, 1936.

Bardet, G. 'Réflexions sur six mois de travaux (novembre 1931–mai 1932)' in *De la récurrence des crises économiques. Centre polytechnicien d'études économiques. Son cinquantenaire 1931–1981*, Paris: Economica, 1981.

Baudoin, C. 1929. *Psychanalyse de l'art*, Paris: Alcan.

Berger, G. 1958. 'Préface', *Prospective* 1, 1–10.

Bergson, H. 1907. *L'Evolution créatrice*, Paris: Alcan.

Bergson, H. 1932. *Les Deux sources de la morale et de la religion*, Paris: Alcan.

Bernège, P. 1928. *Si les femmes faisaient les maisons*, Paris: Mon chez moi.

Bernège, P. 1933. 'L'Agriculture dans les pays du Nord', *Dépêche de Toulouse* 7 June, 1–2.

Bernège, P. 1933. 'L'Aide de l'état à l'agriculture', *Dépêche de Toulouse* 8 June, 1–2.

Bernège, P. 1933. 'L'Enseignement agricole dans les pays du Nord', *Dépêche de Toulouse* 10 June, 1–2.

Bernège, P. 1933. 'Le Mouvement coopératif agricole. L'aide qu'il apporte aux paysans du Nord', *Dépêche de Toulouse* 9 June, 1–2.

Bernège, P. 1933. *J'installe ma cuisine*, Lyon: Editions de la Maison Heureuse.

Bernège, P. 1934. *De la méthode ménagère*, 2nd edition, Paris: Dunod.

Bernège, P. 1935. *Le Ménage simplifié ou la vie en rose*, Paris: Stock.

Bernège, P. 1938. *Encyclopédie de la vie familiale*, Paris: Horizons de France.

Bernège, P. 1943. *Explication: essai de biosociologie dirigée*, Toulouse: Didier.

Bernège, P. 1947. *Guide d'enseignement ménager*, Paris: Librairie de l'Académie d'Agriculture.

Bernège, P. 1950. *J'organise ma petite ferme*, Paris: Editions du Salon des Arts Ménagers.

Bernège, P. 1950. *Le Blanchissage domestique*, Paris: Editions du Salon des Arts Ménagers, 2nd edition.

Bernis, J. 'Le Foyer familial et l'éducation de l'enfant', in P. Bernège, *Encyclopédie de la vie familiale*, Paris: Horizons de France, 1938, 130–52.

Bertillon, J. 1897. *Le Problème de la dépopulation*, Paris: Armand Colin.

Bichelonne, J. 1942. *L'Etat actuel de l'organisation économique*, Paris: Ecole libre des sciences politiques.

Bichelonne, J. 1943. *Conférence de M Bichelonne. Hôtel de Ville de Paris 5 août 1943*, Paris: Imprimerie Municipale.

Billard, Ch. 1942. 'Les Types humains: méthodes et procédés d'investigation', *Leçons de l'Ecole d'organisation scientifique du travail. Leçon No. 162*, Paris: CNOF, 1–26.

Billard, Ch. 1942. 'Les Types humains et les stimulants psycho-physiologiques du travail', *Leçons de l'Ecole d'organisation scientifique du travail. Leçon No. 163*, Paris: CNOF, 11–17.

Bohn, G. 1909. *La Naissance de l'intelligence*, Paris: Flammarion.

Bohn, G. 1934. *Reproduction. Sexualité. Hérédité*, Paris: Hermann, Actualités scientifiques et industrielles.

Bohn, G. 1944. 'Etudes sur la décentralisation de l'industrie aéronautique', *Rapports et travaux sur la décongestion des centres industriels, No.3*, Paris: DGEN.

Bouglé, C. 1907. *Le Solidarisme*, Paris: V. Giard and E. Brière.

Buisson, F. Preface to J. Fontègne, *L'Orientation professionnelle et la détermination de l'aptitude*, Neuchâtel: Delachaux et Niestlé, 1921, 5–8.

Carlioz, J. 1921. *Le Gouvernement des entreprises commerciales et industrielles*, Paris: Dunod.

Carrel, A. 1935. *L'Homme, cet inconnu*, Paris: Plon.

Chayrou, P.-R. 1926. *De l'art d'acheter à l'art d'agir*, Paris: Charles Lavauzelle et Cie.

Chayrou, P.-R. 1938. *Achats rationnels. Caractère du plus avantageux de deux achats semblables*, Paris: Recueil Sirey.

Chevalier, J. 1928. *La Technique de l'organisation des entreprises*, Paris: Librairie française de documentation commerciale et industrielle, Editions Langlois et Cie.

Cheysson, E. Preface to Moll-Weiss et al., *Les Ecoles ménagères à l'étranger et en France*, Paris: A. Rousseau, 1908, i-xii.

Claparède, E. 1922. *L'Orientation professionnelle, ses problèmes et ses méthodes*, Geneva: Bureau international du travail.

Connaissance de l'homme. Revue des sciences de l'homme et de leurs applications pratiques 1 July 1954.

Cousinet, R. Preface to P. Bernège, *Guide d'enseignement ménager*, Paris: Librairie de l'Académie d'Agriculture, 1947, 5–8.

Coutrot, J. 1935. *Le Système nerveux des entreprises*, Paris: Delmas.

Coutrot, J. 1935. *De quoi vivre*, Paris: Grasset.

Coutrot, J. 1936. *Leçons de juin 1936. L'Humanisme économique*, Paris: Editions du CPEE.

Coutrot, J. 1937. *Comment, au XXe siècle, on peut et doit produire*, Paris: COST.

Coutrot, J. 1937. 'Mémoire introductif à la recherche collective', in M. Prélot (ed.), *Entretiens sur les sciences de l'homme*, Paris: Hermann, 15–28.

Coutrot, J. 1937. *Les Méthodes d'organisation rationnelle. Ce qu'elles peuvent apporter à l'activité économique française*, Rennes: Imprimeries réunies (no publisher).

Coutrot, J. 1940. 'Commandes de paix après commandes de guerre', *L'Oeuvre* 15 July.

CSEIC. 1943. *Projet de réforme de l'organisation économique sur le plan national. Rapport de la première session des travaux de la Commission No.1 adopté en séance plénière du Conseil de 6 juillet 1943*, Paris: CSEIC.

Dautry, R. 1937. *Métier d'homme*, Paris: Plon.

de Fréminville, C. Preface to J. Chevalier, *La Technique de l'organisation des entreprises*, Paris: Librairie française de documentation commerciale et industriel, Editions Langlois et Cie, 1928, i-iv.

de Fréminville, C. 1930. *Le Rôle de l'ingénieur dans l'organisation rationnelle du travail. Extrait du numéro du cinquantenaire du Génie civil*, Paris: Publications de Génie Civil.

Decroly, O. 1914. *Initiation à l'activité intellectuelle et motrice par les jeux éducatifs*, Neuchâtel: Delachaux et Niestlé.

Decroly, O. 1928. *La Pratique des tests mentaux*, Paris: Alcan.

de Man, H. 1927. *Au-delà du marxisme*, Brussels: L'Eglantine.

de Man, H. 1930. *La Joie au travail*, Paris: Presses universitaires de France.

Dessus, G. 1944. *Introduction à l'étude de la localisation de l'industrie. Rapports et travaux sur la décongestion des centres industriels, No.1*, Paris: DGEN.

Dessus, G. 1944. 'Conclusions provisoires', *Rapports et travaux sur la décongestion des centres industriels*, 4, Paris: DGEN.

Detoeuf, A. 'Aperçu des services pratiques susceptibles d'être rendus par les syndicats patronaux sur le plan économique et social. Exposé introductif', *Comité central de l'organisation professionnelle. Sous Commission d'études des activités et services syndicaux. Réunion du 18 octobre 1938*, Paris: Editions du CCOP, 1938, 5–7.

Detoeuf, A. 1938. *Construction du syndicalisme*, Paris: Gallimard.

Devinat, P. 1930. 'Les conditions du travail dans une entreprise rationalisée: le système Bat'a et ses conséquences sociales', *Revue internationale du travail* January-February, 48–72.

Devinat, P. 1927. *L'Organisation scientifique du travail en Europe. Bureau international du travail, Etudes et Documents Série B (Conditions économique)*, Geneva: Bureau international du travail.

Dubreuil, H. 1924. *La République industrielle*, Paris: Bibliothèque d'éducation.

Dubreuil, H. 1925. 'Au-delà du salaire', *Information sociale* 3 September, 1.

Dubreuil, H. 1929. *Standards*, Paris: Grasset.

Dubreuil, H. 1931. *Nouveaux Standards: les sources de la productivité et de la joie*, Paris: Grasset.

Dubreuil, H. 1935. *A chacun sa chance: l'organisation du travail fondé sur la liberté*, Paris: Grasset.

Dubreuil, H. 1936. *L'Exemple de Bat'a: la libération de l'initiative individuelles dans une entreprise géante*, Paris: Grasset.

Dubreuil, H. 1938. *La Fin des monstres*, Paris: Grasset.

Dubreuil, H. 1938. *Lettre aux travailleurs français*, Paris: Grasset.

Dubreuil, H. 1942. *La Chevalerie du travail*, Paris: Grasset.

Dubreuil, H. 1942. *L'Organisation de la solidarité nationale*, Paris: Centre Communautaire.

Dubreuil, H. and E. Rimailho. 1939. *Deux hommes parlent du travail*, Paris: Grasset.

Duhamel, G. 1934. *Scènes de la vie future*, Paris: Arthème, Fayard et Cie.

Duthoit, E. 1930. 'La Rationalisation est-elle un progrès? Leçon d'ouverture de la Semaine sociale de Besançon 1929', *Semaines sociales de France. Compte rendu in extenso des cours et conférences*, Lyon: Chronique sociale de France, 37–77.

Ecole supérieure d'organisation professionnelle. Réglement et programme d'enseignement, année scolaire 1941–1942, Centre d'information interprofessionnel.

Ecole supérieure d'organisation professionnelle. Réglement et programme d'enseignement, année scolaire 1942–43, Centre d'information interprofessionnel.

Fayol, H. 1979. *Administration industrielle et générale*, Paris: Bordas.

Fontègne, J. 1920. 'Le Cabinet d'orientation professionnelle de l'Institut J. J. Rousseau', *Orientation professionnelle* March, 38–39.

Fontègne, J. 1921. *L'Orientation professionnelle et la determination de l'aptitude*, Neuchâtel: Delachaux et Niestlé.

Fontègne, J. 1923. *Manualisme et éducation*, Paris: Librairie de l'enseignement technique, Léon Eyrolles Editeur.

Frederick, C. 1918. *La Tenue scientifique de la maison*, Paris: Dunod.

Friedmann, G. 1946. *Problèmes humains du machinisme industriel* translated as *Industrial Society*, New York: Arno Press, 1977 [reprinted from 1955 edition].

Gibrat, J. 1931. *Les Inégalités économiques. Applications aux inégalités des richesses, à la concentration des entreprises, aux populations des villes, aux statistiques des familles etc d'une loi nouvelle: la loi de l'effet proportionnel*, Paris: Recueil Sirey.

Gros, A. 'Avant- Propos' to Degas, *La Mutualité française*, Paris: Bernard Frères, 1943, 3–10.

Gros, A. 1941. *Le Service médico-social d'une usine de métallurgie. Installation et fonctionnement*, Paris: Bernard Frères.

Gros, A. and J. Ménétrier. 1941. *La Médecine du travail*, Paris: Bernard Frères.

Guillaume, E. and G. Guillaume. 1937. *Economique rationnelle. Des fondements aux problèmes actuels*, Paris: Editions du Centre Polytechnicien d'Etudes Economiques, Hermann et Cie.

Halbwachs, M. 1912. *La Classe ouvrière et les niveaux de vie*, Paris: Alcan.

Halbwachs, M. 1933. *L'Evolution des besoins dans les classes ouvrières*, Paris: Alcan.

Halbwachs, M. and A. Sauvy (avec la collaboration de Henri Ulmer et Georges Bournier). 2005. *Le Point de vue du nombre 1936. Edition critique sous la direction de Marie Jaisson et Eric Brian*, Paris: INED.

Hoover Institution on War, Revolution and Peace. 1959. *France during the German Occupation 1940–1944. A collection of 292 Statements on the Government of Maréchal Petain and Pierre Laval*, Stanford, California: Hoover Institution.

Joffre, J. 1932. *Mémoires du Maréchal Joffre, 1910–1917*, Paris: Plon.

Labbé, E. Preface to J. Fontègne, *Manualisme et éducation*, Paris: Librairie de l'enseignement technique, Léon Eyrolles Editeur, 1923, vii-viii.

Lahy, J.-M. 1916. *Le Système Taylor et la physiologie du travail professionel*, Paris: Masson.

Lamirand, G. 1932. *Le Rôle social de l'ingénieur: scènes de la vie d'usine*, Paris: Editions de la Revue des Jeunes.

Lamy, M. 1932. *Bien acheter pour mieux vivre*, Paris: Dunod.

Lamy, M. 1934. *Pour bien faire son marché. Les secrets de la vie moins chère*, Paris: Dunod.

Landry, A. 1934. *La Révolution démographique*, Paris: Sirey.

Le Chatelier, F. 1914. *Le Système Taylor*, Paris: Société pour l'encouragement de l'industrie nationale.

Le Chatelier, H. 1928. *Le Taylorisme*, Paris: Dunod.

Le Chatelier, H. Preface to E. Nusbaumer, *L'Organisation scientifique des usines*, Paris: Nouvelle Librairie nationale, 1924, vii–xiv.

Le Chatelier, H. Preface to J. Amar, *Le Moteur humain*, Paris: H. Dunod et E. Pinat, 1914.

Le Corbusier. 1923. *Vers une architecture*, Paris: Editions Crès.

Lévy, P. 1936. *La Sélection du personnel dans les entreprises de transport*, Paris: Hermann et Cie.

Lyautey, H. Preface to G. Lamirand, *Le Rôle social de l'ingénieur: scènes de la vie d'usine*, Paris, Editions de la Revue des Jeunes, 1932, 7–9.

Lyautey, H. 1891. 'Du rôle social de l'officier dans le service militaire universel', *Revue des deux mondes* 15 March, 443–59.

Martiny, M. 1930. *La Biotypologie humaine et orthogénésique. Sa première application clinique et médico-sociale*, Paris: Masson et Cie.

Martiny. M. 1942. 'Médecine et psychotechnique', in *2e Cycle de perfectionnement des techniques de direction du personnel, 16–20 février 1942*, Paris: CEGOS, 35–47.

Martiny, M. 1948. *Essai de biotypologie humaine*, Paris: Peyronnet.

Mayo, E. 1933. *The Human Problems of Industrial Civilization*, New York: Macmillan.

Moll-Weiss, A. 1902. *Le Foyer domestique, cours d'économie domestique, d'hygiène et de cuisine pratique*, Paris: Hachette.

Moll-Weiss, A. 1907. *La Cuisine rationnelle des malades et des bien portants*, Paris: Doin.

Monin, S. 1933. *La Maison sans domestique*, Lyon: Editions de la Maison Heureuse.

Montessori, M. 1919. *The Montessori Method: Scientific Pedagogy as Applied to Child Education in 'The Children's Houses'*, London: William Heinemann.

Montessori, M. 1932. *Peace and Education*, Geneva: International Bureau of Education.

Nusbaumer, E. 1924. *L'Organisation scientifique des usines*, Paris: Nouvelle Librairie nationale.

Pariset, Mme. 1852. *Manuel de la maîtresse de maison et de la parfaite ménagère*, Paris: Librairie Encyclopédique de Roret.

Parsons, T. 1937. *The Structure of Social Action*, New York: MacGraw Hill.

Philip, A. 1928. *Henri de Man et la crise doctrinale du socialisme*, Paris: J. Gamber.

Planus, P. 1938. *Patrons et ouvriers en Suède*, Paris: Plon.

Ponthiere, M. 1914. *Les Partis de droite*, Paris: Librairie de documentation politique.

Ponthière, M. 1931. *Le Nouvel Esprit des affaires*, Paris: Nouvelle librairie commerciale.

Ponthière, M. 1935. *Le Bureau moteur*, Paris: Delmas.

Ponthière, M. 1942. 'Principes généraux d'OST et leur évolution', *Leçons de l'Ecole d'organisation Scientifique du Travail. Leçon 12*, Paris: CNOF, i–iv, 1–22.

Pouget, E. 1914. *L'Organisation du surménage*, Paris: M. Rivière et Cie.

Prélot, M. (ed). 1937. *Entretiens sur les sciences de l'homme*, Paris: Hermann.

Région économique de l'est. 1942. *Réunion régionale tenu à Nancy, le 20 janvier 1942. Exposés de M. Gérard Bardet, Président du Centre d'information interprofessionnel et de M. de Tavernost, délégué général de ce centre.*

Rimailho, E. 1926. *L'Union entre les collaborateurs de l'industrie par L'Organisation du travail. Conférence faite le 27 janvier 1926 à l'USIC et le 2 février à la Ligue républicaine nationale*, Besançon, no publisher.

Rimailho, E. 1936. *l'organisation à la française*, Paris: Delmas.

Roethlisberger, F. J. and W. Dickson. 1939. *Management and the Worker*, Cambridge, MA: Harvard University Press.

Romier, L. 1927. *Qui sera le maître? L'Europe ou L'Amérique?*, Paris: Hachettte.

Romier, L. 1928. *Explication de notre temps: idées très simples pour les Français*, Paris: Kra.

Rostand, J. 1933. *Les Problèmes de l'hérédité et du sexe*, Paris: Rieder.

Roussy, B. 1916. *Education domestique de la femme et rénovation sociale*, Paris: Delagrave.

Sauvy, A. 1939. *Essai sur la conjoncture*, Paris: Editions du CPEE.

Sauvy, A. 1943. *La Prévision économique*, Paris: Presses universitaires de France.

Sauvy, A. 1943. *Richesse et population*, Paris: Payot.

Sauvy, A. 1956. *L'Opinion publique*, Paris: Presses universitaires de France.

Sauvy, A. 1965. *Mythologies de notre temps*, Paris: Payot

Sauvy, A. 1972. *De Paul Reynaud à Charles de Gaulle: scènes, tableaux et souvenirs. Un économiste face aux hommes politiques 1934–1967*, Paris: Casterman.

Sauvy, A. 1985. *De la rumeur à l'histoire*, Paris: Bordas.

Scelle, G. (ed.). 1943. *Les Comités sociaux d'établissement. Etat présent et vues d'avenir.* Paris: Librairie sociale et économique.

Siegfried, A. 1931. *Les Etats-Unis d'Aujourd'hui*, Paris: A. Colin. [First published 1927].

Taylor, F. W. 1907. *Etudes sur l'organisation du travail dans les usines*, Paris: H. Dunod et E. Pinat.

Taylor, F. W. 1911. *Principes d'organisation scientifique*, Paris: Publication de la Revue de métallurgie.

Taylor, F. W. 1912. *Principes d'organisation scientifique des usines*, Paris: H. Dunod and E. Pinat.

Taylor, F. W. 1913. *La Direction des ateliers*, Paris: H. Dunod and E. Pinat.

Taylor, F.W. 1947. *Scientific Management*, London: Harper and Row.

Tchakotine, S. 1939. *Le Viol des foules par la propaganda politique*, Paris: Gallimard.

Ullmo, J. 1938. 'Recherches sur l'équilibre économique' *Annales de l'Institut Henri Poincaré* 8(1), 3.

Valéry, P. Preface to R. Dautry, *Métier d'homme*, Paris: Plon, 1937, v–xi.

Warnier, J. 1943. *Comment constituer un Comité social d'entreprise*, Paris: Edition Sociale Française.

Warnier. J. 1943. 'Attributions, fonctionnement et financement du comité social d'entreprise', in G. Scelle (ed.), *Les Comités sociaux d'établissement. Etat présent et vues d'avenir. Collection Droit Social* No. 20, Paris: Librairie sociale et économique, 19–21.

Weil, S. 1951. *La Condition ouvrière*, Paris: Gallimard.

Wilbois, J. 1926. *Le Chef d'entreprise: sa fonction et sa personne*, Paris: Alcan.

Wilbois, J. 1934. *La Psychologie au service du chef d'entreprise*, Paris: Alcan.

Wilbois, J. 1939. *Joie au travail et réformes de structure*, Paris: Bloud et Gay.

Wilbois, J. and A. Letixerant. 1928. *Comment faire vivre une entreprise*, Paris: Alcan.

Wilbois, J. and P. Vanuxem. 1919. *Essai sur la conduite des affaires et la direction des hommes*, Paris: Payot.

Wilbois, J. and P. Vanuxem. 1926. *Le Chef d'entreprise: sa fonction et sa personne*, Paris: Alcan.

Winter, P. 1943–1944. 'Cours d'hygiène professionnelle. Introduction. 1.Les services médicaux du travail', *Préparation au concours pour l'emploi d'Inspecteur du Travail. Cahier No.5* Paris: Ministère du Travail, 3–7.

Zamanski, J. 1930. 'La Rationalisation peut-elle influencer les rapports du capital et du travail dans la profession? A-t-elle commencé à les influencer?', *Semaines Sociales de France. Compte rendu in extenso des cours et conférences*, Lyon: Chronique sociale de France, 273–87.

Secondary Sources

Adler, K. H. 2003. *Jews and Gender in Liberation France*, Cambridge: Cambridge University Press.

Amdur, K. E. 1998. 'Paternalism, Productivism, Collaborationism: Employers and Society in Interwar and Vichy France', *International Labor and Working-Class History* 53, 137–63.

Andrieu, C., L. Le Van and A. Prost (dir.). 1987. *Les Nationalisations de la Libération: de l'utopie au compromise*, Paris: Presses de la FNSP.

Aubert, N. 'Du système disciplinaire au système managinaire: l'émergence du management psychique', in J-P. Bouilloud and B-P. Lecuyer (dir.),

L'Invention de la gestion. Histoire et pratiques, Paris: Harmattan, 1994, 119–33.

Azéma, J.-P. and D. Barjot et al. 1991. *Reconstructions et modernisation: la France après les ruines 1918...1945*, Paris: Archives nationales.

Bard, C. 1995. *Les Filles de Marianne: histoire des féminismes 1914–1940*, Paris: Fayard.

Barthes, R. 1957. *Mythologies*, Paris: Seuil.

Barthes, R. 1970 [1st ed. 1957]. 'Poujade et les intellectuels', in Barthes, *Mythologies*, Paris: Seuil, 182–90.

Barthes, R. 2000. *Mythologies*, trans. Annette Lavers, London: Vintage.

Baruch, M.-O. 1997. *Servir l'Etat Français. L'Administration en France de 1940 à 1944*, Paris: Fayard.

Baruch, M.-O. and V. Duclert (dir.). 2000. *Serviteurs de l'Etat. Une histoire politique de l'administration française 1875–1945*, Paris: La Découverte.

Baudouï, R. 1992. *Raoul Dautry 1880–1951: le technocrate de la République*, Paris: Balland.

Beale, M. 1999. *The Modernist Enterprise: French Elites and the Threat of Modernity, 1900–1940*, Stanford: Stanford University Press.

Beausoleil, J. and P. Ory (eds). 1995. *Albert Kahn, 1860–1940: réalités d'une utopie*, Boulogne: Musée Albert Kahn.

Bédarida, F. (ed.), 1976. *Mélanges d'histoire sociale offerts à Jean Maîtron*, Paris: Editions ouvrières.

Belhoste, B. et al. (eds). 1995. *La France des X. Deux siècles d'histoire*, Paris: Economica.

Belhoste, B., A. D. Dalmedico and A. Picon. 1994. *La Formation polytechnicienne 1794–1994*, Paris: Dunod.

Beltran, A. 1991. *La Fée et la servante: la société française face à l'électricité XIXe-XXe siècle*, Paris: Belin.

Beltran, A. 'L'Essor de l'électrodomestique', in M. Lévy-Leboyer and Henri Morsel (dir.) *Histoire générale de l'éléctricité en France. Tome 2. L'Interconnexion et le marché 1919–1946*, Paris: Fayard, 1994, 1232–39.

Beltran, A., R. Frank, H. Rousso (dir.). 1994. *La Vie des entreprises sous l'Occupation. Une enquête à l'échelle locale*, Paris: Belin.

Berthier, G. B. 'Le Comité national d'études sociales et politiques, 1916–1931', in J. Beausoleil, and P. Ory (eds), *Albert Kahn, 1860–1940 : réalités d'une utopie*, Boulogne: Musée Albert Kahn, 1995, 227–36.

Bergeron, L. 2001. *Le Creusot. Une ville industrielle. Un patrimoine glorieux*, Paris: Belin.

Bock, G. and P. Thane (eds). 1991. *Maternity and Gender Policies: Women and the Rise of the European Welfare States, 1880s-1950s*, London: Routledge.

Boltanski, L. 1982. *Les Cadres: la formation d'un groupe social*, Paris: Minuit.

Bouilloud, J-P. and B-P. Lecuyer (dir.). 1994. *L'Invention de la gestion. Histoire et pratiques*, Paris: Harmattan.

Brun, G. 1985. *Techniciens et technocratie en France*, Paris: Albatros.

Buzzi, S., J.-C. Devinck and P-A. Rosental. 2000. *La Santé au travail 1880–2006*, Paris: La Decouverte.

Callu, A., P. Eveno and H. Joly. 2009. *Culture et médias sous l'Occupation: des entreprises dans la France de Vichy*, Paris: Editions du Comité des travaux historiques et scientifiques.

Camiscioli, E. 2001. 'Producing Citizens, Reproducing the 'French Race': Immigration, Demography and Pro-natalism in Early Twentieth-Century France', *Gender and History* 13 (3), 593–621.

Centre des jeunes dirigeants d'entreprise. 1988. *50 ans qui ont changé l'entreprise: 1938–1988*. Paris: Communica International.

Chapman, H. 'France's Liberation Era, 1944–1947: A Social and Economic Settlement', in A. Knapp (ed.), *The Uncertain Foundation: France at Liberation, 1944–1947*, Basingstoke: Palgrave MacMillan, 2007, 103–20.

Chatriot, A. 2002. *La Démocratie sociale à la française. L'Expérience du Conseil national économique 1924–1940*, Paris: La Découverte.

Chessel, M.-E. 2001. *Le Technocrate, le patron et le professeur: une histoire de l'enseignement supérieur de gestion*, Paris: Belin.

Chessel, M.-E. and B. Dumons (eds). 2003. *Catholicisme et modernisation de la société française (1890–1960)*, Lyon: Centre de Pierre Léon d'histoire sociale et économique, Institut des Sciences de l'Homme.

Clark, L. L. 2000. *The Rise of Professional Women in France: Gender and Public Administration since 1830*, Cambridge: Cambridge University Press.

Claude, V. 'Technique sanitaire et réforme urbaine: L'Association générale des hygiénistes et techniciens municipaux, 1905–1920', in Topalov, C. (ed.) *Laboratoires du nouveau siècle: la nébuleuse réformatrice et ses réseaux en France, 1880–1914*, Paris: Editions de l'Ecole des Hautes Etudes en Sciences Sociales, 1999, 269–98.

Cohen, S. R. 1983. 'From Industrial Democracy to Professional Adjustment: The Development of Industrial Sociology in the US, 1900–1955', *Theory and Society* 12(1), 47–67.

Cohen, Y. 1988. 'Mais qui sont donc ces "techniciens sociaux"? Peugeot. Sochaux. 1936–1939', *Vie sociale* 2–3, 41–55.

Cohen, Y. 2001. *Organiser à l'aube du taylorisme: la pratique d'Ernest Mattern chez Peugeot, 1906–1919*, Besançon: Presses universitaires franc-comtoises.

Cohen, Y. 2001–2002. 'Les Chefs, une question pour l'histoire du vingtième siècle' *Cités* 6, 67–83.

Cohen, Y. 2003. 'Fayol, un instituteur de l'ordre industriel' *Entreprises et Histoire* 34, 29–67.

Cohen, Y. and R. Baudouï. 1995. *Les Chantiers de la paix sociale 1900–1940*, Fontenay/St Cloud: ENS Editions.

Costigliola, F. 1984. *Awkward Dominion: American Political, Economic and Cultural Relations with Europe 1919–1933*, Ithaca: Cornell University Press.

Couzon, I. 1997. 'La Place de la ville dans le discours des aménageurs du début des années 1920 à la fin des années 1960', *Cybergéo: European*

Journal of Geography document 37, 1–26.< http://www.cybergeo.eu/ index1979.html> accessed 16 February 2010.

Cross, G. 1989. *A Quest for Time: The Reduction of Work in Britain and France, 1840–1940*, Berkeley: University of California Press.

Dard, O. 1998. *La Synarchie ou le mythe du complot permanent*, Paris: Perrin.

Dard, O. 1999. *Jean Coutrot: de l'ingénieur au prophète*, Besançon: Presses universitaires franc-comtoises.

Dard, O. 'Du privé au public. Des technocrates en quête d'un Etat rationnel et à la conquête de l'Etat républicain dans la France des années trente', in M-O. Baruch and V. Duclert (dir.) *Serviteurs de l'Etat. Une histoire politique de l'administration française 1875–1945*, Paris: La Découverte, 2000, 485–95.

Dard, O. 'Les Technocrates: archéologie d'un concept, généalogie d'un groupe social' in Dard, J.-C. Daumas et F. Marcot (eds), *L'Occupation, l'Etat français et les entreprises*, Paris: Association pour le développement de l'histoire économique, 2000, 213–27.

Dard, O. 2002. *Le Rendez-vous manqué des relèves des années trente*, Paris: Presses universitaires de France.

Dard, O., J.-C. Daumas and F. Marcot (eds). 2000. *L'Occupation, l'Etat français et les entreprises*, Paris: Association pour le développement de l'histoire économique.

Daumas, J.-C. 'La Révolution nationale à l'usine. Les Politiques sociales des entreprises sous l'Occupation', in O. Dard, J.-C. Daumas and F. Marcot (dir.), *L'Occupation, l'Etat français et les entreprises*, Paris: Association pour le développement de l'histoire économique, 2000, 181–95.

Daumas, J.-C. and C. Chevandier. 2007. *Travailler dans les entreprises sous l'Occupation*, Besançon: Presses universitaires de Franche-Comté.

Centre polytechnicien d'études économiques. 1981. *X Crise. De la récurrence des crises économiques. Centre polytechnicien d'études économiques. Son cinquantenaire 1931–1981*, Paris: Economica.

de Rochebrune, R. and J.-C. Hazéra. 1995. *Les Patrons sous l'Occupation*, Paris: Odile Jacob.

Delaunay, Q. 2003. *Société industrielle et travail domestique. L'Electroménager en France XIXe–XXe siècle*, Paris: L'Harmattan.

Denord, F. and O. Henry. 2007. 'La "Modernisation" avant la lettre: le patronat et la rationalisation (1925–1940)', *Sociétés contemporaines* 68, 83–104.

Desrosières, A. 1998. *The Politics of Large Numbers: A History of Statistical Reasoning*, Cambridge, Mass. Harvard University Press.

Diamond, H. and S. Kitson. 2005. *Vichy, Resistance, Liberation: New Perspectives on Wartime France*, Oxford: Berg.

Dockès, P. et al. (dir.). 2000. *Les Traditions économiques françaises*, Paris: CNRS Editions.

Dodge, P. 1966. *The Faith and Works of Hendrik de Man*, The Hague: Martinus Nijhoff.

Donzelot, J. 1984. *L'Invention du social: essai sur le déclin des passions politiques*, Paris: Fayard.

Downs, L. L. 1993. 'Les Marraines-élue de la paix sociale? Les Surintendantes d'usine et la rationalisation du travail en France, 1917–1935', *Mouvement social* 164, 53–76.

Downs, L. L. 1995. *Manufacturing Inequality: Gender Division in the French and British Metalworking Industries 1914–1939*, Ithaca: Cornell University Press.

Drouard, A. 1992. *Une inconnue des sciences sociales: La Fondation Alexis Carrel, 1941–1945*, Paris: Editions de la Maison des Sciences de l'Homme/INED.

Duchen, C. 1991. 'Occupation Housewife: The Domestic Ideal in 1950s France', *French Cultural Studies* 2(4), 1–11.

Duchen, C. 1994. *Women's Rights and Women's Lives in France 1945–1968*, London: Routledge.

Duval, N. 2002. 'L'Education nouvelle dans les sociétés européennes à la fin du XIXe siècle', *Histoire, économie et société* 21(1), 71–86.

Earle, E. M. (ed.). 1951. *Modern France: Problems of the Third and Fourth Republics*, Princeton: Princeton University Press.

Ehrenreich, B. and D. English. 1978. *For Her Own Good: 150 Years of Experts' Advice to Women*, Garden City, NY: Anchor Press.

Ehrmann, H. W. 1957. *Organized Business in France*, Princeton, NJ: Princeton University Press.

Fine, M. 1979. 'Hyacinthe Dubreuil: le témoignage d'un ouvrier sur le syndicalisme, les relations industrielles et l'évolution technologique, 1921–1940', *Mouvement social* 106, 45–63.

Fine, M. 1977. 'Albert Thomas: A Reformer's Vision of Modernization, 1914–1932', *Journal of Contemporary History* 12(3), 545–64.

Foucault, M. 1975. *Surveiller et punir*, Paris: Gallimard.

Fourastié, F. 1947. *La Civilisation de 1960*, Paris: Presses universitaires de France.

Fourastié, F. 1950. *Histoire du confort*, Paris: Presses universitaires de France.

Fourastié, F. 1951. *Machinisme et bien-être*, Paris: Minuit.

Fourastié, F. 1979. *Les Trente Glorieuses où la révolution invisible de 1946 à 1975*, Paris: Fayard.

Frader, L. L. 1999. 'From Muscles to Nerves: Gender, "Race", and the Body at Work in France. 1919–1939', *International Review of Social History* 44(supplement), 123–48.

Frader, L. L. 2008. *Breadwinners and Citizens: Gender and the Making of the French Social Model*, Durham and London: Duke University Press.

Fridenson, P. 1987. 'Un tournant taylorien de la société française (1904–1918)', *Annales ESC* 42(5), 1031–60.

Fridenson, P. and A. Straus (eds). 1987. *Le Capitalisme français, 19e–20e siècle. Blocages et dynamismes d'une croissance*, Paris: Fayard.

Frost, R. 1993. 'Machine Liberation: Inventing Housewives and Home Appliances in Interwar France', *French Historical Studies* 18(1), 109–30.

Furlough, E. 1993. 'Selling the American Way in Interwar France: *Prix Uniques* and the Salon des Arts Ménagers', *Journal of Social History* 26(3), 491–519.

Gardey, D. 2001. *La Dactylographe et l'expéditionnaire: histoire des employés de bureau 1890–1930*, Paris: Belin.

Grunberg, G. and R. Mouriaux. 1979. *L'Univers politique et syndical des cadres*, Paris: Presses de la Fondation nationale des sciences politiques.

Harp, S. L. 2001. *Marketing Michelin: Advertising and Cultural Identity in Twentieth-Century France*, Baltimore: The Johns Hopkins University Press.

Hecht, G. 1998. *The Radiance of France: Nuclear Power and National Identity after World War II*, Cambridge, Mass: MIT Press.

Henry, O. 2004. 'De la sociologie comme technologie sociale: la contribution de Jean Coutrot, 1895–1941', *Actes de la recherche en sciences sociales* 153, 48–64.

Henry, O. 2006. 'L'Impossible Professionnalisation du métier d'ingénieur-conseil (1880–1954)', *Mouvement Social* 214, 37–54.

Herf, J. 1986. *Reactionary Modernism: Technology, Culture and Politics in Weimar and the Third Reich*, Cambridge: Cambridge University Press.

Hesse, P-J. and J-P. Le Crom. 2001. *La Protection sociale sous le régime de Vichy*, Rennes: Presses universitaires de Rennes.

Hoffmann, S. 1961. 'The Effects of World War II on French Society and Politics', *French Historical Studies* 2(1), 28–63.

Hoffman et al. 1963. *In Search of France: The Economy, Society and Political System in the Twentieth Century*, New York: Harper and Row.

Hoffmann, S. 1974. *Decline or Renewal ? France since the 1930s*, New York, Viking Press.

Horn, G.-R. 2001. 'From "Radical" to "Realistic": Hendrik de Man and the International Plan Conferences at Pontigny and Geneva 1934–1937', *Contemporary European History* 10(2), 239–65.

Horne, J. 'L'Antichambre de la Chambre: le Musée social et ses réseaux réformateurs, 1894–1914', in C. Topalov (ed.), *Laboratoires du nouveau siècle: la nébuleuse réformatrice et ses réseaux en France, 1880–1914*, Paris: Editions de l'Ecole des Hautes Etudes en Sciences Sociales, 1999, 121–40.

Horne, J. 2002. *A Social Laboratory for Modern France : The Musée social and the Rise of the Welfare State*, Durham, NC: Duke University Press.

Humphreys, G. 1986. *Taylorism in France 1904–1920: The Impact of Scientific Management on Factory Relations and Society*, New York and London: Garland.

Ipsen, C. 1996. *Dictating Demography: The Problem of Population in Fascist Italy*, Cambridge, Cambridge University Press.

Jackson, J. '« Mal embarqué bien arrivé »: The Strange Story of François Perroux', in H. Diamond and S. Kitson, *Vichy, Resistance, Liberation : New Perspectives on Wartime France*, Oxford: Berg, 2005, 155–69.

Jackson, J. 1985. *The Politics of Depression in France*, Cambridge: Cambridge University Press.

Jackson, J. 1990. *The Popular Front in France: Defending Democracy*, Cambridge: Cambridge University Press.

Jackson, J. 2001. *France: The Dark Years 1940–1944*, Oxford: Oxford University Press.

Jobs, R. I. 2007. *Riding the New Wave: Youth and the Rejuvenation of France after the Second World War*, Stanford: Stanford University Press.

Joly, H. 'Prosopographie des dirigeants des Comités d'organisation', in O. Dard, J-C. Daumas and F. Marcot (dir.), *L'Occupation, l'Etat français et les entreprises*, Paris: Association pour le développement de l'histoire économique, 2000, 245–59.

Joly, H. 2004. *Les Comités d'organisation et l'économie dirigée du régime de Vichy*, Caen: Centre de recherche d'histoire quantitative.

Kalaora, B. 'Le Mysticisme technique de Joseph Wilbois', in Y. Cohen and R Baudouï, *Les Chantiers de la paix sociale 1900–1940*, Fontenay/St Cloud: ENS Editions, 1995, 185–94.

Kalaora, B. 1989. *Les Inventeurs oubliés: Le Play et ses continuateurs aux origines des sciences sociales*, Seyssel: Champ Vallon.

Kalaora, B. et A. Savoye. 1985. 'La mutation du mouvement le playsien', *Revue française de sociologie* 26(2), 257–76.

Kindleberger, 'The Postwar Resurgence of the French Economy', in Hoffmann et al., *In Search of France*, New York: Harper and Row, 1963, 118–58.

Kolboom, I. 1982. 'Patronat et cadres: la contribution patronale à la formation du groupe des cadres (1936–1938)', *Mouvement social* 121 (October-December), 71–95.

Kramer, R. 1976. *Maria Montessori: A Biography*, London: Basil Blackwell.

Kuisel, R. 1967. *Ernest Mercier, French Technocrat*, Berkeley: University of California Press.

Kuisel, R. 1970. 'The Legend of Vichy Synarchy', *French Historical Studies*, 6(3), 365–98.

Kuisel, R. 1975. 'Auguste Detoeuf, Conscience of French Industry: 1926–1947', *International Review of Social History* 20, 149–74.

Kuisel, R. 1977. 'Vichy et les origines de la planification économique 1940–1946', *Mouvement social* 98, 77–101.

Kuisel, R. 1981. *Capitalism and the State in Modern France: Renovation and Economic Management in the Twentieth Century*, Cambridge: Cambridge University Press.

Kuisel, R. 1993. *Seducing the French: The Dilemma of Americanization*, Berkeley: University of California Press.

Laborde, C. 2000. *Pluralist Thought and the State in Britain and France, 1900–1925*, Basingstoke: MacMillan.

Lacroix-Riz, A. 1999. *Industriels et banquiers français sous l'Occupation: la collaboration économique avec le Reich et Vichy*, Paris: Armand Colin.

Lacroix-Riz, A. 2006. *Le Choix de la défaite. Les Elites françaises dans les années 1930*, Paris: Armand Colin.

Landes, D. 'French Business and the Businessman: A Social and Cultural Analysis', in E. M. Earle (ed.), *Modern France: Problems of the Third and Fourth Republics*, Princeton: Princeton University Press, 1951, 334–53.

Landsberger, H. A. 1958. *Hawthorne Revisited:* Management and the Worker, *Its Critics and Developments in Human Relations in Industry*, Ithaca, NY: Cornell University Press.

Lawrence, C. and G. Weisz. 1998. *Greater than the Parts. Holism in Biomedicine, 1920–1950*, Oxford and New York: Oxford University Press.

Le Béguec, G. 1989. 'L'Entrée au Palais-Bourbon: les filières privilégiées d'accès à la fonction parlementaire, 1919–1939', unpublished thesis (doctorat d'Etat), Université de Paris X Nanterre.

Le Béguec, G. 2003. *La République des avocats*, Paris: Armand Colin.

Le Bon, G. 1991. *La Psychologie des foules*, Paris: Quadrige/Presses universitaires de France.

Le Bras, H. 1991. *Marianne et les lapins*, Paris: Olivier Orban.

Le Chatelier, F. 1968. *Henry Le Chatelier, un grand savant d'hier, un précurseur*, Paris: Revue de Métallurgie.

Le Crom, J.-P. 1995. *Syndicats, nous voilà! Vichy et le corporatisme*, Paris: Editions de l'Atelier.

Le Crom, J.-P. 'De la philanthropie à l'action humanitaire' in P.-J. Hesse and J.-P. Le Crom, *La Protection sociale sous le régime de Vichy*, Rennes: Presses universitaires de Rennes, 2001, 183–236.

Le Van-Lemesle, L. 'La « République industrielle » de Hyacinthe Dubreuil (1883–1971), ou la dérive corporatiste', in S. L. Kaplan and P. Minard (éd.), *La France, malade du corporatisme ? XVIII–XXe siècles*, Paris: Belin, 2004, 387–401.

Letté, M. 2004. *Henry Le Chatelier (1850–1936) ou la science appliquée à l'industrie*, Rennes: Presses universitaires de Rennes.

Lévy-Leboyer, M. 'Le Patronat français 1912–1973', in M. Lévy-Leboyer (ed.), *Le Patronat de la seconde industrialisation*, Paris: Les Editions ouvrières, 1979.

Lévy-Leboyer, M. (ed.). 1979. *Le Patronat de la seconde industrialisation*, Paris: Les Editions ouvrières.

Lévy-Leboyer. M. and Henri Morsel (dir.). 1994. *Histoire de l'Electricité en France (vol.2 1919–1946)*, Paris: Fayard.

Leymonerie, C. 2006. 'Le Salon des arts ménagers dans les années 1950. Théâtre d'une conversion à la consommation de masse', *Vingtième siècle* 91, 43–56.

MacBride, T. 1976. *The Domestic Revolution: The Modernisation of Household Service in England and France 1820–1920*, London: Croom Helm.

Macleod, M. 1985. 'Urbanism and Utopia: Le Corbusier from Regional Syndicalism to Vichy', PhD Thesis, Princeton University.

Magraw, R. '"Not Backward But Different"? The Debate on French "Economic Retardation"', in M. Alexander (ed.), *French History since Napoleon*, London: Arnold, 1999, 336–63.

Magri, S. 'La Réforme du logement populaire: la Société française des habitations à bon marché, 1889–1914', in C. Topalov (ed.), *Laboratoires du nouveau siècle:la nébuleuse réformatrice et ses réseaux en France, 1880–1914*, Paris: Editions de l'Ecole des Hautes Etudes en Sciences Sociales, 1999, 239–68.

Magri, S. and C. Topalov. 'L'Habitat du salarié moderne en France, Grande Bretagne, Italie et aux Etats-Unis, 1910–1925', in Y. Cohen and R. Baudouï , *Les Chantiers de la paix sociale 1900–1940*, Fontenay/St Cloud: ENS Editions, 1995, 223–53.

Magri, S. and C. Topalov. 1989. *Villes ouvrières 1900–1950*, Paris: Harmattan.

Maier, C. S. 1970. 'Between Taylorism and Technocracy: European Ideologies and the Vision of Industrial Productivity in the 1920s', *Journal of Contemporary History* 5(2), 31–32.

Maier, C. S. 1987. *In Search of Stability. Explorations in Historical Political Economy*, Cambridge: Cambridge University Press.

Maîtron, J. 1986. *Dictionnaire biographique du mouvement ouvrier. Vol 26*, Paris: Editions ouvrières.

Maîtron, J. 1988. *Dictionnaire biographique du mouvement ouvrier. Vol 33*, Paris: Editions ouvrières.

Margairaz, M. 1991. *L'Etat, les finances et l'économie. Histoire d'une conversion, 1932–1952*, 2 vols, Paris: Comité pour l'histoire économique et financière de la France.

Margairaz, M. 'Les autodidactes et les experts: réseaux et parcours intellectuels dans les années 1930', in B. Belhoste et al. (eds.), *La France des X. Deux siècles d'histoire*, Paris: Economica, 1995, 169–84.

Marpeau, B. 2000. *Gustave Le Bon. Parcours d'un intellectuel 1841–1931*, Paris: CNRS Editions.

Marry, C. 2004. *Les Femmes ingénieurs: une révolution respectueuse*, Paris: Belin.

Martin, M. 1984. 'Femmes et société: le travail ménager (1919–1939)', Thèse de troisième cycle, Université de Paris VII.

Martin, M. 1987. 'Ménagère: une profession? Les dilemmes de l'entre-deux-guerres', *Mouvement Social* 140, 89–106.

Martin, T. (dir). 2000. *Mathémathiques et action politique: études d'histoire et de philosophie de mathématiques sociales*, Paris: INED.

Merkle, J. 1980. *Management and Ideology: The Legacy of the International Scientific Management Movement*, Berkeley: University of California Press.

Milhaud, J. 1956. *Chemins faisant. Tranches de vie*, Paris: Editions Hommes et Techniques.

Mioche, P. 1987. *Le Plan Monnet: genèse et élaboration, 1941–1947*, Paris: Publications de la Sorbonne.

Mission d'étude sur la spoliation des Juifs de France. 2000. *Aryanisation économique et restitutions*, Paris: La Documentation française.

Monnet, F. 1993. *Refaire la République. André Tardieu, une dérive réactionnaire*, Paris: Fayard.

Monnet, F. 1993. *Refaire la République. André Tardieu, une dérive réactionnaire*, Paris: Fayard.

Mouré, K. and M. Alexander. 2002. *Crisis and Renewal in France 1918–1962*, New York and Oxford: Berghahn Books.

Moutet, A. 1975. 'Les Origines du système Taylor en France: le point de vue patronal (1907–1914)', *Mouvement social* 93, 10–45.

Moutet, A. 'La Première Guerre mondiale et le taylorisme', in M. de Montmollin and O. Pastré (eds.), *Le Taylorisme*, Paris: La Découverte, 1984, 67–81.

Moutet, A. 1997. *Les Logiques de l'entreprise. La rationalisation dans l'industrie française de l'entre-deux-guerres*, Paris: Editions de l'EHESS.

Muel-Dreyfus, F. 1996. *Vichy et l'éternel féminin. Contribution à une sociologie politique de l'ordre des corps*, Paris: Seuil.

Murard, L. and P. Zylberman. 1976. *Le Petit Travailleur infatigable. Villes-usines, habitat et intimités au XIX siècle*, Paris: Recherches.

Murard, L. and P. Zylberman. 1983. *Recherche sur la formation et l'histoire des agencements intérieurs de l'habitat*, Paris: CERFI, Ministère de l'urbanisme et du logement.

Noiriel, G. 1999. *Les Origines républicaines de Vichy*, Paris: Hachette.

Nolan, M. 1990. '"Housework made easy:" The Taylorised Housewife in Weimar Germany's Rationalised Economy', *Feminist Studies* 16(3), 549–77.

Nolan, M. 1994. *Visions of Modernity: American Business and the Modernization of Germany*, Oxford: Oxford University Press.

Nord, P. 'Social defence and conservative regeneration: the national revival, 1900–1914', in R. Tombs (ed.), *Nationhood and Nationalism in France: From Boulangism to the Great War, 1889–1918*, London: Harper Collins, 1991, 210–28.

Nye, R. 1975. *The Origins of Crowd Psychology: Gustave Le Bon and the Crisis of Mass Democracy in the Third Republic*, London, Beverly Hills: Sage.

Offen, K. 'Body Politics: Women, Work and the Politics of Motherhood in France 1920–1950', in G. Bock and P. Thane (eds.), *Maternity and Gender Policies: Women and the Rise of the European Welfare States, 1880s–1950s*, London: Routledge, 1991, 138–59.

Ohayon, A. 2003. 'L'Emergence d'un mouvement sexologique français (1929–1939), entre hygiénisme, eugénisme et psychanalyse', *Psychiatrie, sciences humaines, neurosciences* 1(4), 50–61.

Panchasi, R. 2009. *Future Tense: The Culture of Anticipation in France Between the Wars*, Ithaca and London: Cornell University Press.

'Paradoxes français de la crise des années 30', special issue of *Mouvement social* 154, 1991.

Parsons, T. 1937. *The Structure of Social Action*, New York: MacGraw Hill.

Parsons, T. 1951. *The Social System*, New York: Free Press.

Passmore, K. 'Why Did People Believe that the Third Republic Was in Crisis in the 1930s? Anti-southern Prejudice, Anti-Semitism and Anti-communism', paper presented at French Historical Studies, New Brunswick, N.J., 4 April 2008.

Passmore, K. 2004. 'The Construction of Crisis in Interwar France', in Brian Jenkins (ed.), *France in the Era of Fascism*, New York and Oxford: Berghahn Books, 151–99.

Passmore, K. Forthcoming. 'La Droite, l'organisation et la psychologie collective dans l'entre-deux-guerres'.

Passmore, K. Forthcoming. *The Right in the French Third Republic*.

Paxton, R. 1982. *Vichy France: Old Guard and New Order*, New York: Columbia University Press. [1st ed 1972].

Peaucelle, J-L. 2003. 'Saint-Simon, aux origines de la pensée de Henri Fayol', *Entreprises et histoire*, 34, 68–83.

Peer, S. 1998. *France on Display: Peasants, Provincials and Folklore in the 1937 Paris World's Fair*, Albany: SUNY Press.

Perrault, A-S. 1999. *Renault et les Sciences Sociales 1948–1991*, Paris: Seli Arslan.

Perrot, M. 'The Three Ages of Industrial Discipline in Nineteenth-Century France', in J. M. Merriman (ed.), *Consciousness and Class Experience in Nineteenth-Century Europe*, New York and London: Holmes and Meier Publishers Inc. 1979, 149–68.

Perrot, M. 'Travailler et produire: Claude-Lucien Bergery et les débuts du management en France', in F. Bédarida (ed.), *Mélanges d'histoire sociale offerts à Jean Maîtron*, Paris: Editions ouvrières, 1976, 177–90.

Price, M. 1998. 'Bodies and Souls: The Rehabilitation of Maimed Soldiers in France and Germany During the First World War', PhD Dissertation, Stanford University.

Rabinbach, A. 1992. *The Human Motor: Energy, Fatigue and the Origins of Modernity*, Berkeley: University of California Press.

Rabinow, P. 1989. *French Modern: Norms and Forms of the Social Environment*, Cambridge, MA: MIT Press.

Radtke-Delacor, A. 2001. 'Produire pour le Reich. Les Commandes allemandes à l'industrie française (1940–1944)', *Vingtième siècle*, 70, 99–115.

Ragon, M. 1986. *Histoire de l'architecture et de l'urbanisme modernes*, Paris: Casterman.

Reggiani, A. 2002. 'Alexis Carrel, The Unknown: Eugenics and Population Research under Vichy', *French Historical Studies* 25(2), 331–56.

Reggiani, A. 2007. *God's Eugenicist: Alexis Carrel and the Sociobiology of Decline*, New York and Oxford: Berghahn Books.

Reid, D. 1986. 'Genèse du fayolisme', *Sociologie du Travail* 1, 75–93.

Renaud, J. F. 'J. M. Keynes et les économistes français dans l'entre-deux-guerres: quelques éléments explicatifs d'une révolution introuvable', in P. Dockès et al. (dir.), *Les Traditions économiques françaises*, Paris: CNRS Editions, 2000, 925–37.

Reynolds, S. 1996. *France Between the Wars: Gender and Politics*, London: Routledge.

Rials, S. 1977. *Administration et organisation: de l'organisation de la bataille à la bataille de l'organisation dans l'administration française*, Paris: Editions Beauchesne.

Ribeill, G. 'Politiques et pratiques sociales du logement dans les Compagnies de chemin de fer', in S. Magri and C. Topalov, *Villes ouvrières 1900–1950*, Paris: Harmattan, 1989, 155–70.

Ribeill, G. 1980. 'Les Débuts de l'ergonomie en France à la veille de la Première Guerre mondiale', *Mouvement Social* 113, 3–36.

Roberts, M. L. 1994. *Civilization Without Sexes: Reconstructing Gender in Postwar France, 1917–1927*, Chicago: University of Chicago Press.

Rodgers, D. 1998. *Atlantic Crossings: Social Politics in a Progressive Age*, Cambridge, Mass: Harvard University Press.

Rosental, P-A. 2003. *L'Intelligence démographique: sciences et politiques des populations en France 1930–1960*, Paris: Odile Jacob.

Ross, K. 1995. *Fast Cars, Clean Bodies: Decolonization and the Reordering of French Culture*, Cambridge, Mass: MIT Press.

Roussel, C. 1979. *Lucien Romier*, Paris: Editions France Empire.

Rousselier-Fraboulet, D. 1998. *Les Entreprises sous l'Occupation: le monde de la métallurgie à Saint-Denis*, Paris: CNRS Editions.

Rousso, H. 1979. 'L'Organisation industrielle de Vichy (Perspectives de recherches)', *Revue d'histoire de la deuxième guerre mondiale*, 116, 27–44.

Rousso, H. 'Les Paradoxes de Vichy et de l'Occupation. Contraintes, archaïsmes et modernités', in P. Fridenson and A. Straus (eds), *Le Capitalisme français, 19e–20e siècle. Blocages et dynamismes d'une croissance*, Paris: Fayard, 1987, 67–82.

Rousso, H. 'Vichy et la "modernisation"', in J. P. Azéma, D. Barjot et al, *Reconstructions et modernisation: la France après les ruines 1918...1945*, Paris: Archives nationales, 1991, 77–82.

Rutherford, J. W. 2003. *Selling Mrs Consumer: Christine Frederick and the Rise of Household Efficiency*, Athens, Georgia: University of Georgia Press.

Sabin, G. 1991. *Jean Bichelonne: ministre sous l'Occupation 1942–1944*, Paris: Editons France-Empire.

Sauvy, A. 1965–1975. *Histoire économique de la France entre les deux guerres*, 4 vols, Paris: Fayard.

Sauvy, A. 1969. 'The Economic Crisis of the 1930s in France', *Journal of Contemporary History* 4 (4), 21–35.

Schneider, W. H. 1982. 'Toward the Improvement of the Human Race: The History of Eugenics in France', *Journal of Modern History* 54 (2), 268–91.

Schneider, W. H. 1991. 'The Scientific Study of Labor in Interwar France', *French Historical Studies*, 17(2), 410–46.

Segal, H. P. 2005. *Recasting the Machine Age: Henry Ford's Village Industries*, Amherst and Boston: University of Massachusetts Press.

Shennan, A. 1989. *Rethinking France: Plans for Renewal 1940–1946*, Oxford: Clarendon Press.

Shinn, T. 1980. *L'Ecole polytechnique*, Paris: Presses de la Fondation nationale des sciences politiques.

Simonton, D. 1998. *A History of European Women's Work: 1700 to the present*, London: Routledge.

Siwek-Pouydesseau, J. 2006. 'L'Institut technique des administrations publiques, entrepreneur militant de la productivité administrative (1947–1968)', *Revue française d'administration publique* 120, 711–20.

Stanley, A. C. 2008. *Modernizing Tradition: Gender and Consumerism in Interwar France and Germany*, Baton Rouge: Louisiana State University Press.

Sternhell, Z. 1978. *La droite révolutionnaire. Les Origines françaises du fascisme*, Paris: Le Seuil.

Sternhell, Z. 1983. *Ni Droite, ni gauche: l'idéologie fasciste en France*, Paris: Le Seuil.

Thomson, M. 2006. *Psychological Subjects: Identity, Culture and Health in Twentieth-Century Britain*, Oxford: Oxford University Press.

Tombs, R. (ed.). 1991. *Nationhood and Nationalism in France: From Boulangism to the Great War, 1889–1918*, London: Harper Collins.

Topalov, C. (ed.). 1999. *Laboratoires du nouveau siècle: la nébuleuse réformatrice et ses réseaux en France, 1880–1914*, Paris: Editions de l'Ecole des hautes études en sciences sociales.

Verheyde, P. 1999. *Les Mauvais Comptes de Vichy: l'aryanisation des entreprises juives*, Paris: Perrin.

Verheyde, P. 'L'Aryanisation des grandes entreprises juives', in O. Dard, J-C. Daumas and F. Marcot (dir.), *L'Occupation, l'Etat français et les entreprises*, Paris: Association pour le développement de l'histoire économique, 2000, 121–33.

Viet, V. and M. Ruffat. 1999. *Le Choix de la prévention*, Paris: Economica.

Vinen, R. 1991. *The Politics of French Business 1936–1945*, Cambridge: Cambridge University Press.

Weexsteen, A. 'La Commission générale d'organisation scientifique du Travail (CEGOS) sous l'Occupation, 1940–1944', in O. Dard, J-C. Daumas and F. Marcot (dir.), *L'Occupation, l'Etat français et les entreprises*, Paris: Association pour le développement de l'histoire économique, 2000, 197–212.

Werner, F. 1984. 'Du ménage à l'art ménager: l'évolution du travail ménager et son écho dans la presse féminine française de 1919 à 1939', *Mouvement social* 129, 61–87.

Wieviorka, O. 'Replacement or Renewal? The French Political Elite at the Liberation', in A. Knapp (ed.), *The Uncertain Foundation: France at Liberation, 1944–1947*, Basingstoke: Palgrave MacMillan, 2007, 75–86.

Yagil, L. 1992. 'La Synarchie ou le mouvement "Synarchie d'Empire" et Vichy, 1940–1944', *Guerres mondiales et conflits contemporains* 165, 71–89.

INDEX

Lightning Source UK Ltd.
Milton Keynes UK
UKOW05f1534111213

222822UK00004B/50/P